Edward Everett Hale

Stories of War Told by Soldiers

Edward Everett Hale

Stories of War Told by Soldiers

ISBN/EAN: 9783337133788

Printed in Europe, USA, Canada, Australia, Japan

Cover: Foto ©ninafisch / pixelio.de

More available books at **www.hansebooks.com**

Hale, Edward Everett, 1822–1909.

Stories of war told by soldiers. Collected and ed. by Edward E. Hale. Boston, Roberts brothers, 1879.

2 p. l. 264 p. incl. map. 17½ᶜᵐ.

Added t.-p., illustrated.

CONTENTS.—Introduction. Life at Little Crustis.—The first Bull Run.—Fort Henry and Fort Donelson.—General McClellan and the Peninsula. West Virginia.—Antietam.—Pittsburg Landing.—Vicksburg.—Gettysburg.—Chickamauga and Chattanooga.—Grant's advance on Richmond. The Wilderness. Sheridan's ride.—Sherman's great march.—Nashville.—Siege of Richmond. The last week.—The end.

1. U. S.—Hist.—Civil war—Personal narratives. 2. U. S.—Hist.—Civil war—Campaigns and battles.   I. Title.

STORIES OF WAR

TOLD BY SOLDIERS.

COLLECTED AND EDITED

By EDWARD E. HALE.

BOSTON:

ROBERTS BROTHERS.

1879.

UNIVERSITY PRESS:
JOHN WILSON AND SON, CAMBRIDGE.

CONTENTS

STORIES OF THE WAR TOLD BY SOLDIERS.

————◆————

CHAPTER I.

LIFE AT LITTLE CRASTIS.

IT was the third day of a sour northeast storm. Colonel Ingham had a great party of nephews and nieces, and of his old correspondents and of their friends, — all young people, — on a crazy, rollicking visit at his country-house at Little Crastis.

In pleasant weather they all fared very well, — for they were all out of doors. Many of the boys and girls were none too big to pick berries. None were so small but they could be trusted in the boats, of which there were five, on the ponds, of which there were six, within an hour's walk. For the bigger boys and girls there was a catamaran, in which they could make voyages on the ocean. There were plover and yellow-legs, and thirty-one other varieties of sea-birds for the boys who liked to shoot. There were little glens innumerable, ruins of old barns, queer wrecks of old apple-trees, for girls or boys who wanted to

1

make sketches. There were perch, pickerel, and bass for those who liked to fish. There were clethra, and clematis, and coreopsis rosea, and all the rest of the alphabet for those who liked to botanize. There were two tents for those who liked to camp out. There were bows and arrows and targets, and croquet-balls and mallets and hoops, and rackets and nets, and crosses for Lacrosse, and battledores and shuttlecocks, for those who wanted to play games; there were saddles and horses and ponies for those who wanted to ride. But all such amusements, vocations, and avocations fail in a sour northeast storm; — and here were there fifteen young people cooped up in-doors, exhausting the in-door occupations.

"Dear Uncle Fritz," said Horace, — for they all called him uncle, — "what can I read?"

"Read, boy!" said the old gentleman, "there is plenty of reading"; — and he kicked open the door of his own den.

The boy looked in ruefully, but did not pretend to enter. "O, you know, uncle, that there's nothing there. Walter told me how you shipped all those things down here because there was no room for them in C. Street. Who ever read a Congressional document?"

"I have read a good many, Master Horace," said the Colonel, laughing; "and you will read a good many before you have done. It is all in knowing how, my dear boy."

"Well, who ever read a bound-up file of old newspapers, Colonel Ingham?" asked Florence, who had rallied to Horace's assistance as soon as she saw that the Colonel was willing to talk.

"All people of sense read them a great deal," said the Colonel, still laughing. "Now look here, children all," he said, "you were at me, only last night, to tell you stories of my only battle, — the famous action of the Point of Rocks, — in which nobody was killed and nobody was wounded, though we burned up thirty tons of powder. But you would be more glad to have General Grant walk in yonder, with Sherman on one side and Sheridan on the other, and tell you about Vicksburg and Shiloh and Sheridan's ride."

"I am afraid we should, Uncle Fritz," said Horace, bravely.

"Very good. You would be fools if not. Now, in those much despised documents yonder, Master Horace, and in those abominated newspapers, Miss Florence, and beneath that pile of dust in the corner, Master Stephen, are Grant's stories and Sherman's and Sheridan's, as they told them all hot from fight, all mad with defeat, or happy in victory. All that is needed is a boy of sense or a girl of sense to know where to look for them."

"And a real good-natured old Uncle Fritz, with nothing to do but to pet a good-for-nothing set of boys and girls," said Florence, coaxing him and kissing him, "and willing to show those stupid boys and girls where to dig in the dust, and how."

"That's true enough," said the old gentleman, willing to own that he was flattered; "for even I will own that there is more chaff to the wheat in those same newspapers and documents than there is in any other threshing-floor or mill-hopper in the world."

So it happened that these three young folks, with more or less help from three others, whose names will appear as we go on, fell foul of the heap of straw, chaff, and wheat in the inner den. The Colonel led the way loyally. He made them put in marks, red, yellow, and blue, when they found a good dramatic narrative that was worth reading aloud.

There is a sort of fascination about it when you are once started. And before long, even in that first afternoon, five or six of the young people were at work in or near the den. Those who read from bound-up volumes of newspapers preferred on the whole to lie nearly at full length on the floor with the book, or "quarry," as Horace would call it, open before them, or "in a measure," as he said, under them. The others had attitudes more or less elegant, and, in all cases, comfortable, for such was the rule at Little Crastis. At first they began to read aloud little scraps as they lighted on them, and found them too exciting to be enjoyed alone.

But it soon proved that such reading only interests the reader. Uncle Fritz advised them soon to mark with red pencils, which he provided, what was worth reading, and wait till they found fit audience, who really wanted to hear. And this they did.

And so it happened that on that very evening there began a series of readings aloud from the grimiest and stupidest-looking old volumes of documents and newspapers, — readings which were quite largely attended from the little company of visitors. While, in the red parlor, there went on a game at vingt-un, more or less noisy. Those who had tired of vingt-un a little, or thought they had outgrown it, gathered in the gray parlor, and the gleanings for the earlier part of the war of the Rebellion were read, under more or less control from Colonel Ingham, who would not let an eager reader bore the others, or a modest one give up her turn for some one more resolute. As the summer passed, some of the visitors stayed, and some went away and other some came. But it often happened that there was an evening when they fell back on the war papers, — as they came to call them, — and so

THE STORIES OF THE WAR
TOLD BY SOLDIERS

came into being.

CHAPTER II.

THE FIRST BULL RUN.

THE first evening's reading began with the First
Bull Run. Bull Run was the first great battle of the war.

"I tell you, children," said Uncle Fritz, "there
was never anything like it,—no, not in those long
four years. I mean there was nothing that made
people so sick at heart. The truth was that till that
hour we knew nothing of war or what war was. It
was all a piece of stage-play and rhodomontade to
us who were not in the camp, and I was not. We
had hardly advanced on that first notion in which
people supposed that an army on one side was to
walk up in an open field, and another army to walk
up opposite them on the other side, and that they
were to take aim and fire at each other till one side
had all run away. The stuff written home from
Washington and the camps to the newspapers was
such as I cannot now believe we ever read.

"I was away from home on Sunday, the day that
battle was fought. But the church, morning and
afternoon, was all excitement. Telegrams were

coming from Washington all day long; nothing to any real purpose, but all bragging, and nobody thinking of anything but victory. All the anxiety was who might be alive, or who dead. And from that congregation where I was, I suppose some fifty men, the minister among the rest, were in the battle, and we knew it. The next day I went down to Boston. I was in a committee-room, with a committee of the Emigrant Aid Society. The newspapers had had there some cheerful, even jubilant accounts in the morning, and we were eagerly discussing them, when in came Lawrence, who was always well informed.

"'I have a despatch from Washington,' said he. 'We are as badly beaten as an army can be. Washington is full of runaways, and I don't know how soon the Rebels may march in.'

"As it turned out, and as the boys will show you, this was almost as much of an exaggeration as the jubilation of the morning. But if our good friend had walked round the circle and slapped any one of us in the face we should not have been more surprised,—nay, we should not have been so much displeased. It was the end of all business for that day. We went out to the newspaper offices, or where we could, to find more scraps of news. And I know I went home to tell Polly and the children, feeling as sick at body as at heart. It did not seem to me that life was worth living for.

"At that same moment, as I knew years afterwards, almost every house in Richmond was in the depth of sorrow. The Black Horse Cavalry was terribly cut up by the Union army in that action. And all that afternoon, and all the night which followed, every carriage in Richmond — so a negro hackman told me in 1866 — was carrying from the station to his home some wounded soldier. And in so many homes they were lamenting those who would never come! There are two sides to war.

"General McDowell was in immediate command on our side. Horace has made up, from the careful official reports of the battle, a little account of the plan of it, and the way it was fought. He will read you this first, and then you will place the better the scraps which the others have found about the details."

METHOD OF THE BATTLE.

In July, 1861, General McDowell was at Centreville, twenty miles west of Washington, with the "Grand Army" of twenty-eight thousand men. Two miles west of him, encamped behind Bull Run, with his headquarters at Manassas, three miles back, was the Rebel army under Beauregard, twenty thousand strong. To the north, at Harper's Ferry, was another Union army, of eighteen thousand men, under General Patterson, which held in check eight thousand Rebels at Winchester, commanded by General Johnston.

Supposing that Patterson could keep Johnston from joining Beauregard, McDowell on the twentieth of July gave his orders for an advance on Bull Run on the next morning. There were three roads leading from Centreville across the Run, all of which were guarded by the

Rebels; but to the north, at Sudley Springs, was an unguarded ford which could be reached by a detour of three miles from the northern road. By this ford the real attack was to be made by two divisions of the army, reinforced by a third division advancing along the northern road of the three to the Stone Bridge where it crossed the Run, while the other division was to make feints at the two southern roads, and act as a reserve.

But the Rebels had guessed that some advance would be made, and, before the orders for attack had been given by McDowell, a large part of Johnston's army had arrived at Manassas from Winchester by railroad, and had been put into position. The rest of the army was certain to arrive at noon of the next day.

At half past one on the morning of the twenty-first the Union camp was astir. General Tyler's division was under arms, and began its three-mile walk to Stone Bridge. But the troops and officers were raw, and it was dark. They could not see to get their breakfast, men carried off each other's guns, company ran afoul of company, and regiments started in the wrong order. Suffice it to say that it took Tyler six hours to advance three miles and deploy into line; it was as late as half past six when he began firing his thirty-pounder to show that he was ready.

Colonel Hunter, who, with his own and General Heintzelman's division, was to march five miles to Sudley Springs, was still more unfortunate. He had to start after Tyler on the same road; he had to share all his delays, and it was six o'clock before he came to his own three miles of woods. Here the marching was still more difficult, and it was half past nine before his advance reached the ford, with men who for eight hours had been tired by marching, or by waiting, more tiring even than marching.

This delay it was which lost the Union forces the battle; for though the whole Rebel army was massed south of the Stone Bridge, Tyler's firing aroused them to the knowledge of our advance on the right, and at once troops were sent up to sustain the attack. They were drawn up to oppose Tyler; but presently Hunter's men were seen crossing above, and the Rebels faced to the left and advanced to an open field sloping down to the woods, from which he must emerge. They halted within musket-shot of these woods, and when Hunter's advance came to the open ground, it was met by both artillery and infantry fire. Nothing daunted, however, his first regiments formed in the shelter of the woods, and advanced, driving the enemy back, beyond the road on which Tyler was stationed, while the troops in the rear formed to the right and left. When Tyler learned from look-outs in the high trees that Hunter was advancing to the road, he ordered his subordinates, Colonels Sherman and Keyes, with their brigades, across the Run. They forded the stream, as the bridge and road were impassable from the abatis of the Rebels, and faced to the south, forming to the left of Hunter's two divisions. The whole line, advancing, drove the enemy, though strongly reinforced, still farther back, up rising ground upon a plateau, where they made a stand. Here one of Keyes's regiments charged up the hill, capturing a battery, and gaining a position upon the top. This was the turning-point of the battle; the regiment was driven back again after holding the ridge for hardly five minutes. The attack was renewed, with less success, the Rebels advanced and were driven back, and the wave of success swept to and fro.

Meanwhile, in the Rebel lines the prospects were by no means so favorable. Their troops with the greatest difficulty held the hill against the vigorous though spasmodic attacks of our men. Beauregard had hurried up all his troops from the two lower roads, excepting one brigade, and these new troops were pushed to the front, while those who had been broken by the Union attacks were led and driven into shape behind. The time had passed when Johnston's reinforcements were promised. Messengers were sent to the railroad to stop the train at the nearest point to the battle-field, and hurry the men up directly, when they should arrive. The fire of the Union troops, which had slackened, was now reviving, and there were symptoms of a general advance, when, at half past three, on their extreme left, the Rebels heard loud cheering. Anxiously they watched to see if it were friend or foe, when the shout of "Johnston! Johnston!" was heard, and the right of the Union troops was seen to break and run. A general advance was ordered, and the Union line fell back, the two divisions on the right in total disorder, with the exception of the battalion of regulars, which covered their flight. The Rebels pursued them to the Run, where, the reserve under Miles interposing to protect the rout, the Rebels called a halt. The panic spread among the Union camp-followers, and many of the fugitives did not stop till they reached Washington. The whole Union line fell back to their old camp at Centreville, where they passed the night. The next day they retreated to the Potomac.

AN IMPROMPTU LOOK-OUT.

During this period of waiting the thirty-pounder was occasionally used with considerable effect against bodies of infantry and cavalry, which could be seen from time to time moving in the direction of Hunter's column, and out of the range of ordinary guns. Using a high tree as an observatory, we could constantly see the operations of Hunter's and Heintzelman's column from the time they crossed Bull Run, and through one of my staff, Lieut. O'Rourke, of the Engineers, I was promptly notified as to any change in the progress of their columns up to the time when it appeared that the heads of both were arrested, and the enemy seemed to be moving heavy reinforcements to support their troops. At this time I ordered Colonel Sherman with his brigade to cross Bull Run, and to support the two columns already in action. Colonel Sherman, as appears by his reports, crossed the run without opposition, and, after encountering a party of the enemy flying before Hunter's forces, found General McDowell, and received his orders to join in the pursuit. — *Gen. Tyler, 1st Division.*

A SAD MISTAKE.

This movement was effected at "quick" and "double-quick" time, both by the infantry and artillery, during which march the men threw from their shoulders their haversacks, blankets, and most of their canteens, to facilitate their eagerness to engage the enemy. On arriving at the point indicated, being the extreme left of the enemy and the extreme right of our line, and in advance of all other of our troops, and where I was informed officially that two other regiments had declined to charge, we formed a line of battle, our right resting within a few feet of the woods, and the left at and around Rickett's battery, and upon the crest of the hill, within fifty or sixty feet of the enemy's line of infantry, with whom we could have readily conversed in an ordinary tone of voice. Immediately upon Rickett's battery coming into position and we in "line of battle," Colonel Heintzelman rode up between our lines and that of the enemy, within pistol-shot of each, which circumstance staggered my judgment whether those in front were friends or enemies. it being equally manifest that the enemy were in the same dilemma as to our identity. But a few seconds, however, undeceived both, — they displaying the Rebel and we the Union flag. Instantly a blaze of fire was poured into the faces of the combatants, each producing terrible destruction, owing to the close proximity of the forces, which was followed by volley after volley, in regular and irregular order as to time, until Rickett's battery was disabled and cut to pieces, and a large portion of its officers and men had fallen, and until Companies H, I, K, C, G, and those immediately surrounding my regimental flag, were so desperately cut to pieces as to make it more of a slaughter-house than an equal combat, the enemy manifestly numbering five guns to our one, besides being intrenched in the woods and behind ditches and pits plainly perceptible, and with batteries upon the enemy's right, enfilading my left flank, and within three hundred and fifty yards' direct range. After an effort to obtain aid from the Fire Zouaves, then immediately upon our left, two or three different orders came to retire, as it was manifest that the contest was too deadly and unequal to be longer justifiably maintained. —*Col. Gorham, 1st Minn., with 3d Division.*

A BRAVE CAPTAIN.

A further order was then made to advance the colors of the Seventy-first New York to the front, but, as it seemed to be certain death to stand exposed to the tornado which swept the brow of the hill, the color-bearer naturally hesitated for a moment; whereupon several of Company F sprang quickly forward, with the exclamation, "Give us the colors!" But Captain Coles, of Company C, was the foremost in the effort, and, seizing the flag, he ran with it full fifty paces to the front, and held it at arm's length high in the air, and then planted it in the earth. Its folds were hailed in the Rebel battery with a demoniac yell, and in the next instant the bright banner was riddled with a shower of balls. Providentially, the gallant Captain was untouched. —*Capt. Wilkes.*

A LEAP FOR LIBERTY.

The Sixty-ninth New York brought up the rear of the temporarily retiring column; but its gallant Colonel, watchful of its welfare, lingered behind and urged stragglers not to get separated from their commands. He paused for an instant to salute Colonel Tompkins, of the Second, who stood dismounted at a little distance from his regiment, on the opposite side of the road.

Just at this moment a large body of the enemy's Black
Horse were seen making a charge toward them, though
its immediate object was to attack Carlisle's battery,
which, out of ammunition, stood limbered up in the
centre of the road. The two colonels watched the
movement, and, transfixed with excitement as they saw
the dragoons sabre the cannoniers, forgot to take measures for their own protection. It was imminently
necessary that they should, for the quick exploit upon
the battery had scarcely retarded the black column in
the least, and they came pouring upon the unformed
columns of the Schenck Brigade. Promptly, however,
the quick order of McCook shaped the First Ohio, and
the others, following by instinct, showed a firm line,
with bayonets all poised, and ready for the charge.
The Black Horse looked for a moment, but, not liking
that array of steel, they flirted off to the right (receiving a volley as they went), and a squad of them made a
dash to cut off the two colonels who were isolated in the
road. Tompkins, who saw the danger coming, quickly
sprang to a horse near at hand, and calling on Corcoran
to follow, spurred him at a fence. The troopers, however, were too near for Corcoran's tired steed, and,
whirling around the Irish colonel, they took him cap-
tive, and bore him off. A portion of the squad followed
after Tompkins, but his spirited charger leaped two
fences in fine style, and amid the crack of the dragoons' six-shooters, he got safe away. The brigade of
Schenck, being now utterly fagged out, and being moreover entirely without orders, fell back upon the foot-
steps of the Sixty-ninth. — *Capt. Wilkes.*

PIONEERS' WORK.

While this was going on, Captain Alexander, of the
Engineer Corps, brought up the company of pioneers,
or axe-men, which, with its officers and sixty men, had
been entirely detailed from the regiments of my brigade,
to open a communication over the bridge, and through

the heavy abatis which obstructed the passage of troops on our front beyond the Run. — *Gen. Schenck, 2d Brigade, 1st Division.*

KEYES'S SPLENDID CHARGE.

At about two o'clock, P. M., General Tyler ordered me to take a battery on a height in front. The battery was strongly posted, and supported by infantry and riflemen, sheltered by a building, a fence, and a hedge. My order to charge was obeyed with the utmost promptness. Colonel Jameson of the Second Maine, and Colonel Chatfield of the Third Connecticut Volunteers, pressed forward their regiments up the base slope about one hundred yards, when I ordered them to lie down at a point offering a small protection, and load. I then ordered them to advance again, which they did, in the face of a movable battery of eight pieces and a large body of infantry, toward the top of the hill. As we moved forward we came under the fire of other large bodies of the enemy posted behind breastworks, and, on reaching the summit of the hill, the firing became so hot that an exposure to it of five minutes would have annihilated my whole line. . . . . Private Leach is also highly praised for having spiked three abandoned guns with a ramrod, and then bringing away two abandoned muskets. . . . . Lieutenant-Colonel Speidal of the First Connecticut was set upon by three of the enemy, who undertook to make him a prisoner. The Lieutenant-Colonel killed one and drove off the other two of his assailants, and escaped. —*Col. Keyes, 1st Brigade, 1st Division.*

THE FIRST REVERSE.

Griffin's and Rickett's batteries were ordered by the commanding general to the top of the hill on the right, supported with the Fire Zouaves and Marines, while the Fourteenth entered the skirt of wood on their right to pro-

tect that flank, and a column composed of the Twenty-
seventh New York, Eleventh and Fifth Massachusetts,
Second Minnesota, and Sixty-ninth New York moved
up toward the left flank of the batteries ; but so soon as
they were in position, and before the flanking supports
had reached them, a murderous fire of musketry and
rifles, opened at pistol range, cut down every cannonier
and a large number of horses. The fire came from
some infantry of the enemy, which had been mistaken
for our own forces, an officer in the field having stated
that it was a regiment sent by Colonel Heintzelman to
support the batteries.

The evanescent courage of the Zouaves prompted
them to fire perhaps a hundred shots, when they broke
and fled, leaving the batteries open to a charge of the
enemy's cavalry, which took place immediately. The
Marines also, in spite of the exertions of their gallant
officers, gave way in disorder. The Fourteenth, on the
right, and the column on the left, hesitatingly retired,
with the exception of the Sixty-ninth and Thirty-eighth
New York, who nobly stood and returned the fire of the
enemy for fifteen minutes. Soon the slopes behind us
were swarming with our retreating and disorganized
forces, while riderless horses and artillery teams ran
furiously through the flying crowd.

All further efforts were futile. The words, gestures,
and threats of our officers were thrown away upon men
who had lost all presence of mind, and only longed for
absence of body. Some of our noblest and best officers
lost their lives in trying to rally them. Upon our *first
position* the Twenty-seventh was the first to rally, under
the command of Major Bartlett, and around it the other
regiments engaged soon collected their scattered fragments. The battalion of regulars, in the mean time,
moved steadily across the field from left to right, and
took up a position, where it held the entire forces of the
rebels in check until our forces were somewhat rallied. —
Col. Porter, 1st Brigade, 2d Division.

The retreat continued thus until the column was about emerging from the woods and entering upon the Warrenton Turnpike, when the artillery and cavalry went to the front, and the enemy opened fire upon the retreating mass of men. Upon the bridge crossing Cub Run a shot took effect upon the horses of a team that was crossing. The wagon was overturned directly in the centre of the bridge, and the passage was completely obstructed. The enemy continued to play his artillery upon the train carriages, ambulances, and artillery wagons that filled the road, and these were reduced to ruin. The artillery could not possibly pass, and five pieces of the Rhode Island battery, which had been safely brought off the field, were here lost. —*Col. Burnside, 2d Brigade, 2d Division.*

ACTION OF THE RESERVE.

Soon afterward, several squadrons of the enemy's cavalry advanced along the road, and appeared before the outposts. They were challenged, "Who comes here?" and, remaining without any answer, I, being just present at the outpost, called "Union forever!" whereupon the officer of the enemy's cavalry commanded, "*En avant! en avant!* knock him down!" Now the skirmishers fired, when the enemy turned around, leaving several killed and wounded on the spot. About nine prisoners who were already in their hands were liberated by this action. —*Col. Blenker, 1st Brigade, 5th Division.*

A YOUNG COMMANDER.

While the Thirty-second was in this position, the Sixteenth and Thirty-first having passed within its range, a youthful orderly rode up to Colonel Matheson

2

to inform him that the Black Cavalry, sheltered from
his observation by a piece of woods, were coming up
on the right, and, if he would take a cut with his
regiment across the fields, they would be turned back
upon their errand. The evolution was performed,
gave the protection that was desired, and the Black
Horse relinquished its purpose in that quarter. While
the regiment, however, was adhering to this position,
the same youth who had imparted the previous sug-
gestion rode up to the regiment again, and told
Matheson he had better now fall back on Centreville,
as his duty at that spot had been thoroughly performed. As this was about the first sign of orders
(with one single exception) he had received during the
entire day, Matheson felt some curiosity to learn who
this young Lieutenant was, and whence these orders
came; he therefore turned sharply on the youth, who, he
now perceived, could not be more than twenty-two or
three, and said, " Young man, I would like to know
your name." The youth replied that he was a son of
Quartermaster-General Meigs. " By whose authority,
then, do you deliver me these orders?" was the Cali-
fornian's next inquiry. The young man smiled, and
remarked, " Well, sir, the truth is, that for the last few
hours I have been giving all the orders for this division,
and acting as general too, for there is no general on
the field." — *Capt. Wilkes.*

A BRAVE OFFICER.

In addition, I deem it my duty to add that Lieut.
Ames was wounded so as to be unable to ride his horse,
at almost the first fire: yet he sat by his command
directing the fire, being helped on and off the caisson
during the different changes of front or position, refusing
to leave the field until he became too weak to sit up. —
Capt. Griffin, 5th Art., with 2d Division.

A REBEL BATTERY.

While this last battery was forming in our front, a vast column of thousands of infantry marched down in close order, about two hundred yards to its right. I did not then know where the several regiments of our brigade were posted. We heard firing upon our right and left, but too far off to protect us from a sudden charge, as we were in the middle of an open field, and not a single company of infantry visible to us on the right, left, or rear. At the moment the enemy's main column came down the hill, we observed the head of another column advancing down the valley from our left, and therefore concealed by a hill, and not over three hundred and fifty or four hundred yards distant. At first I took them for friends, and ordered the men not to fire on them. To ascertain certainly who they were, I sprang upon my horse and galloped to the top of the hill to our left, when I had a nearer and better view. There were two regiments of them. They halted about three hundred yards in front of their own battery on the hillside, wheeled into line with their backs towards us, and fired a volley, apparently at their battery. This deceived me, and I shouted to my men to fire upon the battery, — that these were friends, who would charge and take it in a moment. Fortunately, my order was not heard or not obeyed by all the gunners, for some of them commenced firing into this line, which brought them to the right-about, and they commenced advancing towards us, when their uniform disclosed fully their character. I instantly ordered the second section of my battery to limber up and come on the hill where I was, intending to open on them with canister. Anticipating this movement, and intending to make the hill to the left too hot for us, or seeing me out there alone, where I could observe their movements and report them, their nearest battery directed and fired all its guns at me at once, but without hitting me or my horse. I galloped back to

my guns, and found that the two guns on our right had
left the field, and we were alone again. My order to
limber up the second section was understood as applying
to the whole battery, so that the drivers had equalized
the teams sufficiently to move all the guns and caissons,
and the pieces were all limbered. On riding back a
short distance, where I could see over the hill again, I
discovered the enemy approaching rapidly, and so near
that I doubted our ability to save the battery; but, by a
very rapid movement up the ravine, we avoided the shells
of the three batteries that were now directed at us,
sufficiently to escape with three guns and all the caissons.
The fourth gun, I think, was struck under the axle by an
exploding shell, as it broke right in the middle, and
dropped the gun in the field. We saved the team.
Their advance fired a volley of musketry at us without
effect, when we got over the hill out of their reach, and
a few moments afterwards heard the infantry engage
them from the woods, some distance to the south of
us. —*Capt. Imboden, Staunton Artillery, C. S. A.*

CHAPTER III.

FORT HENRY AND FORT DONELSON.

YOU can see well enough how eager the whole country was for action, — and how everybody chafed under the delay, which people hardly understood, of preparing for war. In truth, armies had to be clothed, shod, trained to duty. Powder had to be made, — and for this saltpetre had to be bought, even on the other side of the world, — cannon were to be cast, bored, and rifled, — all the other munitions of war were to be made, and this on a scale without precedent. Winter also came on, and winter, in countries where the roads are bad, always arrests the course of war.

This tedious waiting was broken in upon every day by some report or other from the long line of the scene of war. It was not in Virginia only, it was in the State then new made, and now called West Virginia, — a State which was loyal when "Old Virginia" east of the mountains left the Union, — it was in Kentucky, in Missouri, in South Carolina, and in Louisiana, that fighting was going on; so that every day's newspaper had its story of a skirmish

somewhere, and the preparation for battle. And
there were letters — oh, so many letters! — from the
armies, from brothers and sons and husbands and
fathers. Yet, all through the autumn and after the
winter began, there had been no movement of first-
rate importance until the Rebel armies were driven
out of Kentucky and of the greater part of Tennessee by the capture of Fort Henry and Fort Donelson. The joy of the loyal States was out of all
proportion to the numbers engaged, or to the immediate importance of the battles. In truth, those
battles showed a great many things which were not
known before, — though they had been hoped for.
They showed how much might be expected from the
"push" and spirit of the Western troops, though
they had not been trained to war. Men fought in
them, and fought well, who had not had their
muskets a fortnight. These battles showed also
that a commander had appeared who understood
the Western troops, had confidence in them, and
knew how to use them with success.

This officer was Ulysses Simpson Grant, — and
these successes first brought his name prominently
before the country.

You will probably not find Fort Henry or Fort
Donelson on your school maps. They were built
simply for the purposes of the Rebels there, — and
have long since ceased to have any purpose. But
you can place them well enough on your maps,
if you will find where the Cumberland River and

where the Tennessee River cross the line of Kentucky. Just south of this line, on the eastern side of the Tennessee, was Fort Henry, and a few miles from it, on the western side of the Cumberland, was Fort Donelson. General Grant moved with seventeen thousand men, on transports, on the river from Cairo, on the 2d of February, 1862. On the 4th he landed three miles below Fort Henry, and on the 6th began to move by land against the fort. Commodore Foote, of the navy, in command of the gun-boats, moved up by water. Of course he arrived first. His fire silenced the water batteries in an hour and a half, and the fort surrendered at discretion. The garrison, excepting sixty men who were kept to rub the guns, had been marched off to Fort Donelson. So when General Grant arrived with his force, which had a much longer course by land than the boats had had by water, he found the fort had surrendered and the garrison were gone.

Here is his letter announcing the success. Observe the confidence with which he speaks of what he should do next: —

FORT HENRY CAPITULATES.

In a little over one hour all the batteries were silenced, and the fort surrendered at discretion to Flag-Officer Foote, giving us all their guns, camp equipage, etc. The prisoners taken were General Tilghman and staff, Captain Taylor and company, and the sick. The garrison, I think, must have commenced the retreat last night, or at an early hour this morning. Had I not felt it an imperative duty to attack Fort Henry to-day, I should have made the investment complete, and delayed until to-morrow, so as to have secured the garrison. I do not now believe, however, that the result would have been any more satisfactory.

The gun-boats have proved themselves well able to resist a severe cannonading. All the iron-clads received more or less shots, — the flag-ship, some twenty-eight, — without any serious damage to any except the Essex. This vessel received one shot in her boilers that disabled her, killing and wounding some thirty-two men, Captain Porter among the wounded.

I shall take and destroy Fort Donelson on the 8th, and return to Fort Henry with the forces employed, unless it looks possible to occupy the place with a small force, that could retreat easily to the main body. I shall regard it more in the light of an advanced guard than as a permanent post.

For the character of the works at Fort Henry I will refer you to reports of the engineers. . . . .

Owing to the intolerable state of the roads, no transportation will be taken to Fort Donelson, and but little artillery, and that with double teams. — *Gen. Grant.*

Just notice, " I shall take and destroy Fort Donelson on the 8th." This shows what General Sherman alluded to as General Grant's confidence in success.

He did not move on the 8th, however, but on the 12th. And here is his story of what happened then : —

GENERAL GRANT'S HISTORY OF DONELSON.

I am pleased to announce to the Department the unconditional surrender, this morning, of Fort Donelson, with twelve to fifteen thousand prisoners, at least forty pieces of artillery, and a large amount of stores, horses, mules, and other public property.

I left Fort Henry on the 12th instant, with a force of about fifteen thousand men, divided into two divisions, under the command of Generals McClernand and Smith. Six regiments were sent around by water the day before, convoyed by a gun-boat (or boats), and with instructions not to pass it.

The troops made the march in good order, the head of the column arriving within two miles of the fort at twelve o'clock M. At this point the enemy's pickets were met and driven in. The fortifications of the enemy were from this point gradually approached and surrounded, with occasional skirmishing on the line. The following day, owing to the non-arrival of the gun-boats and reinforcements sent by water, no attack was made, but the investment was extended on the flanks of the enemy, and drawn closer to his works, with skirmishing all day. On the evening of the 13th, the gun-boats and reinforcements arrived. On the 14th, a gallant attack was made by Flag-Officer Foote upon the enemy's river batteries with his fleet. The engagement lasted probably one hour and a half, and bade fair to result favorably, when two unlucky shots disabled two of the armored boats, so that they were carried back by the current. The remaining two were very much disabled also, having received a number of heavy shots about the pilot-houses and other parts of the vessels. After these mishaps, I concluded to make the investment of Fort Donelson as perfect as possible, and partially fortify, and await repairs for the gun-boats. This plan was frustrated, however, by the enemy making a most vigorous attack upon our right wing, commanded by Brigadier-General J. A. McClernand, and which consisted of his division and a portion of the force under General L. Wallace.

The enemy were repelled, after a closely contested battle of several hours, in which our loss was heavy. The officers suffered out of proportion. I have not the means of determining our loss, even approximately, but it cannot fall far short of twelve hundred, killed, wounded, and missing. Of the latter, I understand, through General Buckner, about two hundred and fifty were taken prisoners. I shall retain here enough of the enemy to exchange for them, as they were immediately shipped off, and not left for re-capture.

About the close of this action the ammunition and cartridge-boxes gave out, which, with the loss of many of the field-officers, produced great confusion in the ranks. Seeing that the enemy did not take advantage of it, convinced me that equal confusion, and consequently great demoralization, existed with him. Taking advantage of this fact, I ordered a charge upon the left (enemy's right) with the division under General C. F. Smith, which was most brilliantly executed, and gave our arms full assurance of victory. The battle lasted until dark, and gave us possession of part of the in-trenchment. An attack was ordered from the other flank, after the charge by General Smith was commenced, by the divisions under McClernand and Wallace, which, notwithstanding hours of exposure to a heavy fire in the fore part of the day, was gallantly made, and the enemy further repulsed. At the points thus gained, night having come on, all the troops encamped for the night, feeling that a complete victory would crown their efforts at an early hour in the morning. This morning, at a very early hour, a note was received from General Buckner, under a flag of truce, proposing an armistice. A copy of the correspondence which ensued is herewith enclosed.

I could mention individuals who especially distinguished themselves, but will leave this to division and brigade commanders, whose reports will be forwarded as soon as received.

Of the division commanders, however, Generals Smith, McClernand, and Wallace, I must do the justice to say that all of them were with their commands in the midst of danger, and were always ready to execute all orders, no matter what the exposure to themselves.

At the hour the attack was made on General McClernand's command I was absent, having received a note
from Flag-Officer Foote, requesting me to go and see
him, he being unable to call on me in consequence of a
wound received the day before. — *Gen. Grant, Official
Report.*

THE REBEL ATTACK.

Again the Rebels move towards the right flank of our
new line, and again the battle rages. Cruft's brigade,
of Lewis Wallace's division, is ordered down upon this
flanking column at a run. Thus checked, the enemy
might have been driven back and pursued, had it not
been for a new and unexpected foe, or rather the fear of
one, swarming from their intrenchments, and passing
the rifle-pits like a surge of the sea. Buckner's force
came out to attack the left flank and crotchet of our
new line. As soon as they were discovered, Wallace
strengthened the flank thus threatened, and two of
Taylor's guns, coming rapidly into action, dealt grape
and canister on his advance. Buckner was easily repulsed, for his attack was very feebly delivered, and
his troops behaved in the most cowardly manner. When,
at eleven o'clock, Pillow rode over to Buckner's position,
he found them huddled together under cover, from
which it was only after a good deal of artillery firing
that their general could persuade them to emerge. In
speaking of the repulse, Buckner says his attacking
regiments " withdrew without panic, but in some confusion, to the trenches."

But the moral effect of Buckner's attack was not without its value. Beset on all sides, Pillow thundering
upon our new front, the cavalry threatening our rear,
Johnson's well extended upon our right, checked but
not driven off by Cruft, our men were somewhat demoralized by Buckner's demonstration; many became dis-
heartened; the fugitives from the front became a crowd.
A mounted officer galloped down the road, shouting,

"We are cut to pieces." The ammunition had given out. Our line, including Cruft, who had borne the brunt of the battle for some time, was again forced back. Logan, Lawler, and Ransom were wounded,—many field-officers and large numbers of subalterns killed. The crisis of the battle had indeed arrived, when General Wallace posted Colonel Thayer's (Third) brigade across the road, formed a reserve of three regiments, placed Wood's battery in position, and awaited the attack. The retiring regiments formed again in the rear, and were supplied with ammunition. The Rebel attack upon this new line was extremely vigorous. They had delayed for a while to plunder the dead and pick up what they could find in McClernand's camp, and Pillow sent back an aid to telegraph to Nashville that, "on the honor of a soldier," the day was theirs. The new attack, which he was about to make, was only the finishing stroke. Again he moved upon Thayer's brigade; but by their unflinching stand and deliberate fire, and especially by the pioneers of the First Nebraska, and the excellent handling of the artillery, he was repulsed. — *Gen. Coppee.*

SMITH'S ATTACK.

Wallace was already on his war-path, as we have just described, when General Smith organized his column of attack. Cook's brigade is posted on his left, and is designed to make a feint upon the work. Cavender's heavy guns are posted in rear to the right and left, having a cross-fire upon the intrenchments, and also playing upon the fort; but the attacking force — the forlorn hope — is Lanman's brigade, formed in close column of regiments, and composed of the Second Iowa, the Fifty-second Indiana (temporarily attached), the Twenty-fifth Indiana, the Seventh Iowa, and the Fourteenth Iowa.

Cook's feigned attack is already begun; Cavender's guns are thundering away. It is nearly sunset, when

Smith, hearing Wallace's guns far to the right, puts himself at the head of Lauman's brigade, and, climbing the steep hill-side, bursts upon the ridge on which the enemy has constructed his outer works. Before advancing, and when the force was just in readiness to move, Smith had ridden along the line, and in a few but emphatic words had told them the duty they were to perform. He said that he would lead them, and that the pits must be taken by the bayonet alone. Perhaps during the whole war, full as it is of brilliant actions, there is none more striking than this charge.

At the given signal, the lines are put in motion, Smith riding in advance, with the color-bearer alongside of him, his commanding figure, gray hair, and haughty contempt of danger, acting upon his men like the white plume of Navarre at Ivry. Not far has he moved before his front line is swept by the enemy's artillery with murderous effect. His men waver for a moment, but their general, sublime in his valor, reminds them, in caustic words, that while he, as an old *regular*, is in the line of his professional duty, this is what they have *volunteered* to do. With oaths and urgency, his hat waving upon the point of his sword, by the splendor of his example, he leads them on through this valley of death, up the slope, through the abatis, up to the intrenchment — and over. With a thousand shouts, they plant their standards on the captured works, and pour in volley after volley, before which the Rebels fly in precipitate terror. Battery after battery is brought forward, Stone's arriving first, and then a direct and enfilading fire is poured upon the flanks and faces of the work. Four hundred of Smith's gallant column have fallen, but the charge is decisive. Grant's tactics and Smith's splendid valor have won the day. — *Gen. Coppee.*

CHAPTER IV.

GENERAL McCLELLAN AND THE PENINSULA.— WEST VIRGINIA.

MEANWHILE, on the Atlantic side,—in front of Washington, as soldiers say—they did not mean to make the mistake of Bull Run again. General Scott, who was an old man, withdrew from the command of the army. General McClellan, comparatively a young man, had the credit of the one success so far attained by the National army. This was in West Virginia. He was an accomplished officer, and people hoped he would be the young Napoleon again. You shall see, as an engineer officer tells the story, how that success in Western Virginia came about. McClellan was appointed to command the army of the Potomac. He was not afraid to conquer by delay, if he could, as Washington and Fabius had done before him. So, from the 1st of August, 1861, all through the winter, and until the next May, he was engaged on the southern side of the Potomac in bringing the Northern army into discipline,—in arranging its several parts so that they should work as one machine, and in accustoming men and officers to their duties and to their relations with each other. As nine out of ten of these soldiers had never been soldiers before, — indeed, had scarcely dreamed of such a thing, — the time was none too much for the enterprise. At first the country behind the army was well enough satisfied, for the lesson of Bull Run had been a tremendous one. But people observed that the Western army did not seem to require such long preparation, and when spring came of the year 1862 they were impatient, as the army itself was indeed, for action. Still, from the army itself there came back the word that nothing could be done till the roads were dry. The mud of the Virginia road is indeed a protection against invaders for many months of the year, almost equal to any batteries.

At last, however, the army moved; not directly across the country, as in the march which resulted so badly at Bull Run, but by steamboats and barges down Chesapeake Bay, to land at Fort Monroe, opposite Norfolk, at the mouth of James River, and so to drive the Rebels from Yorktown, — where Cornwallis surrendered eighty years before, — and then to march up " the Peninsula," as it was called, 'to attack Richmond from the east.

The " Peninsula " means the peninsula between James River and York River. It was the country first settled in America. In one of Captain John Smith's letters, written from the infant colony at the old Jamestown, he says it is all of America that

there will ever be any need to settle, and proposes
to build a line of little forts across the isthmus, to
keep out the Indians forever from it. It was in the
swamps of the Chickahominy that he was lost
when the Indians took him prisoner, and where he
pretended that Pocahontas rescued him. She was
then a child, seven years old. In these same
swamps McClellan's army encamped, and here
were the "battles of the six days" fought. These
were battles in which he withdrew his army from
that side of Richmond, after many severe fights
before that city, and changed the base of his supplies from the York River to the James. That
means, that he received his supplies afterward by
James River.

General McClellan's own report of these movements makes a book much larger than this which
you are reading. Horace and Walter were very
much interested in it, and for a while they became
very strong "McClellanites." They said that no
novel had scenes so pathetic as his descriptions of
his disappointments when troops were withheld
that he hoped for, or ordered away from him to
the defence of Washington when he needed them
for attack. But other readers and other people
have not greatly praised him.

Here is the detail of the success in West Virginia,
by which he earned his command. You will see
that, if he had had his way, the victory would not
have been won.

And for nearly a week, we watched this road to the north, and those to the right and left, along the north face of the mountain, as ordered by McClellan; it being understood (as was stated by him) that *he* was to take care of the road *south*, over the mountain; by which road Garnett eventually escaped. We had daily skirmishing, — now and then a man killed, and some two to five wounded each day, on either side, — for the five or six days we lay there; from time to time routing out Garnett's camp with our artillery, which I had placed on the different near hills as they could reach him. This continued until about seven, on the morning of the 12th of July; when a sergeant of the command (a preacher at home), who had been on picket, (or scouting on his own account,) came rushing into Morris's head-quarters at Eliot's House, crying out, "They are gone, they are all gone! We can see no one in their camp." I mounted at once, and went forward to Garnett's camp, reconnoitring carefully as we came near, and entered the works, which I found were in a *continuous line* from the woods at the north to the mountain on the west. I there saw manifest signs of their leaving in great haste. Many articles of value, even, had been abandoned, and much that was useful. I sent back at once to request that General Morris would send forward two regiments, and a wagon-load or two of biscuit, for the pursuit. And *while waiting for these* in Garnett's camp, about nine A. M., I received from General Morris an order sent to him by General McClellan, informing him of the rout of Pegram, and *forbidding him to attack Garnett.*

As soon as the first regiment arrived, we started to go over the Laurel Mountain, and reach the south side, about three or four miles distant, between one and two P. M. Here General Morris joined us; and, after remaining an hour or so, he returned to camp to bring up

3

the rest of his men. But he directed me not to move from that position until he rejoined us, as he expected to some time that afternoon.

.   ..   .   .   .

About nine or ten P. M. General Morris joined us, and was quite indignant at Milroy's disobedience, saying he should not lead the march in the pursuit on the next day to punish him for this disobedience of his order; by which he had found everything — artillery, wagons, and all — were in the greatest confusion on this narrow mountain-path at midnight.

About ten P. M. orders came from McClellan, then at Beverly (in response to my report), for us to pursue with the earliest light, and stating that General Hill had orders sent him to intercept Garnett where he was expected to pass at the " Red House," near Oakland, some twenty-five or thirty miles to the northeast of us.

At daylight of the 13th, I started in command of the advance column, ... there being some eighteen hundred men in all. On reaching New Interest, at six to seven A. M., we began to find the camp equipage scattered along the road; first tent-poles, then tents, and then camp furniture. And soon we made sure that Garnett had turned off over a winding, hilly road, to his right, which passed over several mountain spurs to branches of the Cheat River, and led to the village of St. Georges, some fifteen to twenty miles to the northeast, on its right bank; and, later, we found, as we entered this mountain road, that the more valuable camp furniture was then being left behind, and among the first (probably as an example), the fine camp-stools, &c. (as marked) of General Garnett himself. We then came upon barricades of trees felled across the roads upon the mountain slopes, and at all defiles and steep " hill-sides" : some eighteen or twenty such obstructions, from eighty to three hundred yards in extent on the road, were encountered in the march of some eight to ten miles over two spurs of the mountains. The Rebels, fortunately for us, left their axes as they fled from our advance skirmishers, sometimes by twos and threes, struck into the trees woodman-like, sometimes by the boxful even; and thus we were soon enabled, with our Western woodsmen, to clear these roads even for our artillery: so that, when we eventually reached the Cheat River, near noon, our guns joined our advance regiment (Steedman's) within twenty to thirty minutes after.

On this route, about ten to eleven A. M., after passing the second mountain spur, we came upon the last camp of Garnett, deserted in such haste that the provisions were actually cooking upon the fires, and were soon devoured by our half-famished men. . . . .

About ten to eleven A. M. we came upon some wagons loaded with clothing, drab overcoats, &c.; with which I at once equipped our advance skirmishers, to deceive the enemy, as well as to protect ourselves from the violent storm which had been raging for several hours. . . . . We finally discovered the Rebel wagon-train resting in a field in the river-bottom, about five hundred yards in advance, and apparently entirely un-suspicious of our approach. I at once directed Colonel Steedman soon as he could learn that our guns were near his regiment, and Dumont well up behind them, that he should cross carefully: and, passing along by the road on the right bank, as it curved to our left, and was screened by the thick trees and bushes on the right of this road, he was to endeavor to pass to the right and rear of their wagons, without, as appeared possible, his being discovered.

These guns of Barnett were reported to be well up, and Dumont just behind them, ready to close in some fifteen or twenty minutes after; and the movement of Steedman commenced with every prospect of his getting to their rear unseen, and of capturing the whole train, as he moved with much boldness and discretion. But at this juncture a scoundrel straggler, who had crossed without permission, fired off his musket in the air, towards the wagon-train, as I could only suppose on

purpose to drive them forward, and avoid a fight. I
endeavored to gallop over him with my horse; but he
escaped down the steep bank into the river. But the
enemy's train, for this time, was saved; for we saw the
wagons move on immediately after, and then two lines
of infantry draw out to protect them; and they started
on the run for the next ford.

I delayed Steedman there until most of our troops
had closed up; and then we moved on as rapidly as
possible, crossing this second ford after covering with
our fire the adjacent hills to prevent a suspected ambus-
cade. And about two miles farther on, from a high
hill, we came in sight of their regiments, on a regular
run, and so near, that I ordered up the guns, directing
the *vis a tergo* of a few discharges to expedite their
movement, already characterized by one of our Western
captains as a " long dog-trot."

This force was still followed as rapidly as possible;
although two messages had already reached me from
General Morris, each with a contingency, fortunately,
" to stop the pursuit." I had the first message before I
came to the first ford: it was brought by young Pritch-
ard (son of lieutenant-colonel of Sixth Indiana), who
had been sent back with the first flag, captured, as it
was, under my horse's feet. This order required, that,
if I " was not sure of reaching the enemy within two or
three hours," I " must halt, and rest my men." The
second message, by Sergeant-Major Fletcher of the
Sixth Indiana, directed me to stop, and rest my men,
unless I " was immediately upon the enemy." A third,
by General Morris's aid (Lieut. Hines), reached me as
I was arranging for action at Corrick's Ford, and was,
to " stop at once, unless" I " was ready to strike";
to which my reply simply was, " Wait five minutes!"
General Morris afterwards told me, another (a fourth)
message had been sent, — a positive order to stop at
once (and, as I understood, by Whitelaw Reid, a Cincinnati reporter); but, as the General said, "This was
not delivered, as you were found to be fighting." These

orders were sent because General Morris had seen only the stragglers who " fell by the wayside "; while I had the " whalebone " with me.

Our march thus continued for about three miles from the second ford, till we came to another field of river-bottom land, and another ford. Here we saw that the Rebel troops had crossed, and that a part of their train was in the river, apparently balked; and we soon found that they were making dispositions to defend this train, from the steep, elevated ground (about sixty to eighty feet above the river) on the opposite side; the river being some hundred and twenty yards wide and three feet deep at this ford.

The advance regiments (Steedman's and next Dumont's), with Barnett's artillery, were soon arranged along the river-bank, behind a rail fence, partially covered by a slight screen of trees; and our fire first opened at them across the river upon their more advantageous position; and I could not force our gallant fellows, so unused to the danger, to take the slight cover of the bank of an old channel-way, a few rods in their rear, — a cover such as before the war closed, however, with just as much of bravery, our men, on other fields, had learned to appreciate, and to seize on all occasions. We received a strong musketry-fire in return; and soon their cannon opened on us, with the usual effect, or rather non-effect, from a much more elevated position, fortunately for us, for the most part; and we replied more effectively with our riflemen and artillery. As, however, in the course of some ten to fifteen minutes, I discovered a break in the hill on their left, which indicated an easier ascent than by the steep bank in our front, I sent orders to Dumont to cross at our right, and move up this valley-gorge to attack them. This was soon proved to be impossible, (as I found afterwards, this slope was strewn with dead cedars,) and the steepness was too great directly in front. I saw the men flat on the ground, endeavoring to crawl up the bank; and Colonel Milroy, who followed Dumont closely, rode up to me, and reported the hill to be entirely impracticable. I sent word by him to Dumont to go down the river with his regiment, and to hug the cover of the bank, on the side of the enemy: and that he would certainly find the road below them, opposite our left. The firing still continued for some fifteen to twenty minutes longer, between our main body and the Rebels on the hill; our men picking off their gunners whenever seen through the branches of the trees. And at length I saw the men of Dumont moving down as directed, until they passed the Rebel front at the foot of the bank, and turned inland, to the right of the enemy, bringing themselves at once in rear of their position; when the Rebels hastily retreated past the next ford, some five hundred yards distant, leaving their cannon, and their dead and wounded, behind them. And they were closely followed by Dumont's regiment skirmishing in their rear.

. . . . .

At about the time of this retreat of the enemy from his position on the hill, the leading regiment (the Sixth Indiana) of General Morris's main column, which had hurried up, hearing the firing, joined us, though too late to share in the action.

I crossed over immediately after Dumont's success, finding twenty-two heavily-loaded wagons stalled in the river, and a like number in the roadway made through an impracticable laurel-thicket on the other side, — all with their horses and harnesses attached. And ascending by the rear, to the plateau they had just occupied, we found their cannon and caisson, with the dead gunners (seven or eight men) lying around the piece, mostly shot in the head, some directly above the mouth, the only sight our men had being through the bush embrasures.

The position Garnett had selected here was one of the best natural defensive sites I ever saw. It was a cleared field of some two hundred yards square, with a steep bank sixty to eighty feet down to the river. The bank was covered with thick undergrowth, and fringed at the top with trees whose branches had been cut away to give firing views, — embrasures, in fact, for their guns. On their left, a steep ravine of a V cross-section, filled with dead cedars, as stated, protected them, as we had found, completely from assault; and on their right flank, as this plateau dropped to near the river level, they were covered by the broad laurel-thicket, impracticable to man or beast, even to the smaller animals, except by roadways cut through by the axe.

While examining the dead at this position, Major Gordon (just recently sergeant-major of the Ninth Indiana) came up to me, asking if I knew Garnett, saying an officer had just been killed at the next near ford, who had " stars on his shoulders." I at once accompanied him, crossing the ford; and, about twenty yards beyond, I found the Rebel general, R. S. Garnett, lying dead, and near him the body of a young lad, in the uniform of the Georgia troops (gray with black facings, like that of our Indiana regiments). No other signs of strife were near; and I learned that they had been killed from a clump of bushes on our side the river-bank, by the fire, at about the same time, of three of our advanced scouts. Recognizing Garnett at once, who, six years before, received the majority I had declined in the Ninth U. S. Infantry, I had Major Gordon remove and take care of his sword, watch, and purse (of Confederate money), reserving for our use, as much needed, a fine map of Virginia, and his field-glass.

.   .   .   .   .

The killed and wounded on our side were limited to five or six only, as they mostly fired upon us down hill. Of the Rebels we found about fifteen bodies, and some twenty to thirty wounded. There were also taken three flags, a fine rifled cannon, a military chest with bank money ready for signing, and — besides a large amount of valuable private property — the train to the number of forty-four heavily-loaded wagons, with their horses and harnesses even (some hundred and fifty to two hun-

dred in all) ; and, in the pursuit next day and the day
after, about fifteen more loaded wagons were captured,
or about sixty in all. They were loaded with clothing,
blankets, tents, &c., and at an estimated value, as far
as we could judge, of at least some two hundred and
fifty thousand dollars. The quartermaster at the Graf-
ton depot afterwards told me, that there had reached
that station, within the next two or three weeks (and
by difficult or mountain roads), an amount of property
worth at least a hundred thousand dollars. And this
was after weeks of plundering by the occupants of the
adjacent farms, and after nearly all the horses and large
amounts of other property, as I was told, had been run
across the Ohio River, by these retiring troops, whose
three months of service expired, for the most part,
within one or two weeks after this action, which ended
the first campaign in West Virginia.

The report of the action was written and sent to
General McClellan from Corrick's House, on the morn-
ing of the 14th, and received by him at Huttonsville,
Va., about thirty-five miles southeast, at "eleven
P. M."; when he at once telegraphed this success to
Washington in glowing colors.

.   .   .   .   .

Upon the evening of the 16th, Major Marcy, chief of
staff of General McClellan, came to Eliot's (*en route* to
Washington) with McClellan's reports, and the flags
from Philippi, and requiring also those just captured,
which, being still with the regiments in camp, he would
not wait for, but ordered to be "sent express to Washington."

Major Marcy had with him at this time four flags that
had been captured at Philippi, which, with considerable
difficulty and management, I had recovered from the
colonels of the regiments who had them, and sent to
General McClellan some time previously. One of them,
I recollect, was an elegant green silk cavalry flag, or
guidon, with gold bullion tassels and fringe, that had
within the week been presented to the Highland Guards

by the ladies of Highland County; when the captain,
as we were told, had promised "to defend that flag
with the last drop of his blood," &c. I presume, however, he forgot his promise, as no one was killed in this
rout. As this banner had on it in gold letters the
motto, "GOD DEFEND THE RIGHT," I had the pleasure,
soon after, of sending word to the ladies of Highland
County "that God had heard and answered their
prayer."

Of the three flags taken at Corrick's Ford, one was a
large flag of Colonel Taliaferro's Twenty-third Virginia
Regiment; another was a silk flag of Colonel Ramsey's
Georgia Regiment; and the third, taken just after the
action, was an elegant white silk color, with silver tassels and fringe, and over the arms of Georgia the motto,
"COTTON IS KING," surmounting the temple. This beautiful and unique banner has proved too much for the
honesty of some of the people about the White House
or the War Department; for in the winter of 1863 and
1864, when I found most of these other flags in the War-
Office, this white banner had disappeared, as had also
the green silk cavalry guidon taken at Philippi.

Major Marcy proceeded to Washington, reaching
there a day or two before the defeat of Bull Run, and
at a most fortunate moment, as it proved, for himself
and his chief; for though it is certain, I believe, that
neither McClellan nor any of his staff (not on detached
service) had been within the range of a hostile cannon,
if they had even heard its sound, in all these actions
and skirmishes, yet within that week McClellan's chief
of staff, Major Marcy, was made Inspector-General, and
McClellan himself the Major-General and *active chief of
our whole army.* — *Gen. H. W. Benham.*

When McClellan advanced up the Peninsula,
the first resistance was made at Yorktown, the
same place which Lord Cornwallis held.

THE REBEL ARMY AT YORKTOWN.

It is clear that the forces stationed here had more than enough to eat, — many luxuries, — and were provided for in all that was necessary for mere camp comfort, such as it is. The whole place is strewed with heaps of oyster-shells, empty bottles, and cans of preserved fruit and vegetables, and, strange to say, there are an enormous number of sardine-boxes lying around. Privates and all seemed to have enjoyed the luxury of sardines in profusion. They had the excellent Richmond flour, from the Gallego mills, and Louisville packed beef and pork. Their exit was so sudden that their bread was left in their kneading-troughs, their pork over the fire, and biscuits half baked; but attempts were made, more or less generally, to spoil the food. Here and there a bottle of turpentine or some other vile fluid was emptied over the food they could not take. The tents are standing, but are slashed by knives.

The equipments and clothing of the rebel dead were of the most miserable kind. No attempt at uniformity of dress could be seen. Here and there some officer had a flannel stripe sewed to his pantaloons. Their buttons were simple bone and black fly buttons, such as are used for waistcoats. Here and there an officer had a gilt or United States artillery button. The men were dressed in common linsey butternut, and cotton suits, of the commonest and coarsest materials. They had few knapsacks, being generally supplied with a school-boy's satchel, sometimes of flimsy leather, but more commonly of cotton osnaburg, with here and there a rope to sling over the shoulders. Immense numbers of these were scattered about the woods, generally containing a few articles of clothing and a hoe-cake. — *Boston Journal Correspondence.*

TAKEN AND LEFT.

In the course of the guerilla fighting of course there were many very singular scenes. Captain Montgomery,

General Newton's Chief of Staff, and Lieutenant Baker, of General Franklin's staff, ventured too far into the woods and soon found themselves close up with the Hampton Legion. A question put by one of them revealed their character, and instantly a number of muskets were discharged at them. Lieutenant Baker escaped; Captain Montgomery's horse, pierced by half a dozen bullets, fell with his rider. The Captain feigned dead, but when the rebels commenced robbing his body, he was moved to come to life, and to give the Secessionists the benefit of some testamentary opinions, — as Mr. Choate said when he spoke in behalf of the remains of the Whig party. Just at that moment a shell from one of our batteries — which I can't undertake to say, as the officers of three companies have positively assured me that they did it — burst upon the party. Then the cry was raised, "Shoot the Yankee!" "Wherefore?" queried the Captain, "I didn't fire the shell." Then another shell, — whereupon the whole party skedaddled, Rebels in one direction, and the Captain in the other. — *Capt. Montgomery.*

CAPTURING A GUN.

There is an old chap in the Berdan Sharp-shooters, near Yorktown, known as "Old Seth." He is quite a character, and is a crack shot, one of the best in the regiment. His "instrument," as he terms it, is one of the heaviest telescopic rifles. The other night at roll-call, Old Seth *non est.* This was somewhat unusual, as the old chap was always up to time. A sergeant went out to hunt him up, being somewhat fearful that the old man had been hit. After perambulating around in the advance of the picket-line, he heard a low "hollo." "Who's there?" inquired the sergeant. "It's me," responded Seth, "and I've captured a Secesh gun." "Bring it in," said the sergeant. "Can't do it," exclaimed Seth.

It soon became apparent to the sergeant, that Old

Seth had the exact range of one of the enemy's heaviest guns, and they could not load it for fear of being picked off by him. Again the old man shouted. " Fetch me a couple of haversacks full of grub, as this is my gun, and the cussed varmints sha'n't fire it again while the scrimmage lasts." This was done, and the old patriot has kept good watch over that gun. In fact, it is a " captured gun." — *N. Y. Tribune.*

THE SIAMESE TWINS.

It is not often that two regiments, camping side by side for months, fall desperately in love. On the contrary, quite the reverse. But between the Ninth Massachusetts and the Sixty-second Pennsylvania there exists a very romantic attachment. The shanty of the Sixty-second is always open to the patronage of the Ninth, however scanty may be its supply. Does the Sixty-second find itself short of provisions on a march? Every haversack in the Ninth is opened. The men of the Ninth may pass through the camp of the Sixty-second at all times, but when one of the Three Hundred and Thirty-third New York, or any other man, comes up to the lines, he is ordered away.

" How will we take Richmond?" says one of the Sixty-second the other day. " Why, don't you know? The Sixty-two-th will fire, and the Ninth will charge!"— *Boston Journal.*

FRIENDLY PICKETING.

We were stationed on Warwick Creek, and the enemy's pickets were on the opposite side, about six hundred yards above. They kept up a constant fire during the afternoon, and the way some of their bullets whistled past our heads, if we poked them from behind a tree, inclined us to believe that they had good arms, and understood their use. Our orders were not to fire back, but, in violation of orders, a stray shot would once in a while find its way to the opposite side, to let them know that we still lived. This firing was kept up until dark when the tongue superseded the rifle. Now came the tug of war. Epithets were hurled spitefully across Warwick's turbid waters. The burden of their song appeared to be, "We will give you Bull Run." "What do you think of Corinth?" "You can have Yorktown if you can take it." "You are five to one, but you can't whip us"; — to which latter accusation one of our boys replied that it was so, as it took four Yankees to catch one of them for one of us to whip. They finally came to the conclusion, they could not out-talk us in that style, so they tried another tack, made all manner of inquiries, of how we lived, what State we were from, etc. They informed us that they were from South Carolina, and if we would not fire upon them in the morning, they would come out and talk with us.

Morning came, and with it a friendly conversation, at first under cover of trees; and as they gained confidence, both parties came out from cover. They told us that they lived principally upon fresh meat and "sponge," — soft bread; "shingles" — hard bread — had played out with them. Salt was not within their limits, it being twenty dollars a sack. Coffee could not be got, — it being a luxury not enjoyed by a soldier. We asked them if they had any "salt-junk." No, they had not got down to pickled mule yet. — *A Fall River Soldier.*

The "change of base" closed in the battle of Malvern Hill. Here is General McClellan's own account of it, and there follows the narrative of an artillery officer.

GEN. McCLELLAN'S ACCOUNT OF MALVERN HILL.

The position selected for resisting the further advance of the enemy, on the 1st of July, was with the left and centre of our lines resting on Malvern Hill, while the right curved backward through a wooded country toward a point below Haxall's, on James River. Malvern Hill is an elevated plateau, about a mile and a half by three fourths of a mile in area, well cleared of timber, and with several converging roads running over it. In front are numerous defensible ravines, and the ground slopes gradually to the north and east to the woodland, giving clear range for artillery in those directions. Toward the northwest the plateau falls off more abruptly into a ravine which extends to James River. From the position of the enemy his most obvious line of attack would be from the direction of Richmond and White-Oak Swamp, and would almost of necessity strike in upon the left wing. Here, therefore, the lines were strengthened by massing the troops and collecting the principal part of the artillery. Porter's corps held the left of the line, — Sykes's division on the left, Morrell's on the right, — with the artillery of his two divisions advantageously posted, and the artillery of the reserve so disposed on the high ground that a concentrated fire of some sixty guns could be brought to bear on any point in his front or left. Colonel Tyler had also, with great exertion, succeeded in getting two of his siege-guns in position on the highest part of the hill. Couch's division was placed on the right of Porter's; next came Kearney and Hooker; next Sedgwick and Richardson; next Smith and Slocum; then the remainder of Keyes's corps, extending by a backward curve nearly to the river. The Pennsylvania Reserve Corps was held in reserve, and stationed behind Porter's and Couch's position. One brigade of Porter's was thrown to the left, on the low ground, to protect that flank from any movement direct from the Richmond road. The line was very strong along the whole front of the upper plateau, but thence to the extreme right, the troops were more deployed. This formation was imperative, as an attack would probably be made upon our left. The right was rendered as secure as possible by slashing the timbers, and by barricading the roads. Commodore Rodgers, commanding the flotilla on James River, placed his gunboats so as to protect our flanks, and to command the approaches from Richmond. Between nine and ten A. M., the enemy commenced feeling along our whole left wing with his artillery and skirmishers, as far to the right as Hooker's division. About two o'clock a column of the enemy was observed moving toward our right, with the skirt of woods in front of Heintzelman's corps, but beyond the range of artillery. Arrangements were at once made to meet the anticipated attack in that quarter, but though the column was long, occupying more than two hours in passing, it disappeared, and was not again heard of. The presumption is, that it retired by the rear, and participated in the attack afterwards made on our left. About three P. M., a heavy fire of artillery opened on Kearney's left and Couch's division, speedily followed up by a brisk attack of infantry on Couch's front. The artillery was replied to with good effect by our own, and the infantry of Couch's division remained lying on the ground until the advancing column was within short musket range, when they sprang to their feet and poured in a deadly volley, which entirely broke the attacking force, and drove them in disorder back on their own ground. This advantage was followed up until we had advanced the right of our lines some seven or eight hundred yards, and rested upon a thick clump of trees, giving us a stronger position and a better fire. Shortly after four o'clock, the firing ceased along the whole front, but no disposition was evinced on the part of the enemy to withdraw from the field. Caldwell's brigade, having been detached from Richardson's division, was stationed upon Couch's right by General Porter, to whom he had been ordered to report. The whole line was surveyed by the General, and everything held in readiness to meet the coming attack. At six o'clock the enemy suddenly opened upon Couch and Porter with the whole strength of his artillery, and at once began pushing forward his column of attack, to carry the hill. Brigade after brigade formed under cover of the woods, started at a run to cross the open space, and charged our batteries; but the heavy fire of our guns, and the cool and steady volleys of our infantry, in every case, sent them reeling back to shelter, and covered the ground with their dead and wounded. In several instances our infantry withheld their fire until the attacking columns, which rushed through the storm of canister and shell from our artillery, had reached within a few yards of our lines. They then poured in a single volley, and dashed forward with the bayonet, capturing prisoners and colors, and driving the routed columns in confusion from the field. About seven o'clock, as fresh troops were accumulating in front of Porter and Couch, Meagher and Sickles were sent with their brigades, as soon as it was considered prudent to withdraw any portion of Sumner's and Heintzelman's troops, to reinforce that part of the line, and hold the positions. These brigades relieved such portions of Porter's corps and Couch's division as had expended their ammunition, and batteries from the reserve were pushed forward to replace those whose boxes were empty. Until dark the enemy persisted in his efforts to take the position so tenaciously defended; but despite his vast numbers, his repeated and desperate attacks were repulsed with fearful loss, and darkness ended the battle of Malvern Hill, though it was not until after nine o'clock that the artillery ceased its fire. During the whole, Commodore Rodgers added greatly to the discomfiture of the enemy by throwing shells among his reserves and advancing columns. As the army, in its movement from the Chickahominy to Harrison's Landing, was continually occupied in marching by night and fighting by day, its commanders found no opportunity for collecting data which would enable them to give exact returns of casualties in each engagement. — *McClellan's Official Report.*

THE BATTLE OF MALVERN HILL, AS SEEN BY AN OFFICER OF ARTILLERY.

The July sun shone clear and bright over Malvern Hill, — in the words of General McClellan's Report, "an elevated plateau about a mile and a half by three fourths of a mile in area." Through this plain ran the road from White-Oak Swamp and the Chickahominy region, along which the Rebel advance would come. To the left, much below the plateau on which the Malvern mansion-house stood, was the Richmond road, and to the left and rear, by Turkey Island Bend, the James River was laid like a bed of silver under the warm morning sun. Woods skirted the northern side of these fields, and about two thirds of a mile from this boundary our main line of defence was posted. Here the light field-batteries were stationed, with their infantry supports lying on the ground between their several positions. The earth swelled up to this line, then fell gently, northerly and through the open plain rising again toward the line of woods. But the woods were somewhat lower than the swell on which the guns stood, thus giving the vantage, so dear to the artillery, of a slightly plunging fire. This position was on the left of the Chickahominy road, and was held by Porter's Fifth Corps. On the right of the road the woods intruded more upon the position, and Couch held this ground, looking rather obliquely toward the main field, where the brunt of the Rebel attack afterwards was felt. Porter's troops had been severely punished at Gaines's Mills, and, smarting under this defeat, they were in a good fighting mood, though they had lost heavily.

We, that is Porter's corps, had bivouacked on the hill near Malvern House, and his arrangements were made after an early breakfast. McClellan with his staff and General Barnard rode over the field, and inspected the order of battle, as the corps commanders and engineers had laid it out. " Very well, Fitz," (i. e. Fitz

4

John Porter,) "there will be some axes up presently, and you may cut and slash wherever you please." This was said in the familiar, almost affectionate tone he used with the old West Point comrades whom he knew, and who trusted in him. McClellan never lost his hold upon the affections of the Army of the Potomac, an organization which grew up under his forming hand.

The General's counsel referred to some timber upon the left, which was soon " slashed " to prevent the enemy from turning the position by a flank attack.

It is hard to comprehend that, while you have a new world created on the moment within the lines of your own army, there is just beyond the skirmish lines and pickets another world, — your enemy's, — differing from and yet very like to your own. While we had been marching up the above-mentioned road and spreading our lines for miles on either side the main field, — much as if a lobster should spread his claws, then convert his tail into more claws spreading wider and wider, — the enemy had been busy within his territory. Between these two sections, busy with life and action, there is a debatable land, dark under the coming storm-cloud, quiet amid the forces hurrying on either side, heavy with the mists of death.

The skirmishers are men deployed at wide intervals, elastic feelers the army puts forth, to meet — it knows not what. The assailants push, the defenders recoil, until the main body receives them, and feels the force of the attacking party. About nine o'clock we felt the enemy's approach, and for five or six hours he was occupied in running his feelers along our lines, seeking the weakest points, and making his dispositions of attack. Meanwhile the gunboats from the James River and our heavy guns posted in the rear threw great shells over our heads. These shells sometimes accidentally damaged ourselves, but generally they burst in the woods where the Rebels were forming, or along the line of their march, and with excellent effect. The direction of the fire was controlled by the Signal Corps.

"What did you do, in all these six hours?" That is the hardest question of all. To be dressed for an evening party and to wait a half-hour for the guests, is not easy; to be ready and to wait five or six hours, when the guests bring Minies, and the chance of a bayonet-thrust, tries all the powers of a man. The line of privates were kept at their fixed posts; the company officers must be near by; the field-officers took a little wider range; general and staff officers strolled about at will, when not busy with the minor details of the plan of defence. Every bit of shade, a steep bank, closed and deserted houses, fence covers, single trees, — each became coignes of vantage where groups of waiting officers could while away the weary interval. Criticism of battles and generals flies fast and furious. Men sore with a week's fighting, or exhausted by night marches, are not gentle in their estimates of men or things. Every incident is made much of. General Hooker comes up the road with his staff. His reputation was then making, and a bright halo rightly followed the admirable field-officer. He had not then been tried and found wanting in the higher, the highest qualities of a general. His presence, so gallant and soldier-like, was just becoming known through the whole army. "That man, — don't you know Fighting Joe Hooker? Give him a division, — he knows what to do with it. I like to see a general who knows what he is about. I am sick of the indecision of a man who is always pulling at his whiskers." This allusion to the well-known habits of a worthy and most respectable Brigadier, never born to command, caused a general smile. The speaker never criticised another battle, for at sunset he was wrapped in his blanket.

What good fellows they were! — Griffin with the best "soldier's eye"[1] of them all, now in his first week with his brigade; Butterfield, the one volunteer who mastered the *technique* of field tactics, even better than the regulars did; — and the Colonels, Woodbury of Michi-

---

[1] Jomini thus characterizes the true soldierly intuition.

gan, a tight-made red-bearded Saxon at the head of a model regiment, and McQuaid, a solid New-Yorker. Cass, the Irish leader of a full Irish American regiment, had fallen at Gaines's; so had Gove, the thoroughly educated Massachusetts Colonel; so had Black, of Pennsylvania, with "Forward, Sixty-ninth! Ch——" on his lips. The awful word was never syllabled, and another led his regiment to the charge. And among the lesser officers, lesser in rank, but not in the importance of their service, for they wielded the mighty arm in this fight, were the Lieutenants commanding batteries of field artillery; — Ames, one of the model officers from West Point onward, Kingsbury, and Hazlitt, — afterwards killed at Antietam, now handling the old battery of instruction from West Point, which Griffin had vacated for his promotion to a brigade of infantry. Waterman of Rhode Island and Phillips of Massachusetts are among the volunteers. Porter was himself an old officer of artillery; he knew the latent power of that arm, and to-day would use it to turn back the last attack Lee and Jackson would have the strength to make.

There was a farm-house over on the left, and just in rear of the line of batteries. The ice-house had been opened, a pitcher and glasses had been seized from the household, abandoned by the housekeeper, and thirsty warriors cooled themselves with the best of all drinks, now made better and more precious by rarity. Even whiskey or the strength-giving brandy could not compete with ice-water here. Haversacks were opened, and he who found a sandwich or a cold mutton-chop was happy; he who had hard-tack made the most of it.

The day wears on; a breeze from the river tempers the fierce heat of the Southern sun. The sound of our great guns mingles with the scattering shots of skirmishers, and the stealthy bullets of Rebel sharp-shooters now beginning to take effect as the intervals lessened. By three o'clock the enemy had reached his positions, and his artillery opened a brisk fire upon our right and centre. Almost immediately, the woods bordering our main field swarmed with gray and butternut coats, and regiments stepped briskly forward, firing as they moved. Our batteries spoke quick and often. Shrapnell shells and case shot, fired with time fuses, burst and scattered their bullets just in front of the advancing ranks. Here and there a wide rent opens in the ordered files; it never closes, for another gap disorders the men who would try to fill the first. On the left, where our infantry are solid and not impeded by the artillery, they move obliquely forward, and add their galling fire to the crash of the shells from the guns.

I have said that the woods came forward nearer to Couch, and his position obliqued somewhat upon the main field of battle. His infantry were also bearing upon the Rebel lines now coming from the woods and seeking to push forward to the line of batteries on the swell of ground which was the main position to be held. Couch's men rushed gallantly forward, with shouts and cheers, and went beyond the intended lines of defence. The General, alert and brave, but cool, was not carried away by the enthusiasm. After the enemy were repulsed, riding up, and switching his horse with a little stick, he said eagerly, "That charge was all wrong! Captain, if I am killed, be sure to say that I never commanded that movement."

No troops can stand such a fire, and the Rebel brigades fell back under the cover of the woods after half an hour or more of courageous effort. They came out singly and picked up the wounded. On our side we had not as yet suffered much. This was a smart little action, but only the prelude to the battle of Malvern Hill.

Comrades now meet again and exchange experiences. The different arms congratulate each other for deeds, observed perhaps better from points a little distant from their actual occurrence. The jealousies of camp life melt away in the more cordial service of the field; the three arms become as one in supporting the whole body. The cavalry is the wings and eyes of the army.

The infantry is the back-bone, the enduring frame, the ready fingers which never fail in the constant service required of it. On its firm courage and patient endurance the final success of all troops and of every campaign must depend. But in certain contingencies, not many, but important, the artillery becomes the leading arm, and turns the fortune of the day. When a great force is to be concentrated on one point, either for attack or defence, then the power of guns and the skill of the men who handle them become conspicuous.

There was no better soldier on the field than Colonel Woodbury, commanding the Fourth Michigan regiment. We met in this pause. "Now, Colonel, you see what the artillery can do!" "Yes, I am glad to see an artillery fight. I never saw the power of field guns before." At sunset his body was borne to the rear, and two days after, his spirited little bay, christened "Baby," was sent to his widow, sorrowing in her home at the West.

The field was now comparatively quiet, but not comfortable. The gun-boats had ceased firing as the lines joined battle. The Rebels had crept up and gained little points of cover, from which sharp-shooters might give you that most miserable of deaths by one single assassinating bullet. An officer would hardly lift his field-glass when "whizz" would sing a minie, — "phtt" it would thud into the brown earth, and a tiny column of dust would mark the spot. This was not pleasant.

Lee's army, as well as McClellan's, had been roughly handled in the half-dozen engagements of the week. Magruder's and Huger's divisions were fresh, and they meant to carry Malvern Hill by fiery valor and the sheer force of their onset. All the afternoon their troops were massing, and our infantry sent us word that the rebels were bringing up batteries in the woods directly on our left front. We began to shell the woods. Soon their guns opened fire from the shelter of the trees bordering the main field, where the first attack had been repulsed. This artillery fire was intended to cover and assist Magruder's final attack. It was a pretty range, hardly twelve hundred yards. Our shells burst regularly, sometimes at the very muzzles of their guns, now marked by their own surging smoke.

The sun's rays were drooping, but at six o'clock there was time to win or lose a battle. The masses of men who had been gathering opposite the main field poured out from the woods. Regiments in line reached out until they became brigades, and the brigades multiplied into divisions. All in good order they came, colors flying, officers at their posts, men elbow to elbow, marching as if on parade, the front lines firing as they marched. But a thousand yards under your enemy's cool and regular fire makes a long course of attack. The steps are many, and at every step men drop. The brave are wounded, cowards faint. Our guns, which had been elevated at three degrees, were lowered to two and a half, to two, to one and a half, and were trained in the faces of the great mass drawing nearer and nearer. Shrapnell shells and case shot, bursting just in front of the coming lines, showered down leaden balls and fragments of broken iron. The ranks were rent open; men were winged and hipped; but worse than the individual losses was the disorder, physical and moral, the breaking and jangling of the nice machine built up with such careful skill. Regiments lost their regimen; colors were stricken down, officers killed or disabled, men bewildered, made hopeless, scattered under the merciless shells and the converging bullets of the infantry. It seemed like thrusting a fagot of icicles against white-heated iron. Your weapon fails, and you know not where or how. The force and organization, well enough when not overtasked, become naught before a vastly superior force.

The sight was dreadful; the sound was worse. The air was torn by explosions; not split, but rent and torn, by so many discharges, into jagged vibrations, — weird and terrible. All these sounds swelled into one mighty roar.

Toward sunset, the wind, which had purified the

afternoon, died away, and left the guns and musketry in their own atmosphere. The increasing volumes of smoke rolled over the field and hung over the tree-tops, murky, dark, and dismal. The cheery light of day was gone, and the evening was beclouded with this infernal darkness, lighted by blazing gunpowder. The attacking party did better under these conditions. They crept up under cover of the smoke until within one or two hundred yards of our guns. Then the batteries rattled out canister shot, deadly at close range, and drove them back. Gradually the enemy's fire slackened, as his gallant but ill-planned effort failed.

About twenty guns did the most of the work; but they were relieved in some cases two and three times, as the batteries expended their ammunition. Ames had light twelve-pounders, the very best field gun for a close encounter. Kingsbury's West Point battery was relieved by Weeden's of Rhode Island, commanded by Lieut. Waterman, and a section of Phillips's.

These few minutes of description cover some three hours of work. And, frightful as it seems in imagination, it was done much as other work is done. Resolute men worked together, performing simple acts under pressure of the most exciting circumstances. Mistakes were made, and righted. The result was a great achievement and heroic, but the deeds of individuals were simple, and done in a simple way. A soldier doing his duty thinks little of himself. Even the horses submit patiently to the inevitable. My own horse dragged wearily about. It did not seem strange, as his week's service had been hard, that he would not answer to the spur. But General Griffin, coming up, says, "Captain, your horse is wounded." Looking down, I saw that one hinder leg was soaked in blood. He went to the rear carrying the ball, which was afterward extracted.

One forgets the more horrible scenes, or perhaps rather ignores them. I could not have said whether the livid corpses were Caucasian or African, for I did

not look at them as I rode among them. And little
bits of action which were dramatic live in the memory,
though they might be trifles in historic importance. A
section of New York guns was on our right, beginning
Couch's left. Their position obliqued their direction
over the heads of some infantry. The fire looked high
as the shells swept across. "At what elevation are
you firing, Lieutenant?" "Five degrees!" "Five degrees, you might as well turn around and fire into the
James River." "'T is General Couch's order, sir!"
Just then the General rode along. "General, these
guns are wasting their ammunition away over the heads
of the enemy." "But the infantry sent word the shells
burst among our own ranks." "General, the infantry
always think themselves hurt when fired over, whether
we point high or low. If you want to hurt the enemy,
you must take the risk, and put the guns down where
they will tell." "Well, Captain, do as you think best
with them." And they were laid at a degree and a half.

My own command had been relieved, battery by
battery. I went up to the centre of the line and
found General Porter, to know if there were any further commands. Beside the corps commander was
General Hunt, chief of the artillery reserve of the Army
of the Potomac. At the rear there was a battery of
thirty-two-pounder howitzers, big light pieces, which
throw canister by the hatful. Porter wanted them
brought up, but Hunt was doubtful whether the can-
noneers were experienced enough to be trusted in the
thick of that fight. They were talking quietly, even
in the din around them. Porter said very earnestly,
"Why, Hunt, the sound of those guns will fill their
ears with terror." It was so unconscious, and so melo-
dramatic, that the humor of the scene has always lingered in my mind.

It was late in the evening. I turned down the road
toward Malvern House, in the rear. There were steep
banks on either side as the way descended. Bang!
bang! a battery on my left was firing a whole round.

I shivered with horror; and almost with the thought
my horse sprang up the bank and bounded into the
space between guns and limbers.   "Who is in command here?"   A sergeant gave the well-known name
of a crack officer in the horse artillery, and he came up,
almost at the moment.   "Captain, you are firing right
through our own line."   "D—n it, I can't help it.   I
was ordered to fire when I was fired on, and the bullets came in here; I could not see."   "Cease firing!"
No serious harm came from it.   A second line of guns
had been posted with orders to open on friend and foe
alike if our first line had given way.

After nine o'clock, the uproar ceased.   I found my
own mess, and ate a rude but welcome supper.   We
lay down on a tarpaulin gun-cover, but not to sleep;
for the adjutant-general soon found his way, by the light
of a lantern, to this uneasy couch.   He brought orders
to move, and before midnight and for all night we were
marching to Harrison's Landing.

We brought off our own wounded and dead.   In the
early morning, Averill held the line our batteries had
defended so well, and then quietly left the field of
Malvern Hill, thickly strewn with the Rebel dead. —
Capt. Weeden, First R. I. Artillery.

During the same summer Banks was in command
in the valley of the Shenandoah.   Here is a story
of that campaign : —

FIGHT AT WINCHESTER.

Though our men were exhausted, when we came by
General Banks, and were ordered by him to the double-
quick, the whole regiment seemed electrified and went
on with a will for the fight.   We passed the Twenty-
seventh Maryland drawn up in line of battle, and things
looked serious.   Companies A and C were thrown out
as skirmishers, and the rest of the battalion acted as

supports to the line of skirmishers and to the batteries. As we came into the street a battery at the other end opened upon us with shells, that came raking along furiously in perfect range. We stove in the street fences and pushed along under some shelter. On we passed through people's gardens, and gave the natives some new notions on the subject of demolishing fences. Bert's regular battery and Cotheau's New York soon got into position, and we drove the enemy like sheep a mile or two out of the town, — not without some compliments from their guns. The firing was good on both sides. At one time we noticed some Rebel cavalry pouring round on our flank ; a piece was sent out to treat their case, and the first shell struck in the very centre of them, — it would have hit the bull's-eye. — *A member of the 2d Mass.*

HOW GENERAL BANKS'S ARMY WAS SAVED.

You have probably heard by this time of the three days' fighting from Strasburg and Front Royal to Martinsburg. Our company and Company B were ordered to Front Royal, in the mountains, twelve miles from Strasburg, last Friday, and when we got within two miles of our destination we heard cannonading. The Major ordered the baggage to stop, and our two companies dashed on, and found several companies of our infantry and two pieces of artillery engaged with several thousand of the enemy. Just as we arrived on the field, Colonel Parem, who had command of our forces, rode up to me and ordered me to take one man and the two fastest horses in the company and ride for dear life to General Banks's head-quarters in Strasburg for reinforcements. The direct road to Strasburg was occupied by the enemy, so I was obliged to ride round by another, seventeen miles. I rode the seventeen miles in fifty-five minutes. General Banks did n't seem to think it very serious, but ordered one regiment of infantry and two pieces of artillery off. I asked General

Banks for a fresh horse to rejoin my company, and he
gave me the best horse I ever rode, and I started back.
I came out on the Front Royal turnpike, about two miles
this side of where I left our men. Saw two men standing in the road, and their horses standing by the fence.
I supposed they were our pickets. They did n't halt me,
so I asked them if they were pickets. They said no.
Says I, "Who are you?" "We are part of General
Jackson's staff." I supposed that they were only joking.
I laughed and asked them where Jackson was. They
said he was in the advance. I left them and rode to
Front Royal, till I overtook a soldier, and asked him
what regiment he belonged to. He said he belonged to
the Eighth Louisiana. I asked how large a force they
had, and the reply was "twenty thousand." I then
turned back and drew my revolver, expecting a desperate fight or a Southern jail; but the officers in the
road didn't stop me, and I was lucky enough not to
meet any of their pickets. But if it was not a narrow
escape, then I don't know what is. When I got out of
the enemy's lines I rode as fast as the horse could carry
me to General Banks, and reported what I had seen
and heard. He said I had saved the army. In less
than an hour the whole army was in motion towards
Winchester. — *C. H. Greenleaf, 5th N. Y. Cav.*

CHAPTER V.

ANTIETAM.

AFTER the six days' change of base, General McClellan made Harrison's Landing his base of supplies; — but he afterwards occupied Malvern Hill again, and on the 5th of August wrote from that place to Washington, that with reinforcements he could march his army to Richmond in five days.

To which General Halleck, in command at Washington, replied by telegraph, " I have no reinforcements to send you," and immediately afterwards bade him send cavalry and artillery up to the Potomac at Acquia Creek again, saying, " It is reported that Jackson is moving North with a very large force." He had been already ordered to withdraw the whole army to Acquia Creek (below Washington), and had, on the 4th of August, protested against this change.

The country and the President took the strategic " change of base " as an acknowledgment of defeat, and as in fact defeat. This General McClellan never acknowledged. General Pope, who had been summoned from the West, was directed to defend Washington; and as fast as the army could be hurried back from the James River, which was now open to the Union steamboats, it was placed under his command. Meanwhile, the Rebel army again threatened Washington. The forts erected by McClellan on the southern side of the Potomac were its protection. But beyond them, — with his army but just back from the James River, — on almost the same ground as the battle of the year before, General Pope fought Generals Stonewall Jackson and Longstreet, and was badly beaten. Meanwhile General Lee, who probably never intended to attack that strong line of forts, had taken the larger part of his army northward, so as to march around them, and to attack the Northern Capitol, or the Northern States, as he might find best, by crossing the Potomac, and moving thence either on Washington or on Philadelphia.

A second defeat at Bull Run discouraged the country, and perhaps the army, as much as that of a year before. Rightly or wrongly, the army and the country conceived a great contempt for General Pope, who had lost this battle. It was supposed — as it proved very unjustly — that General Fitz John Porter, one of the ablest officers in the army, had refused his best assistance in the battle. President Lincoln, with the magnanimity which always showed itself in his character, was willing to acknowledge that he had made a mistake, — and placed McClellan again at the head of the army, which now had to defend Washington on the west. Under him the battle of Antietam was fought on the 17th of September.

OPENING OF THE BATTLE.

The night of the 16th was passed by both armies with the expectation of a heavy battle in the morning. Few officers found relief from anxiety, for it was believed by many that it might be a turning-point in the war. Only the commander-in-chief of the National army seems to have had a lofty faith that all would be well. He retired to his room at a little past ten o'clock, and did not leave it until eight o'clock the next morning, when the surrounding hills had been echoing the sounds of battle which had been raging within a mile of head-quarters for three hours. Then, with some of his aids, he walked to a beautiful grove on the brow of a declivity near Pry's, overlooking the Antietam, and watched the battle on the right for about two hours, when he mounted his horse and rode away to Porter's division, on the right, where he was greeted, as usual, by the hearty cheers of his admiring soldiers.

The contest was opened at dawn by Hooker, with about eighteen thousand men. He made a vigorous attack on the Confederate left, commanded by Jackson. Doubleday was on his right, Meade on his left, and Ricketts in his centre. His first object was to push the Confederates back through a line of woods, and seize the Hagerstown road and the woods beyond it in the vicinity of the Dunker church, where Jackson's line lay. The contest was obstinate and severe. The National batteries on the east side of the Antietam poured an enfilading fire on Jackson that galled him very much, and it was not long before the Confederates were driven with heavy loss beyond the first line of woods, and across an open field, which was covered thickly in the morning with standing corn.

Hooker now advanced his centre under Meade, to seize the Hagerstown road and the woods beyond. They were met by a murderous fire from Jackson, who had just been reinforced by Hood's refreshed troops, and had brought up his reserves. These issued in great numbers from the woods, and fell heavily upon Meade in the cornfield. Hooker called upon Doubleday for aid, and a brigade under the gallant General Hartsuff was instantly forwarded at the double-quick, and passed across the cornfield in the face of a terrible storm of shot and shell. It fought desperately for half an hour unsupported, when its leader fell severely wounded. In the meanwhile, Mansfield's corps had been ordered up to the support of Hooker, and while the divisions of Williams and Greene of that corps were deploying, their brave commander was mortally wounded.[1]

This brave and good man was killed, almost immediately after the battle began, and General Williams took command of the Twelfth Corps. For about two hours the battle raged with varied success. But the Union troops gradually drove the left wing of their enemy back into a line of woods. At about nine o'clock General Sedgwick's division arrived, as a reinforcement. It passed diagonally to the front across an open space before General Williams's first division, and this division was withdrawn for a time. Entering the woods and driving the enemy before them, the first line was met in the woods by heavy musketry and a fire of shell. Meanwhile a stray column of the

---

[1] I take this concise statement of the opening of the battle from Mr. Lossing's admirable book, because he had the advantage, which I have not had, of personal acquaintance with the scene. — E. E. H.

enemy had crowded back General Greene, so that their left flank was exposed. General Howard faced the third line to the rear preparatory to a change of front to meet this advancing column. But his men, exposed, both in front and on the left, to a destructive fire which they could not return, gave way, and were soon followed by the first and second lines.

General Gorman's brigade, however, and one regiment of General Dana's, soon rallied, and checked the enemy's advance on the right. On General Gorman's left the second and third lines formed, and met the advance of the enemy with a heavy fire. This fire and the Union batteries on the left, which were able to open as soon as the infantry withdrew, threw the enemy back into the woods again. As these movements went on, Generals Sedgwick and Dana and Hooker were all wounded and were taken from the field. General Howard took General Sedgwick's command, and General Meade took General Hooker's.

General McClellan's report of the continuation of the battle is in these words: —

FRENCH AND RICHARDSON.

While the conflict was so obstinately raging on the right, General French was pushing his division against the enemy still further to the left. This division crossed the Antietam at the same ford as General Sedgwick, and immediately in his rear. Passing the stream in three columns, the division marched about a mile from the ford, — then, facing to the left, moved in three lines towards the enemy. . . . The division was first assailed by a fire of artillery, but steadily advanced, driving in the enemy's skirmishers, and encountered the infantry in some force at the group of houses near Roulette's farm. General Weber's brigade gradually advanced with an unwavering front, and drove the enemy from their position about the houses.

While General Weber was hotly engaged with the first line of the enemy, General French received orders to push on with renewed vigor to make a diversion in favor of the attack on the right. Leaving the new troops, who had been thrown into some confusion from their march through cornfields, over fences, &c., to form as a reserve, he ordered the brigade of General Kimball to the front, passing to the left of General Weber. The enemy were pressed back to near the crest of the hill, where he was encountered in greater strength, posted in a sunken road, forming a natural rifle-pit, running in a northwesterly direction. In a cornfield in rear of this road were also strong bodies of the enemy. As the line reached the crest of this hill, a galling fire was opened upon it from the sunken road and cornfield. Here a terrific fire of musketry burst from both lines, and the battle raged along the whole line with great slaughter.

The enemy attempted to turn the left of the line, but were met by the Seventh Virginia and One Hundred Thirty-second Pennsylvania Volunteers and repulsed. Foiled in this, the enemy made a determined assault on the front, but were met by a charge from our lines, which drove them back with some loss, leaving in our hands some three hundred prisoners and several stand of colors. The enemy, having been repulsed by the terrible execution of the batteries and the musketry fire on the extreme right, now attempted to assist the attack on General French's division by assailing him on his right, and endeavoring to turn his flank; but this attack was met and checked by the Fourteenth Indiana and Eighth Ohio Volunteers, and by canister from Captain

Tompkins's battery, First Rhode Island Artillery. Having been under an almost continuous fire for nearly four hours, and their ammunition being nearly exhausted, this division now took position immediately below the crest of the heights on which they had so gallantly fought, the enemy making no attempt to regain their lost ground.

On the left of General French, General Richardson's division was hotly engaged. Having crossed the Antietam about 9.30 A. M., at the ford crossed by the other divisions of Sumner's corps, it moved on a line nearly parallel to the Antietam, and formed in a ravine behind the high grounds overlooking Roulette's house; the Second (Irish) Brigade, commanded by General Meagher, on the right, the Third Brigade, commanded by General Caldwell, on his left, and the brigade commanded by Colonel Brooks, Fifty-third Pennsylvania Volunteers, in support. As the division moved forward to take its position on the field, the enemy directed a fire of artillery against it, but, owing to the irregularities of the ground, did but little damage.

Meagher's brigade, advancing steadily, soon became engaged with the enemy posted to the left and in front of Roulette's house. It continued to advance under a heavy fire nearly to the crest of the hill overlooking Piper's house, the enemy being posted in a continuation of the sunken road, and cornfield, before referred to. Here the brave Irish brigade opened upon the enemy a terrific musketry fire. All of General Sumner's corps was now engaged, General Sedgwick's on the right, General French in the centre, and General Richardson on the left. The Irish brigade sustained its well-earned reputation. After suffering terribly in officers and men, and strewing the ground with their enemies as they drove them back, their ammunition nearly expended, and their commander, General Meagher, disabled by the fall of his horse, shot under him, this brigade was ordered to give place to General Caldwell's brigade, which advanced to a short distance in its rear. The lines were passed by the Irish brigade, breaking by company to the rear, and General Caldwell's, by company to the front, as steadily as on drill. Colonel Brooks's brigade now became the second line.

The ground over which General Richardson's and French's divisions were fighting was very irregular, intersected by numerous ravines, hills covered with growing corn, enclosed by stone walls, behind which the enemy could advance unobserved upon any exposed point of our lines. Taking advantage of this, the enemy attempted to gain the right of Richardson's position in a cornfield, near Roulette's House, where the division had become separated from that of General French. A change of front by the Fifty-Second New York and Second Delaware Volunteers, of Colonel Brooks's brigade, under Colonel Frank, and the attack made by the Fifty-third Pennsylvania Volunteers, sent further to the right by Colonel Brooks to close this gap in the line, and the movement of the One Hundred Thirty-second Pennsylvania and Seventh Virginia Volunteers, of General French's division, before referred to, drove the enemy from the cornfield, and restored the line.

The brigade of General Caldwell, with determined gallantry, pushed the enemy back opposite the left and centre of this division, but sheltered in the sunken road they still held our forces on the right of Caldwell in check. Colonel Barlow, commanding the Sixty-first and Sixty-fourth New York regiments, of Caldwell's brigade, seeing a favorable opportunity, advanced these regiments on the left, taking the line on the sunken road in flank, and compelled them to surrender, capturing over three hundred prisoners and three stand of colors.

The whole of the brigade, with the Fifty-seventh and Sixty-sixth New York regiments of Colonel Brooks's brigade, who had moved these regiments into the first line, now advanced with gallantry, driving the enemy before them in confusion into the cornfield beyond the sunken road. The left of the division was now well advanced, when the enemy, concealed by an intervening ridge, endeavored to turn its left and rear. Colonel Cross, Fifth New Hampshire, by a change of front to the left and rear, brought his regiment facing the advancing line. Here a spirited contest arose to gain a commanding height, — the two opposing forces moving parallel to each other, giving and receiving fire. The Fifth, gaining the advantage, faced to the right and delivered its volley. The enemy staggered, but rallied and advanced desperately at a charge. Being reinforced by the Eighty-first Pennsylvania regiment, these regiments met the advance by a counter charge. The enemy fled, leaving many killed, wounded, and prisoners, and the colors of the Fourth North Carolina in our hands. — *Gen. McClellan's Official Report.*

GREENE'S CHARGE.

At last their line began to waver, and General Greene shouted, "Charge!" With a yell of triumph we started, with levelled bayonets; and, terror-stricken, the Rebels fled. Like hounds after the frightened deer, we pursued them fully three fourths of a mile, killing, wounding, and taking prisoners almost every rod. Their colors fell: a private soldier leaped forward, and tore them from the staff.

Across the fields we pursued the foe, who again took shelter in a heavy piece of timber, flanked by their artillery. A battery of twelve-pounder howitzers came to our support, and most efficient service it rendered. We formed in two lines in rear of the battery, and lay behind a low ridge, sufficiently high to protect from a direct shot, but which offered no shelter from the fragments of shells bursting near and over us; these were continually striking amongst us, often grazing a cap or an arm, but doing no particular harm. The howitzers were doing splendidly, when suddenly we heard, "But eight rounds left!" Twenty more rounds would silence the Rebel battery, but we had them not. Soon the

Rebel fire was more rapid, and a yell in the distance denoted an advance of their infantry. Shall we retreat? No! we will hold our ground or die! On they come, yelling defiantly: 't is Hill's division, second to none but Jackson's. We look anxiously for another battery. It comes! it comes! · We are safe! — *Maj. Wood, 7th Ohio.*

THOUGHT FOR THE WOUNDED.

As we neared the grove, — it was at the corner of the field, — a regiment of Rebels, who had lain concealed among the tall corn, arose and poured upon us the most withering volley we had ever felt. Another and another followed, and a continuous rattle rent the air. We could not stop to reply, — we could but hurry on. The slaughter was fearful; I never saw men fall so fast; I was obliged to step over them at every step. . . . . .

We reached the grove, and drove the Rebels from it. They retired obliquely into the corn-field, keeping up a retreating fire. I observed, not thirty yards from me, two stout Rebels assisting a wounded comrade from the field, supporting his fainting form between them. I could have killed one of them; their backs were presented toward me very temptingly. I was going to fire, but at that moment I heard the wounded man groan. I hesitated. Could I shoot one of the men who were bearing him away, and allow him again to fall to the earth? I could not. I sought another mark; and seeing a Rebel in the act of loading his gun, just at the edge of the cornfield, I fired at him. — *Serg. Hill, 8th Penn. Reserves.*

MAINE AT ANTIETAM.

The Maine Seventh was ordered to drive the enemy from a strong position about nine hundred yards in front of the line of battle. Every private in the ranks knew that a brigade of the enemy was massed there with a battery of artillery, and that an awful blunder had been made, but obedience is the first duty of a soldier. The order was given to the regiment to advance. On they went across the field under a shower of bullets, halting twice to return the fire of the enemy. After halting the second time to deliver their fire, the regiment rushed forward with such a cheer as only the "Seventh" can give, driving the enemy before them.

The Rebels now took refuge behind a stone wall and opened a galling fire of musketry. At this point the regiment had arrived within range of one of our batteries, which had been playing upon the enemy, and, not aware of the advance, our forces continued firing. The Rebels opened their battery with grape and canister. The regiment seemed now devoted to destruction, yet the men delivered their fire with steadiness and terrible effect as they moved by the left flank to gain the cover of an orchard. Thence through a cornfield, by a circuitous route, they returned to their old position in line of battle. Not a man had straggled, all that the bullets had spared were there; but how thinned the ranks! Only sixty-five men now constitute the gallant "Seventh Maine." — *Portland Press.*

BURNSIDE'S ATTACK ON THE LEFT.

The Antietam in front of Burnside was deep, not fordable, flowing in the bottom of a charming valley, and overshadowed by trees. There was a solid stone bridge over it, with three arches rising picturesquely in the centre, with stone parapets on the sides, the parapets spreading at both ends of the structure. One would almost imagine that it was an old Italian bridge, transported to our modern building land. The side of the valley held by the Rebel troops rises sharply, not densely wooded, but covered by large trees thickly placed as in an old English park. Along the top of this ridge ran a solid stone wall, thicker and of heavier stones than any we saw in the neighborhood. Where the wall ended rifle-pits had been dug. Behind the massive trunks, and in the branches of the old trees, behind this wall, and in the pits, were crowded the sharp-shooters of the Rebels. The ascent from the bridge out of the valley on the enemy's side was too steep for a straight road up the ridge. If ever a bridge could be defended, that should have been; the only disadvantage the Rebels were under was that they could not sweep it with artillery.

Our left had vainly attempted to cross the bridge; twice had they been repulsed. On the right our troops were hard pressed; much of the ground gained in the morning had been lost; Hooker had been wounded, Sumner's corps routed, Mansfield killed, and his corps beaten back. Then McClellan ordered Burnside to take the bridge, and hold it any cost. Burnside sent some troops further down the river where it was fordable. He called up one of his old brigades that had been with him in North Carolina, saying, if any brigade could take the bridge, that one would. It was composed of the Fifty-first New York, Fifty-first Pennsylvania, Twenty-first Massachusetts, and a Rhode Island regiment; on their colors were inscribed "Roanoke," "Newbern," two of our most glorious victories. With these veteran troops was the Thirty-fifth Massachusetts, a new regiment that had left home only a month before, but who nobly did their part. Down went the Fifty-first Pennsylvania in column in the advance, at the run, shouting and crowding and firing as they hurried across the bridge, bringing down the Rebels from the trees, suffering themselves, but never halting. They crossed and deployed on the other side. Next came the Thirty-fifth Massachusetts over the bridge, up the valley, then forming in line of battle on the top of the small hill commanding the stream. The enemy were drawn up before them, quite a distance off, on the top of the next hill. Every inch of ground between was commanded by the Rebel fire; but our brave fellows charged on up this hill, driving the foe before them. Nothing daunted, they followed up their charge, and drove the enemy from this hill and took this most commanding position. There they halted, close to Sharpsburg, almost in the rear of the Rebels. Some of our troops even penetrated to Sharpsburg itself, and were taken prisoners. A short distance farther would have cut off the enemy's direct retreat to the Potomac. Rebel troops were seen hurrying on the road to the river. Our men were now fired upon by artillery, and attacked by fresh bodies of infantry coming up, as the enemy say in their account, from Harper's Ferry. Our brave fellows, however, stood their ground waiting for reinforcements, which .Burnside called for. But McClellan, unfortunately, dared not throw in his reserves; his object had probably been gained in making a diversion from the hard contested field on our right. Our gallant fellows had to stand there unsupported, until their ammunition gave out. They fired their sixty rounds of ammunition, collecting all they could from their dead and wounded comrades, and then began to retreat. Benjamin's battery of artillery was also short of ammunition, and could not support them. Our brave boys only retreated to the next hill, not to the hill above the Antietam, and there lay on their arms during the night, and there they stayed during the next day, expecting the order to advance. — *C. W. Loring, in the Continental Magazine.*

CHAPTER VI.

PITTSBURG LANDING.

"TOM," said Uncle Fritz, "you are an old-fashioned sort of boy. Do you remember anything about Washington's success at the battle of Trenton?"

"Why, yes," said Tom; — "it says that they had driven him across the Delaware, and had stretched their army all over New Jersey; and that Washington said, 'This is the time to clip their wings, now they are so spread.' So he turned round and took all the Hessians at Trenton, — and a few days after cut in on them at Princeton. And they say he might have taken another set at Brunswick, but his council of war would not let him. I hate councils of war."

"They are pretty much out of fashion now," said Uncle Fritz. "Just that sort of thing, which Washington did there, is what the Southern Generals Johnston and Beauregard tried to do with Grant's army on the Tennessee. If you will look on the map, you will see that, at the western part of its course, the Tennessee River flows nearly north.

When General Grant took command of the National army, on the 17th of March, 1862, he found it in five 'divisions,'[1] ranged along this river. General Sherman and General Hurlbut, with about half the army, were at Pittsburg Landing, on the west side of the river. They commanded two 'divisions,' and were farthest south, which is to say nearest the enemy. General Lew Wallace, with another division, was on the same side of the river, about five miles farther north. General McClernand and General Charles F. Smith, with two more divisions, making about half the army, were at Savanna, or in transports near it, — still farther north. As soon as Grant took command, he gave orders to concentrate this force. On the other side, as soon as Johnston felt strong enough, he meant to attack its advance, under Hurlbut and Sherman, before it was strengthened, and this he did in the beginning of April. It was precisely what Washington did, with much smaller forces, at Trenton, but that the English army there was at posts separated by land, and here a navigable river gave Grant's divisions easy methods of movement. The Rebel army had been concentrated around Corinth, which is in the northern part of Mississippi. There was some skirmishing between outposts as early as the 2d of April. On the 4th, Johnston 'felt Sherman's front,' as soldiers say,

---

[1] By "division" was meant a separate command, of which the officers reported to the general at the head.

in force. But both Grant and Sherman thought
there was no probability of an immediate engagement. Here they were mistaken. For on the 6th
of April came one of the most terrible battles of
the war, or any war, — which did not end, indeed,
till the final retreat of the defeated Rebel force on
the 7th. Johnston and Beauregard attacked with
their whole force the divisions of Hurlbut and
Sherman. Lew Wallace did not succeed in bringing
up the support of his division till night of the 6th.
At night McClernand's and Smith's divisions began to arrive from Savanna, and with the morning
Grant was able to move these fresh troops against
the enemy, who had been fighting all the day before. They gave way slowly, and he drove them
back to Corinth. On the first day they had driven
back Sherman's and Hurlbut's lines so far, as
to take possession of their camps. On the 7th
they were themselves driven back. But many of
the prisoners whom they took the first day were
not recaptured. The loss, in both days, of the
National army was twelve thousand two hundred
and seventeen. The loss of the Rebels was ten
thousand six hundred and ninety-nine.

"Remember that the battle-field reaches back from
the bluffs at Pittsburg Landing two or three miles.
It is a thickly-wooded and broken country, mixed
with some patches of cultivation. The river was
very high, so that back-water filled deep the little
streams which run into it. As the battle began,

Sherman·commanded at the extreme right, and a little stream called Owl Creek protected him from any attack from the west or the rear. Between him and the Tennessee were McClernand's and Prentiss's forces, with Stuart nearest the river. In a second line, behind these troops were General Hurlbut and General W. H. L. Wallace, — whom you must not confound with General Lew Wallace, who was five miles away. These officers were so near that their men could be moved up at once to support the front. The troops were all Western troops, some of whom had never been under fire.

"Now I think you will understand these stories of parts of the battle. The very earliest attack, at three o'clock in the morning, was made on General Prentiss's men. Colonel Everett Peabody, of the Twenty-fifth Missouri, 'by one of those undefinable impulses or misgivings which detect the approach of catastrophe without physical warning of it, became convinced that all was not right.' He commanded the first brigade of General Prentiss's division. Very early Sunday morning, therefore, he sent out three companies of his own regiment, and two of the Twelfth Michigan, under the command of Major Powell of that regiment, to reconnoitre."

Here is the report of that movement, as it is told by the senior surviving officer : —

The regiment occupied the right of the first brigade, commanded by Colonel Peabody, acting brigadier-general, and had the honor of opening the fight on the 6th, the attack being made on its front at three o'clock in the morning. By Colonel Peabody's orders three companies were despatched to engage the enemy's advance, which was successfully done until reinforced by the Twenty-first Missouri. The fighting now became general and heavy, and I was ordered to support with the whole regiment. The enemy had now come within half a mile of the encampment, where they were checked and held until near seven o'clock, when our force fell back to the line of encampment, where another stand was made. The fighting was very severe until eight o'clock, when we were compelled to fall back still further, behind our encampments, on the division which had by this time formed in line of battle on an elevation in our rear. My regiment had, by this time, become badly cut up, but they rallied and took position on the right of the Twelfth Michigan, with the loss of several of my most valuable officers. The fighting now became most determined, and continued with little intermission for three hours. The enemy, being thrice repulsed, finally moved to our left. It was in this part of the engagement that Major Powell fell mortally wounded, and Sergeant Euler, color-bearer, was killed, clinging to the staff till it had to be detached from his grasp by Sergeant Simmons, who took his place. — *Lieut.-Col. Van Horn.*

The Rebels, you see, were steadily gaining ground here. General Prentiss with a part of his command stood too firmly, for they were taken prisoners, being surrounded by the Rebel advance.

Now here is the account which the Twenty-first Missouri give, — who, as you see, reinforced these companies.

On the 5th with three companies I made a reconnoissance over three miles, which failed to discover the enemy. I returned to my encampment about eleven P. M. On Sunday morning, the 6th, at about six o'clock, by order of Colonel Everett Peabody, commanding the first brigade, sixth division, I advanced with five companies of my command a short distance from our encampment. I met the retreating pickets bringing in their wounded. I ordered and compelled those who were able for duty to return to their posts, — and, learning that the enemy was advancing in force, I sent for the remaining five companies of my regiment. With them I ordered an advance, and attacked the enemy, who were commanded by General Ruggles. A terrific fire was opened upon us from the whole front of the four or five regiments forming the enemy's advance, which my gallant soldiers withstood until I had communicated the intelligence of the movement against us to my commanding general. About this time, being myself severely wounded, the bone of the leg below the knee being shattered, I was compelled to retire from the field, leaving Lieut.-Col. Woodyard in command. — *Col. Moore.*

Now here is Colonel Woodyard's story of what happened there : —

I then assumed command of the regiment, and formed a line of battle on the brow of a hill on the cotton-field, facing nearly west. I held this position for some half or three quarters of an hour, — and kept the enemy in check. He fell back, and attempted to outflank me. Discovering this, I moved my line to the north of the hill again, joined by four companies of the Sixteenth Wisconsin infantry. Having no field-officers with them, I ordered them to a position to the east of the field, and as soon as this was done joined them with my command. This line of battle, formed facing south, behind a small incline, enabled my men to load and be out of the range of the enemy's fire. The position proved a strong one, and we managed to hold it for upwards of an hour. Finding they could not dislodge us, the enemy again tried to outflank us and deal a cross-fire. We then fell back in good order, firing as we did so, to the next hill. Colonel Peabody, commanding first brigade, here came up with the Twenty-fifth Missouri regiment. I requested him to bring his men up to the hill on our right, as it would afford protection to his men and be of assistance to my command. He did so, — but the enemy coming by heavy main centre, and dealing a cross-fire upon our right and left, we could not maintain this position for over thirty minutes. We gradually began to fall back, and reached our tents, when the ranks got broken in passing through them. We endeavored to rally our men in the rear of our tents, and formed as well as could be expected, but my men got much scattered, a great many falling into other regiments under the immediate command of General Prentiss; others divided to other divisions, but continued to fight during the two days. — *Col. Woodyard.*

We cannot follow everybody's account of what he and his men did, in this fashion. But I believe Tom and Walter read all the despatches, and down on the beach the next day they fought it all out by putting lines of white stones for our men, and black stones for the Rebels. But this is enough to show you how they tell the story. You will see that Prentiss was being steadily driven back. This being so, General Hurlbut moved up to aid him. Here is a part of his report : —

A single shot from the enemy's batteries struck in Meyers's Thirteenth Ohio battery, when officers and men, with a common impulse of disgraceful cowardice, abandoned the entire battery, horses, caissons, and guns, and fled, and I saw them no more until Tuesday. I called for volunteers from the artillery: the call was answered, and ten gallant men from Mann's battery and Ross's battery brought in the horses, which were wild, and spiked the pieces. The attack commenced on the third brigade, through the thick timber, and was met and repelled by a steady and continuous fire, which rolled the enemy back in confusion, after some half-hour of struggle, leaving many dead and wounded.

The glimmer of bayonets on the left and front of the first brigade showed a large force of the enemy gathering, and an attack was soon made on the Forty-first Illinois and Twenty-eighth on the left of the brigade, and on the Thirty-second Illinois and Third Iowa on the right. At the same time a strong force of very steady and gallant troops formed in columns, doubled on the centre, and advanced over the open field in front. They were allowed to approach within four hundred yards, when fire was opened from Mann's and Ross's batteries, and from the two right regiments of the first brigade, and the Seventeenth and Twenty-fifth Kentucky, which were thrown forward slightly so as to flank the column. Under this withering fire they vainly attempted to deploy, but soon broke, and fell back under cover, leaving not less than one hundred and fifty dead and wounded as evidence how our troops maintained their position.

The attack on the left was also repulsed; but, as the ground was covered with trees, the loss could not be judged. General Prentiss having succeeded in rallying a considerable portion of his command, I permitted him to pass to the front of the right of my third brigade, where they redeemed their honor by maintaining that line for some time, while ammunition was supplied to my regiments. A series of attacks upon the right and left of my line were readily repelled, until I was compelled to order Ross's battery to the rear, on account of its loss in men and horses. During

all this time Mann's battery maintained its fire steadily,
effectively, and with great rapidity, under the excellent
handling of Lieut. E. Brotzmann.

For five hours these brigades maintained their position under repeated and heavy attacks, and endeavored,
with their thin ranks, to hold the space between Stewart and McClernand, and did check every attempt to
penetrate the line; when, about three o'clock, Colonel
Stewart, on my left, sent me word that he was driven
in, and that I would be flanked on the left in a few
moments. It was necessary for me to decide at once
to abandon either the right or left. I considered that
Prentiss could, with the left of General McClernand's
troops, probably hold the right, and sent him notice to
reach out toward the right, and drop back steadily
parallel with my first brigade, while I rapidly moved
General Laumann's from the right to the left, and
called up two twenty-pound pieces of Major Cavender's
battalion to check the advance of the enemy upon the
first brigade. These pieces were taken into action by
Doctor Cornine, the surgeon of the battalion, and
Lieut. Edwards, and effectually checked the enemy for
half an hour, giving me time to draw off my crippled
artillery and to form a new front with the third brigade.
In a few minutes two Texas regiments crossed the
ridge separating my line from Stewart's former one,
while other troops also advanced. Willard's battery
was thrown into position under command of Lieut.
Wood, and opened with great effect upon the lone-star
flags, until their line of fire was obstructed by the
charge of the third brigade, which, after delivering its
fire with great steadiness, charged full up the hill, and
drove the enemy three or four hundred yards. Perceiving that a heavy force was closing on the left,
between my line and the river, while heavy fire continued on the right and front, I ordered my line to fall
back. The retreat was made quietly and steadily, and
in good order. I had hoped to make a stand on the
line of my camp; but masses of the enemy were press-

ing rapidly on each flank, while their light artillery were closing rapidly in the rear. On reaching the twenty-four-pounder siege-guns in battery, near the river, I again succeeded in forming line of battle in rear of the guns, and, by direction of Major-General Grant, I assumed command of all the troops that came up. Broken regiments and disordered battalions came into line gradually upon my division. Major Cavender posted six of his twenty-pound pieces on my right, and I sent my aid to establish the light artillery — all that could be found — on my left. Many officers and men unknown to me, and whom I never desire to know, fled in confusion through the line. Many gallant soldiers and brave officers rallied steadily on the new line.

I passed to the right, and found myself in communication with General Sherman, and received his instructions. In a short time, the enemy appeared on the crest of the ridge, led by the Eighteenth Louisiana, but were cut to pieces by the steady and murderous fire of our artillery. Dr. Cornine again took charge of one of the heavy twenty-four-pounders, and the line of fire of that gun was the one upon which the other pieces concentred. General Sherman's artillery, also, was rapidly engaged; and, after an artillery contest of some duration, the enemy fell back. Captain Gwinn, United States Navy, had called upon me, by one of his officers, to mark the place the gun-boats might open their fire. I advised him to take position on the left of my camp-ground, and open fire as soon as our fire was within that line. He did so; and from my own observation, and the statement of prisoners, his fire was most effectual in stopping the advance of the enemy on Sunday afternoon and night.

About dark the firing ceased. I advanced my division one hundred yards to the front, threw out pickets, and officers and men bivouacked in a heavy storm of rain. — *Gen. Hurlbut.*

General Hurlbut's report is thus indorsed by General Grant: —

" This is a fair, candid report, assuming none too much for officers or men of the division.

"U. S. GRANT,
Major-General."

Thus we have traced the history of the division which met the very earliest attack, from three in the morning to the end of that bloody day. Stewart's brigade, detached at the left of Prentiss's main force, had been driven back, as you have seen. The Rebels in front of General Prentiss were under the command of General Bragg. These accounts have been by regimental officers and by General Hurlbut. Uncle Fritz chose them as illustrations of the way soldiers tell their story. Now you shall have General Sherman's view of the whole, and of what passed under his eye, stationed as he was on Prentiss's right. To understand the time, you should observe that it was a full hour after Peabody's outposts gave warning before they were driven into Prentiss's camps. About seven the Rebel General Gladden moved upon Prentiss's centre, Chalmers's brigade on the left, and Jackson on the right. Gladden was killed by a cannon-shot. Peabody was mortally wounded in our lines. Before nine o'clock the Confederates had driven Prentiss from his camps. The attack on Sherman's front had been made at the same time, by

General Hardee. By eight o'clock the battle was raging on both these lines of attack.

About eight A. M., I saw the glistening bayonets of heavy masses of infantry to our left front in the woods beyond the small stream alluded to, and became satisfied, for the first time, that the enemy designed a determined attack on our whole camp. All the regiments of my division were then in line of battle at their proper posts. I rode to Colonel Appler and ordered him to hold his ground at all hazards, as he held the left flank of our first line of battle. I informed him that he had a good battery on his right, and strong supports to his rear. General McClernand had promptly responded to my request, and had sent me three regiments, which were posted to protect Waterhouse's battery and the left flank of my line. The battle began by the enemy opening a battery in the woods to our front, and throwing shells into our camp. Taylor's and Waterhouse's batteries promptly responded, and I then observed heavy battalions of infantry passing obliquely to the left, across the open field in Appler's front; also other columns advancing directly upon my division. Our infantry and artillery opened along the whole line, and the battle became general. Other heavy masses of the enemy's forces kept passing across the field to our left, and directing their course on General Prentiss. I saw at once that the enemy designed to pass my left flank, and fall upon Generals McClernand and Prentiss, whose line of camps was almost parallel with the Tennessee River, and about two miles back from it. Very soon the sound of musketry and artillery announced that General Prentiss was engaged, and about nine A. M. I judged that he was falling back.

About this time Appler's regiment broke in disorder, soon followed by fugitives from Mungen's regiment, and the enemy pressed forward on Waterhouse's battery, thereby exposed.

The three Illinois regiments in immediate support of

this battery stood for some time; but the enemy's advance was so vigorous, and the fire so severe, that when Colonel Raith, of the Forty-Third Illinois, received a severe wound and fell from his horse, his regiment and the others manifested disorder, and the enemy got possession of three guns of this (Waterhouse's) battery. Although our left was thus turned and the enemy was pressing on the whole line, I deemed Shiloh so important that I remained by it and renewed my orders to Colonels McDowell and Buckland to hold their ground, and we did hold those positions till about ten o'clock A. M , when the enemy got his artillery to the rear of our left flank, and some change became absolutely necessary.

Two regiments of Hildebrand's brigade, Appler's and Mungen's, had already disappeared to the rear, and Hildebrand's own regiment was in disorder, and therefore I gave directions for Taylor's battery, still at Shiloh, to fall back as far as the Purdy and Hamburg road, and for McDowell and Buckland to adopt that road as their new line. I rode across the angle, and met Behr's battery at the cross roads, and ordered it immediately to unlimber and come into battery, action right. Captain Behr gave the order, but he was almost immediately shot from his horse, when drivers and gunners fled in disorder, carrying off the caissons, and abandoning five out of six guns without firing a shot. The enemy pressed on, and we were again forced to choose a new line of defence. Hildebrand's brigade had substantially disappeared from the field, though he himself bravely remained. McDowell's and Buckland's brigades still retained their organization, and were conducted by my aids so as to join on General McClernand's right, thus abandoning my original camps and line. This was about half past ten A. M., at which time the enemy had made a furious attack on General McClernand's whole front. Finding him pressed, I moved McDowell's brigade directly against the left flank of the enemy, forced him back some

distance, and then directed the men to avail themselves of every cover, — trees, fallen timber, and a
wooded valley to our right. We held this position for
four long hours, sometimes gaining and at other times
losing ground, General McClernand and myself acting
in perfect concert, and struggling to maintain this line.
While we were so hardly pressed, two Iowa regiments
approached from the rear, but could not be brought
up to the severe fire that was raging in our front, and
General Grant, who visited us on that ground, will remember our situation about three P. M.; but about four
P. M. it was evident that Hurlbut's line had been driven
back to the river, and, knowing that General Lew Wallace was coming from Crump's Landing with reinforcements, General McClernand and I, on consultation,
selected a new line of defence, with its right covering
the bridge by which General Wallace had to approach.[1]
We fell back as well as we could, gathering, in addition
to our own, such scattered forces as we could find, and
formed a new line.

During this change the enemy's cavalry charged
us, but was handsomely repulsed by an Illinois regiment, whose number I did not learn at the time or
since.[2] The Fifth Ohio battery, which had come up,
rendered good service in holding the enemy in check
for some time; and Major Taylor came up with a new
battery, and got into position just in time to get a good
flanking fire upon the enemy's columns as he pressed
on General McClernand's right, checking his advance,
when General McClernand's division made a fine charge
on the enemy, and drove him back into the ravines on
our front and right. I had a clear field, about two
hundred yards wide, in my immediate front, and con-
tented myself with keeping the enemy's infantry at
that distance during the rest of the day. In this position we rested for the night. — *General Sherman.*

[1] But General Lew Wallace took the wrong road at starting,
and did not arrive before night.
[2] It was the Twenty-ninth.

And this must be all we can read of that terrible first day at Shiloh, except one plucky little report from an Illinois captain, who suspected that his company had been accused of cowardice. As his company lost even more than he says, — namely, six men killed and thirty-one wounded, — more than half the number he took into action, he might have left that record to speak for itself. But he could not bear to have the living or the dead maligned, so he sent in, "on his own hook," this spirited little narrative.

Dear Sir : — Enclosed please find list of killed, wounded, and missing. I will avail myself of this opportunity to give you a correct statement of things that happened on the battle-field after our order to go to the left (as to what happened before, there is no dispute). I was ordered there by our colonel, who led the way in person to the hollow, where we had the severest part of the action, in which I participated. We fought there until ordered to leave by the colonel in person; then I moved off with my company in as good order as the nature of the case would admit, and can say that a large part of the regiment could have been *rallied* anywhere from two hundred yards of our position to our quarters (where all assembled), if we had had only one field-officer to have directed the movement. I will also state that my men had shot away all their ammunition, and in several instances had robbed the boxes of the dead and wounded. Had we not been compelled by the enemy to fall back, we could not have held our position longer for want of ammunition. After my arrival in camp, I beat towards the river with all my company, — all that was not detached to take care of the wounded. When we arrived at the guard I was pleased, for that was the first thing I had seen that looked like a place to stop; here I stopped with my squad, and with others formed and joined other fragments of regiments and marched to the right, where we lay on our arms all night. The next morning, I picked up until I had sixteen men and my first-lieutenant, and with Captain Davidson (our surgeon captain) reported to you for duty; as to what occurred after this, you know as well as I do. I have only to add that I went into the action with fifty-four men and three officers; lost, in killed, wounded, and missing, one lieutenant and thirty men, leaving only twenty-four to fight and take care of the wounded. And let me say that a braver or better-behaved company of men never lived on this continent; you may stigmatize me as a coward, but please make an exception to the brave men under my command. I am getting old, and my fighting time is almost done, consequently it makes but little difference about me. I have a son and neighbor in this action that his parent never expected to be disgraced under my command. I also wear a sword presented to me by an aged soldier father, who is still living to look over the history of the Thirty-Second regiment Illinois volunteers. What I say of my conduct, I suppose to be true of other commanders of companies. . . . And now allow me to say, to take everything into consideration, I believe the Thirty-Second behaved as well, or better, than any other regiment on the field that I have heard of. I have only to add, that I expect never to behave better in action while I live, and never expect a better set of companies, consequently you need not expect any better work of the Thirty-Second than they have done. — *Capt. Campbell, 32d Illinois.*

Night found the lines of Sherman and Prentiss forced back with their left on the river at the Landing. But at the Landing a battery of great force had been formed, and the gun-boats had moved up so as to shell the enemy in the woods.

Lew Wallace had at last arrived with his division by land, and General Buell with his by water, so that the next day the tired regiments of Sunday's fight and the newly arrived reinforcements had only to advance to drive the enemy back to Corinth.

The Southern army had put all its men into the battle. General Johnston, their commander-in-chief, as well as Generals Gladden and Hindman, were killed. On the Northern side, Prentiss had been taken prisoner, and General W. H. L. Wallace had been killed.

Of the second day the story is thus told by General Coppee : —

The fresh troops were placed in line as they came upon the field, far in advance upon the ground abandoned by Beauregard after the failure of his last attack. Nelson was on the left ; then, in order, Crittenden, McCook, Hurlbut, McClernand, Sherman, and Lew Wallace, the new line on the left nearly a mile in advance of our position on Sunday evening. . . . . .

The battle of Monday began by a determined advance on our left and centre ; simultaneously with which, Beauregard, having formed a strong rear-guard, and whipping in all stragglers, undertook a vigorous assault upon our left. He was still deceived into the hope that he might capture the landing. The assault upon Nelson was tremendous ; but while his troops were wavering, in spite of all his efforts, the regular battery of Captain Mendon had, detached by Buell from Crittenden's division, come into action, unlimbering at a jump, while the Rebels were rushing forward, and, by rapid discharges of grape and canister, hurled them back. Again and again fresh troops were formed upon our left, but only to be driven back. At length Hazen's brigade charged, captured a Rebel battery, and turned it upon the astonished enemy.

Once more a Rebel charge, and Hazen is driven back, when Terrill's battery, of McCook's division, being in search of its position, is posted by General Buell at the contested point. He opens with shell from his ten-pounders, and grape and canister from his brass twelves, and the brunt of the battle burns low in Nelson's front. Buell has admirably posted his artillery, and the guns have been splendidly served. Nelson can move forward. On his right, Crittenden and Mc-Cook advanced abreast, but to meet with a stubborn resistance. Throughout the war, as numerous examples could testify, the Rebel generals always sought to pierce our line at its weakest point, — at some joint in the armor. It was so now. In the slight interval between Crittenden and McCook they endeavored to force a passage. Rousseau, partially flanked, is driven back, but rallies upon the support of Kirk's and Gibson's brigades.

On the right, Sherman and Wallace have advanced with ardor to the same ridge occupied by the former on Sunday morning. But here again furious battle was to be joined, for the Rebels, when satisfied that they could effect nothing on the left, had countermarched their troops to try the right once more, and the little log church of Shiloh was again to witness a desperate struggle. By well-concerted movements, our troops are kept well abreast throughout the whole line, and when at length a concerted advance was made, in spite of the great efforts of the enemy, it was successful. By four o'clock the rebel commander had seen the uselessness of further effort; by half past five he was in full retreat. — *Gen. Coppee.*

We cannot follow the details of the Western campaign of that year; but must pass to the siege and capture of Vicksburg.

CHAPTER VII.

VICKSBURG.

THE control of the Mississippi River was, for each party, one of the most important objects of the war. The navigation of that river by steamboats is very important for the States which border upon it and its branches. It also gives a very easy method for the movement of troops. The city of New Orleans grew to be the great city it was, before the days of railroads, when almost all the articles of trade produced in these great States were sent down the river on their way to the markets where they were sold. Cotton, pork, sugar, hemp, tobacco, corn, wheat, and other productions of the fertile Western and Southwestern States, were sent down the river by steamboats to New Orleans. As railroads have been built from the Mississippi, across the country eastward to the ocean, the river is not now the only means these States have of sending their produce to market. Still the Mississippi River is a very important channel for trade, and so it was in the time of the war.

The United States government had therefore seized Cairo, at the mouth of the Ohio, in the very beginning of the war, and this had become an important central point, as a depôt of troops, food, and ammunition. The Rebels had seized Memphis, which stands on a high bluff on the eastern side of the river and commands the passage. By this word "commands," this is meant, — that the bluff is so high that cannons placed there are easily fired downward upon vessels which try to pass, while it is impossible for them to fire guns up, so as to strike such batteries on the shores with any great effect. When the Rebel armies were driven towards the south, they could not hold Memphis, and they withdrew their forces there. But in place of Memphis they fortified Vicksburg, a city of Mississippi, and it became what President Jefferson Davis called the "Gibraltar of America." [1]

On the next page is a map, to show you how admirably Vicksburg is situated for stopping the passage of the river. The Mississippi, in one of its winding frolics, doubles right in front of Vicksburg. The river itself is less than half a mile wide. The little neck just opposite the city is three quarters of a mile wide. The bluff on which the city stands is abrupt, and rises two hundred feet above the river. A steamboat, therefore, which tried to pass down the Mississippi in front of Vicksburg would have to pass the batteries twice, — once northward, and again

[1] Vicksburg is just below Walnut Hills, and just above the site of Fort Adams. These places are often alluded to in the history of the beginning of the century.

close to the city southward. For, with guns as
high as two hundred feet above the object to be
struck, the distance even of a mile and three quarters, which would be the farthest which a steam-

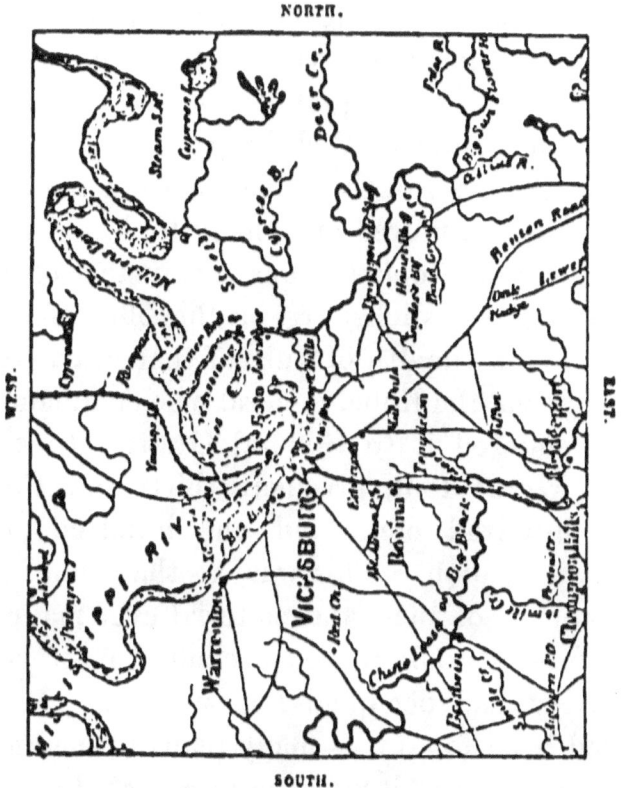

boat could take, would not be greater than the shot
could be thrown. Of course, when the boat turned
to go south, it would be close under the batteries.
The Rebels availed themselves carefully of these
advantages. They also fortified Port Hudson, in
Louisiana, lower down, for the purpose of preventing boats from coming up the river.

To open the river again General Grant was to take Vicksburg, and General Banks to take Port Hudson. Each army had the assistance of what President Lincoln called "our web-footed allies," by which he meant the vessels of the navy. With Grant was Admiral Porter, who had sixty vessels of all sorts, mostly river steamers; this fleet carried eight hundred men and two hundred and eighty guns. At the beginning of the year 1863, when the operations against Vicksburg began, Grant's army, at all the posts of the Department of the Tennessee, was one hundred and thirty thousand men.

General Grant took personal command of the movement against Vicksburg on the 30th of January, 1863. On the 4th of July of that year, General Pemberton, the Rebel general who commanded there, surrendered it to General Grant. In that surrender Grant took prisoners thirty-one thousand six hundred men, and one hundred and seventy-two cannon. This was, at that time, the largest capture of men and material ever made in war. Before it took place, a campaign of very great variety had occupied five months. Many battles had been fought, — many plans formed and failed, — and the result was due to one of the most ingenious, as it was one of the boldest, military combinations. It will always be a campaign which young soldiers will study with great interest. It is the campaign in which General Grant won his reputation as one of the first soldiers of this time,

—in which he conciliated the regard of his most skilful subordinates,—and won the respect and admiration of his superiors, General Halleck and President Lincoln.

So I shall let you boys, and any girls who have sense enough to read stories of war, have a longer chapter about the campaign against Vicksburg, than we have yet had about any other single event in this history.

The first plan made was to dig a canal across the neck of land, or peninsula in front of Vicksburg,—below the city,—at a point where the isthmus was only a mile and a fifth in width. This had been begun before General Grant's arrival. If a canal could have been made large enough for large steamboats, then, no matter how strong were the fortifications of Vicksburg, the boats would pass through, far away from their fire. So a canal ten feet wide and six deep was made here, in the hope that the freshets of the river would widen it, and so make it large enough for large steamers. But very little came of the canal. When the river did rise, it would not flow where it was meant to do. It flooded the camps of the workmen. Meanwhile, the Rebels had made new batteries below it. Thus ended plan number one. Another similar plan, to open a route by Lake Providence and Bayou Baxter, Bayou Maçon, and the Washita and Red River, did not succeed better. The canals attempted here were both on the west of the river. A very bold attempt was made on the east side, by what was known as the Yazoo Pass, into the Tallahatchee and Yazoo River. The expeditions sent by this route would come out above Vicksburg; but it was hoped that thus the Rebel gunboats on the Yazoo River might be destroyed. If a practicable route were made here, the whole army could be moved to Haine's Bluff, — above Vicksburg, — an upland region very desirable for occupation. But nothing came of this movement, though some hard work and some hard fighting were done in it. What resulted of importance was, that the troops found their way into the granary from which Vicksburg had been fed; and in the resistance, many of the Rebel stores were destroyed. In such attempts February and March passed away. Meanwhile, Admiral Farragut, of the navy, ran by the Rebel batteries at Port Hudson, so that he communicated with Grant below Vicksburg, — and Grant could communicate with General Banks, who was trying to do at Port Hudson what Grant was trying to do above. The distance from Vicksburg to Port Hudson is about one hundred and twenty miles in a straight line, and more than twice that by the crooked river.

Grant now determined to pass the city of Vicksburg on the west side of the river by marching his army by land — with the help of boats on some bayous if possible — from Milliken's Bend, which is twenty miles above Vicksburg, to New Carthage, which is about as far below. At his request Admiral Porter sent seven of his iron-clads, with three steamers and ten barges, down the river, past the Rebel batteries. They were well laden with forage and supplies. The crews of all but one refused to go. But volunteers from the army offered, enough to man a hundred vessels had they been needed. On a dark night, of the 16th of April, led by Admiral Porter, they steamed down, with the barges in tow. They turned the bend without being noticed. Then the first batteries opened on them. The Rebels set fire to houses so as to light up the scene ; and from the ships the crews could see the men at the batteries and in the streets of Vicksburg. Though every vessel was hit, all got by, except the Henry Clay steamer. Finding she was sinking, her commander cut off the barge he was towing, which drifted safely down, and, soon after, the vessel herself took fire. The crew escaped in their boats, — the vessel blazed up and lighted up all around. At last, however, after the boats had been under fire two hours and forty minutes, the whole fleet except the Henry Clay arrived safely below the batteries. Grant had thus secured, not only forage and stores, but the means of transportation. On the 26th of April five more vessels passed successfully, one being lost as before. Grant was now strong enough to cross the Mississippi River. His army had to march seventy miles on the west side by muddy roads, scarcely above the river line. He feared he might have to go as far down as a little town called Rodney for a good landing-place on the east side. But a friendly negro man, who knew the country, brought in information that there was a good road inland from Bruinsburg, — and so it proved. Grand Gulf, on the river, where the Rebels had a post, was still between Grant and Bruinsburg. Porter attacked it with his gun-boats, and Grant was ready to land ten thousand troops to storm the place if the batteries were silenced. But Porter did not succeed. Grant therefore marched his troops down on the west side of the river. Porter ran by Grand Gulf with transports in the night, and, on the morning of the 30th of April, Grant crossed the river with ten thousand men. They did not carry a tent nor a wagon. General Grant and his staff went without their horses. It was said afterwards that his whole baggage was a toothbrush!

Other divisions followed, and on the 3d of May he left the river, and marched, not directly on Vicksburg, but more inland, to cut off all communication with that city. His army took three days' rations with them, and relied principally for provisions on the stores in the rich country through which they marched. In the twenty days which followed, they fought the battles of Port Gibson, of Raymond, and of Jackson, and took the city of Jackson, the capital of Mississippi. Then Grant turned back upon Vicksburg, and before

May ended fought a very severe battle at Champion Hill, and in another gained the passage of Black River. By these actions, in all of which he succeeded, he separated General Pemberton and his army in Vicksburg from General J. E. Johnston, who was trying to relieve him. Pemberton was obliged to fall back into Vicksburg.

Grant assaulted it, without success, on the 19th of May, hoping to take it by storm. The works were too strong, and the assaulting parties, after gaining some few outworks, were all thrown back. A regular siege then began, and Vicksburg surrendered, as has been said, on the 4th of July.

Now you are ready for some scraps of letters and despatches which will give details of some of these all-important movements and battles.

First you shall read one of General Sherman's and then one of General Grant's brief histories. After these come as many other accounts as we can make room for.

THE YAZOO RIVER.

On Sunday morning, March 21st, as soon as daylight appeared, we started, following the same route which Giles A. Smith had taken the day before; the battalion of the Thirteenth United States Regulars, Major Chase, in the lead. We could hear Porter's guns, and knew that moments were precious. Being on foot myself, no man could complain, and we generally went at the double-quick, with occasional rests. The road lay along Deer Creek, passing several plantations; and occasionally, at the bends, it crossed the swamp, where the water came above my hips. The smaller drummer-boys had to carry their drums on their heads, and most of the men slung their cartridge-boxes around their necks. The soldiers generally were glad to have their general and field-officers afoot, but we gave them a fair specimen of marching, accomplishing about twenty-one miles by noon. Of course, our speed was accelerated by the sounds of the navy guns, which became more and more distinct, though we could see nothing. At a plantation near some Indian mounds, we met a detachment of the Eighth Missouri, that had been up to the fleet, and had been sent down as a picket to prevent any obstructions below. This picket reported that Admiral Porter had found Deer Creek badly obstructed, had turned back; that there was a Rebel force beyond the fleet, with some six-pounders, and nothing between us and the fleet. So I sat down on the door-sill of a cabin to rest, but had not been seated ten minutes when, in the wood just ahead, not three hundred yards off, I heard quick and rapid firing of musketry. Jumping up, I ran up the road, and found Lieut.-Col. Rice, who said the head of his column had struck a small force of Rebels with a working gang of negroes, provided with axes, who in the first fire had broken and run back into the swamp. I ordered Rice to deploy his brigade, his left on the road and extending as far into the swamp as the ground would permit, and then to sweep forward until he covered the gun-boats. The movement was rapid and well executed, and we soon came to some large cotton-fields and could see our gun-boats in Deer Creek, occasionally firing a heavy eight-inch gun across the cotton-fields into the swamp behind. About that time a Major Kirby, of the Eighth Missouri, galloped down the road on a horse he had picked up the night before, and met me. He explained the situation of affairs, and offered me his horse. I got on *bare-back*, and rode up the Levee, the sailors coming out of their iron-clads and cheering most vociferously as I rode by, and as our men swept forward across the cotton-field in full view. I soon found Admiral Porter, who was on the deck of one of his iron-clads, with a shield made of the section of a smoke-stack, and I doubt if he was ever more glad to meet a friend than he was to see me. He explained that he had almost reached the Rolling Fork, when the woods became full of sharp-shooters, who, taking advantage of trees, stumps, and the Levee, would shoot down every man that poked his nose outside the protection of his armor; so he could not handle his clumsy boats in the narrow channel. The Rebels had evidently despatched a force from Haines's Bluff up the Sunflower, to the Rolling Fork, had anticipated the movement of Admiral Porter's fleet, and had completely obstructed the channel of the upper part of Deer Creek by felling trees into it, so that further progress in that direction was simply impossible. It also happened that, at the instant of my arrival, a party of about four hundred Rebels, armed, and supplied with axes, had passed around the fleet, and had got below it, intending in like manner to block up the channel by the felling of trees, so as to cut off retreat. This was the force we had struck so opportunely at the time before described. I inquired of Admiral Porter what he proposed to do, and he said he wanted to get out of that scrape as quickly as possible. He was actually working back when I met him, and, as we then had a sufficient force to cover his movement completely, he continued to back down Deer Creek. He informed me at one time things looked so critical that he had made up his mind to blow up the gun-boats, and to escape with his men through the swamps to the Mississippi River. There being no longer any sharp-shooters to bother the sailors, they made good progress; still it took three full days for the fleet to back out of Deer Creek into Black Bayou, at Hill's plantation, whence Admiral Porter proceeded to his post at the mouth of the Yazoo, leaving Captain Owen in command of the fleet. I reported the facts to General Grant, who was sadly disappointed at the failure of the fleet to get through to the Yazoo above

Haines's Bluff, and ordered us all to resume our camps at Young's Point. We accordingly steamed down, and regained our camps on the 27th. — *Gen. Sherman.*

GEN. GRANT'S LETTER TO GEN. HALLECK.

GRAND GULF, Miss., May 3, 1863.

On the 29th of April, Admiral Porter attacked the fortifications at this place with seven iron-clads, commencing at eight o'clock A. M., and continuing until half past one, engaging them at very close quarters, many times not being more than one hundred yards from the enemy's guns. During this time, I had about ten thousand troops on board transports and barges, ready to land them, and carry the place by storm the moment the batteries bearing upon the river were silenced, so as to make the landing practicable. From the great elevation the enemy's batteries had, it proved entirely impracticable to silence them from the river; and when the gun-boats were drawn off, I decided immediately upon landing my forces on the Louisiana shore, and marching them across the point below Grand Gulf.

At night the gun-boats made another vigorous attack, and in the mean time the transports safely ran the blockade, and on the following day the whole force with me was transferred to Bruinsburg, the first point of land below Grand Gulf where the interior can be reached, and the march immediately commenced for Port Gibson. General McClernand was in the advance, with the Thirteenth Army Corps. About two A. M., on the 1st of May, when about four miles from Port Gibson, he met the enemy. Some little skirmishing took place before daylight, but not to any great extent. The Thirteenth Corps was followed by Logan's division of McPherson's corps, which reached the scene of action as soon as the last of the Thirteenth Corps was out of the road. The fighting continued all day, and after dark, over the most broken country I ever saw. The whole country is a series of irregular ridges, divided by deep and impracticable ravines, grown up with heavy timber, undergrowth, and cane. It was impossible to engage any considerable portion of our force at any one time. The enemy were driven, however, from point to point, towards Port Gibson, until night closed in, under which, it was evident to me, they intended to retreat. The pursuit was continued after dark, until the enemy was again met by Logan's division, about two miles from Port Gibson. The nature of the country is such, that further pursuit in the dark was not deemed prudent or advisable. On the 2d, our troops moved into the town without finding any enemy except their wounded. The bridge across Bayou Pierre, about two miles from Port Gibson, on the Grand Gulf road, had been destroyed, and also the bridge immediately at Port Gibson, on the Vicksburg road. The enemy retreated over both these routes, leaving a battery and several regiments of infantry at the former, to prevent a reconstruction of the first bridge. One brigade, under General Stevenson, was detached to drive the enemy from this position, or occupy his attention, and a heavy detail set to work, under Lieut.-Col. Wilson and Captain Tresillian, to reconstruct the bridge over the other. This work was accomplished, a bridge and roadway (over a hundred and twenty feet long) made, and the whole of McPherson's two divisions marched over before night. This corps then marched to the north fork of Bayou Pierre, rebuilt a bridge over that stream, and was on the march by five and a half A. M. to-day. Soon after crossing the Bayou, our troops were opened on by the enemy's artillery. It was soon demonstrated that this was only intended to cover the retreat of the main army. On arriving at Willow Springs, General McPherson was directed to hold the position from there to the Big Black with one division, and General McClernand, on his arrival, to join him in this duty. I immediately started for this place with one brigade of

Logan's division, and some cavalry (twenty men). The brigade of infantry was left about seven miles from here, contrabands and prisoners taken having stated that the last of the retreating enemy had passed that point. The woods between here and the crossing of the Big Black are evidently filled yet with the detachments of the enemy, and some artillery. I am in hopes many of them will be picked up by our forces.

Our loss will not exceed one hundred and fifty killed, and five hundred wounded. The enemy's loss is probably about the same. We have, however, some five hundred of their men prisoners, and may pick up many more yet. Many stragglers, particularly from the Missouri troops, no doubt have fallen out, and will never join their regiments again.

The move by Bruinsburg undoubtedly took the enemy by surprise. General Bowen's (the Rebel commander's) defence was a good one, and well carried out. My force, however, was too heavy for his, and composed of well-disciplined and hardy men, who know no defeat and are not willing to learn what it is.

This army is in the finest health and spirits. Since leaving Milliken's Bend, they have marched as much by night as by day, through mud and rain, without tents or much other baggage, and on irregular rations, without a complaint, and with less straggling than I have ever before witnessed.

Colonel Grierson's raid from La Grange, through Mississippi, has been the most successful thing of the kind since the breaking out of the Rebellion. He was five miles south of Pontotoc on the 19th of April. The next place he turned up at was Newton, about thirty miles east of Jackson. From there he has gone south, touching at Hazlehurst, Bahala, and various places. The Southern papers and Southern people regard it as one of the most daring exploits of the war. I am told the whole State is full of men paroled by Grierson. — *Gen. Grant.*

THE ATTACK OF THE 22D OF MAY.

GRANT'S CADET.

Lawler's brigade in Carr's division, which had carried the *tête-du-pont* on the Big Black River, dashed forward with its old impetuosity, supported by Landrum's brigade of Smith's division ; and, in less than fifteen minutes, a part of one regiment, the Twenty-second Iowa, succeeded in crossing the ditch and parapet of a Rebel outwork ; but, not receiving the support of the rest of the column, could not push further, nor drive the enemy from the main work immediately in the rear. A hand-to-hand fight here ensued, lasting several minutes ; hand-grenades also were thrown by the Rebels in the rear, while the National troops still commanded the outer parapet. Every man in the party except one was shot down. Sergeant Joseph Griffith, of the Twenty-second Iowa, fell at the same time with his comrades, stunned, but not seriously hurt. On his recovery, he found a Rebel lieutenant and sixteen men lying in the outwork, still unwounded, though exposed to the fire of both friend and foe. He rose, and bade them follow him out of the place, too hot for any man to stay and live. The Rebels obeyed, and, calling to the troops outside to cease their firing, Griffith brought his prisoners over the parapet, under a storm of Rebel shot that killed four of those so willing to surrender. For this act of gallantry, Griffith was next day promoted by Grant to a first lieutenancy, thus literally, like a knight of the Middle Ages, winning his spurs on the field. He was not twenty years old, and shortly afterwards received an appointment to the Military Academy at West Point, where he was known as "Grant's Cadet," and graduated in 1867, fifth in his class. — *Gen. Badeau.*

THE FLAGS ON THE PARAPET.

The colors of the One Hundred and Thirtieth Illinois were now planted on the counterscarp, and those of two other regiments were also raised on the exterior slope of the parapet. The work, however, was completely commanded by others in the rear, and no real possession of it was gained by the National soldiers. But the troops remained in the ditch for hours, although hand-grenades and loaded shells were rolled over on them from the parapet. The colors were not removed; as often as a Rebel attempted to grasp the staff, he was shot down by soldiers in the ditch; and the National flags waved all day on the Rebel work, neither party able to secure them, but each preventing their seizure by the other. After dark, a National soldier climbed up stealthily and snatched one of the flags away; the other was captured by a Rebel, in the same manner, leaning over suddenly from above. — *Gen. Badeau.*

A HOT PLACE.

General A. J. Smith had been ordered by McClernand to get two guns up to this position, and called upon five or six batteries successively; but the captains all protested that it was impossible to drag guns, by hand, down one slope and up another under fire. Smith however, exclaimed, "I know a battery that will go to hell if you order it there." So he sent for Captain White, of the Chicago Mercantile Battery, and told him what he wanted. White replied, "Yes, sir, I will take my guns there." And his men actually dragged the pieces over the rough ground, by hand, carrying the ammunition in their haversacks. One gun was stuck on the way, but the other they hauled up so near the Rebel works, that it was difficult to elevate it sufficiently to be of use; finally, however, White succeeded in firing it into an embrasure, disabling a gun just ready to be discharged, and scattering death among the Rebel can-noneers. A detachment here got into the work, but the Rebels rallied and captured every man. These were the only troops that actually carried or gained possession even for a moment of any portion of the enemy's line. — *Gen. Badeau.*

CAVE LIFE IN VICKSBURG. — THE CAVES.

Our new habitation was an excavation made in an earth-bank and branching six feet from the entrance, forming a cave in the shape of a T. In one of the wings my bed fitted; the other I used as a kind of dressing-room; in this the earth had been cut down a foot or two below the floor of the main cave. I could stand erect here; and when tired of sitting in other portions of my residence, I bowed myself into it, and stood im-passively resting at full height, — one of the variations in the still, shell-expectant life. . . . .

THE SHELLS.

My heart stood still as we would hear the reports from the guns, and the rushing and fearful sound of the shell as it came toward us. As it neared, the noise became more deafening; the air was full of the rushing sound; pains darted through my temples, my ears were full of the confusing noise; and, as it exploded, the report flashed through my head like an electric shock, leaving me in a quiet state of terror, the most painful that I can imagine, — cowering in a corner, holding my child to my heart, — the only feeling of my life being the choking throbs of my heart, that rendered me almost breathless. As singly they fell short, or beyond the cave, I was aroused by a feeling of thankfulness that was of short duration. Again and again the terrible fright came over us in that night.

I saw one fall in the road without the mouth of the cave, like a flame of fire, making the earth tremble, and, with a low, singing sound, the fragments sped on in their work of death.

Morning found us more dead than alive, with blanched faces and trembling lips. We were not reassured on hearing, from a man who took refuge in the cave, that a mortar shell in falling would not consider the thickness of the earth above us a circumstance.

Some of the ladies, more courageous by daylight, asked him what he was in there for, if that was the case. He was silenced for an hour, when he left. . . . .

PRECAUTIONS.

The night was so warm, and the cave so close, that I tried to sit out at the entrance; George [the servant] saying he would keep watch, and tell when they were falling toward us. Soon the report of the gun would be heard, and George, standing on the hillock of loose earth near the cave, looked intently upward; while I, with suspended breath, would listen anxiously, as he cried, " Here she comes ! going right over ! " then again, " Coming, — falling, — falling right dis way ! " Then I would spring to my feet, and for a moment hesitate about the protection of the cave. Suddenly, as the rushing descent was heard, I would beat a precipitate retreat into it, followed by the servant. . . . .

A RESCUE.

I ran to the little dressing-room, and could hear them striking around us on all sides. I crouched closely against the wall, for I did not know at what moment one might strike within the cave. A man came in much frightened, and asked to remain until the danger was over. The servants stood in the little niche by the bed, and the man took refuge in the small cell where I was stationed. He had been there but a short time, standing in front of me, and near the wall, when a Parrott shell came whirling in at the entrance, and fell in the centre of the cave before us all, lying there smoking. Our eyes were fastened upon it, while we expected every moment the terrific explosion would ensue. I pressed my child closer to my heart, and drew nearer to the wall. Our fate seemed almost certain. The poor man who had sought refuge within was most exposed of all. With a sudden impulse, I seized a large double blanket that lay near, and gave it to him for the purpose of shielding him from the fragments; and thus we remained for a moment, with our eyes fixed in terror on the missile of death, when George, the servant boy, rushed forward, seized the shell, and threw it into the street, running swiftly in the opposite direction. Fortunately, the fuse had become nearly extinguished, and the shell fell harmless, — remaining near the mouth of the cave, as a trophy of the fearlessness of the servant and our remarkable escape. . . . .

Nor was this all. I had occasion to go to the mouth of the cave one evening to speak to George; and there, with an enlightened audience of servants from the surrounding caves collected near him, George was going through a grave pantomime of the whole affair. It seems that he expected the refugee to act the part of preserver in our extremity, and throw out the shell; but, as he was disappointed in the matter, he represented him in the most ridiculous manner possible to the audience.

Pressing up closely to the wheel of a wagon near by, George extended his eyes, holding out his hand as with a shell, and shrinking with the semblance of extreme terror, that amused his spectators vastly; then, changing the whole character, he put on the bravest port imaginable, pushing his hat, with an independent air, on the side of his head, and, assuming a don't-carish look, he sauntered forward to a large piece of shell that lay conveniently near, caught it with both hands, gave it a careless swing and throw far different from the reality, turned on his heels, walked back to the wagon, with the peculiar swinging step of a proud negro; then, leaning his arm on the wheel, carelessly surveyed his audience with a look that plainly said, " What do you think o' dat, niggers?" . . . .

IN THE RIFLE-PITS.

So they sat cramped up all day in the pits, their ·rations cooked in the valley and brought to them, — scarcely daring to change their positions and stand erect, for the Federal sharp-shooters were watching for their heads; and to rise above the breastworks was almost certain death. . . . .

They amused themselves, while lying in the pits, by cutting out little trinkets from the wood of the parapet and the Minie balls that fell around them. Major Fry, from Texas, excelled in skill and ready invention; . . . . he sent me one day an arm-chair that he had cut from a Minie ball, — the most minute affair of the kind I ever saw, yet perfectly symmetrical. At another time he sent me a diminutive plough, made from the parapet work, with traces of lead, and a lead point made from a Minie ball. . . . .

SHRAPNEL.

There is one missile, were I a soldier, that would totally put me to rout, — and that is a Shrapnel shell. Only those who have heard several coming at a time, exploding near, and scattering several hundreds of small balls around, can tell how fearful is the noise they make, — a wild scream, — a clattering and whizzing sound that never fails in striking terror to my heart! It seemed sometimes that as many as fifty balls fell immediately around our door. I could have sent out at any time, near the entrance of our cave, and had a bucketful of balls from Shrapnel and the Minie rifle, picked up in the shortest possible time. — *A Southern Lady.*

CONDUCT OF THE SIEGE.

The lack of engineer officers gave the siege one of its peculiar characteristics; at many times, and at different places, the work to be done depended on officers and men without either theoretical or practical knowledge of siege operations, and who had, therefore, to rely, almost exclusively, on their native good-sense and ingenuity. Whether a battery was to be constructed by men who had never built one before, or sap-rollers made by those who had never heard the name, or a ship's gun-carriage put together by infantry soldiers, it was always done, and, after a few trials, well done. This fertility of resource and power of adaptation to circumstances, possessed in so high a degree by the volunteers, was, however, displayed while a relieving force was gathering in Grant's rear. Officers and men had to learn to be engineers while the siege was going on. Much valuable time was in this way lost, and many a shovelful of earth was thrown that brought the siege no nearer to an end.

One result of this scarcity of engineers was, that Grant gave more personal attention to the supervision of the siege than he would otherwise have done. His military education fitted him for the duty, and he rode daily around the lines, directing the scientific operations, infusing his spirit into all his subordinates, pressing them on with energy to the completion of their task, and, with unflagging persistency, devising and employing every means to bring about the great end to which all labor, skill, and acquirement was made to tend. . . . .

At one point the enemy's salient was too high for the besiegers to be able to return the hand-grenades which were thrown into the trenches so freely. There were no Cohorn mortars with the army, and wooden mortars were therefore made, by shrinking iron bands on cylinders of tough wood, and boring them out for six and twelve pound shells. These mortars stood firing well, and gave good results at a distance of one hundred or one hundred and fifty yards. — *Gen. Badeau.*

GRANT'S CONFIDENCE IN HIMSELF.

He was one day riding around his lines, and stopped for water at the house of a Rebel woman who had remained within her shattered walls, not changing her disloyal sentiments. She asked Grant, tauntingly, if he expected ever to get into Vicksburg. "Certainly," he replied. "But when?" "I cannot tell exactly when I shall take the town, but *I mean to stay here till I do, if it takes me thirty years.*" The woman's heart seemed to fail her at the reply. Apparently, she had hoped that her friends would be able to tire out the besiegers, even if they could not drive them off; but this waiting thirty years, if necessary, was a greater persistency than she had contemplated. — *Gen. Badeau.*

THE MINES.

Meanwhile the head of sap had reached the enemy's lines, on the Grave-yard and Jackson roads, and in Ransom's front as well as on the Baldwin and Hall's Ferry roads. Mining had been resorted to by both besiegers and besieged, and, on the Jackson road, Grant fired a heavy mine on the 25th of June. It extended thirty-five feet from the point of starting; fifteen hundred pounds of powder were deposited in three different branch mines, and seven hundred in the centre one; fuses were arranged so as to explode them all at the same instant, and the mine was tamped with cross-timbers and sand-bags. Troops were disposed so as to take advantage of any result. At three and a half P. M. the explosion took place, and a heavy artillery-fire opened along the line at the same moment. Huge masses of earth were thrown up in the air, and the ground was shaken as if by a volcano. As soon as the earth was

8

rent, a bright glare of fire issued from the burning powder, but quickly died away, as there was nothing combustible in the fort. A few Rebel soldiers were hurled into the air, one or two of whom came down alive inside the National lines. The enemy, however, had detected the building of the mine, and, in anticipation of the explosion, removed most of his troops behind a new line in the rear. Countermining had also been resorted to by the Rebels, and several sappers who were in the lower shaft were buried; all the troops in the neighborhood were jarred by the shock.

The cavity made was large enough to hold two regiments, and, as soon as the partial destruction of the parapet was discovered, a column of Grant's infantry, which had been concealed in a hollow beneath the fort, rushed forward with loud cheers to gain possession of the breach. The ditch and slope were gained, and a desperate struggle ensued in the crater, but the Rebels soon retired to their interior line, only a few feet back. Pioneers went to work at once, clearing an entrance to the crater; but both sides were reinforced promptly, and no further result was attained. The loss to the National side was thirty men in killed and wounded, and to the besieged about the same.

The crater was cone-shaped, and entirely exposed to field projectiles or loaded shells thrown by hand, but McPherson's men rushed into the gulf, lighting and throwing grenades in return. The enemy, however, from his higher position, could throw ten shells to their one, and, in nearly every case, with deadly effect; indeed, the Rebels had only to lay the lighted missiles on the parapet and roll them down. But, on the night after the explosion, details from Leggett's brigade relieved each other in the attempt to hold the crater. No systematic attempt could be made to carry the enemy's work, or to take possession of his parapet and run boyaux along the exterior slope; yet, all night long, parties of men, fifty, sixty, or eighty at a time, stood in the crater, along its sides not shaped into banquettes, and fired at an enemy they could not see ; for after the first hour the Rebels ceased to appear on the parapet at all, contenting themselves with the use of the grenades.

After a while, feathered grenades were given to the National troops, and thrown inside the Rebel line with some effect ; but many of these failed to explode, and were hurled back by the Rebels with terrible results. Boxes of field-ammunition were also brought out by the enemy, who lighted them with port-fires and threw them by hand into the crater. Nearly every one took effect, killing and wounding sometimes half a dozen men. The crater was called by the soldiers the " death-hole " ; but the ground that had been gained was held through all the horrors of the night, and rifle-pits next day were built across the aperture. A covered gallery was also at once commenced, from which further mines or counter-mines might lead.

As it was found impossible to continue the work until the Rebels were driven from the outer face of the opposing parapet, another mine was at once begun. This was sprung on the 1st of July. The result was the destruction of an entire redan, leaving only an immense chasm where the Rebel work had stood. The greater portion of the earth was thrown towards the National forces, the line of least resistance being in that direction. The Rebel interior line, however, was much injured, and many of those manning the works were killed or wounded. But no serious attempt to charge was made, the result of the assaults on the 25th having been so inconsiderable. — *Gen. Badeau.*

FROM A REBEL ACCOUNT.

Among the casualties during the siege were three women and three children, and four men [non-combatant]. Among the troops the casualties were greater. Most of these were sick or wounded, and in the hospitals. A number were severely injured, and numerous limbs were lost. Some most remarkable and ludicrous escapes were made.

I remember that one man had his head blown off while in the act of picking up his child. One man had a shell explode close by him, and lift him some distance in the air. Many strange escapes and incidents are spoken of, — so many that they have not been specially noticed.

One shell fell and exploded between two officers as they were riding together on the street, and lifted both horses and riders into the air without hurting either man or beast. One woman had just risen from her chair when a shell came through the roof, took her seat, and shattered the house without injuring the lady; and a hundred other similar cases. A little girl, the daughter of Mr. Jones, was sitting at the entrance of a cave, when a Parrott shell entered the portal and took her head right off. Surely this is terrible warfare which dooms the innocent lambs to inhuman slaughter.

THE TOWNSMEN'S PROTECTION.

The greatest curiosities are the caves hewn into the banks of earth, in which the women and children and non-combatants crept during the heat of the bombardment. At night, and sometimes during an entire day, the whole of the people would be confined to these caverns. They are constructed about the height of a man and three feet wide, a fork Y shaped into the bank. There are perhaps five hundred of these caves in the city around the works. As many as fifteen have been crowded into one of them. — *St. Louis Republican.*

THE MEETING OF GRANT AND PEMBERTON.

Thousands of soldiers looked upon the strange scene. Two men who had been lieutenants in the same regiment in Mexico, now met as foes, with all the world looking upon them. . . . . When they had approached within a few feet there was a halt and silence. Colonel Montgomery spoke : " General Grant, General Pemberton." They shook hands politely, but Pemberton was evidently mortified. He said : "I was at Monterey and Buena Vista. We had terms and conditions there." General Grant here took him aside, and they sat down on the grass and talked more than an hour. Grant smoked all the time ; Pemberton played with the grass and pulled leaves. It was finally agreed to parole them, allowing the officers each his horse. This was a politic thing. The dread of going North and fear of harsh treatment had deterred them from capitulating sooner.

Our men treated the Rebels with kindness, giving them coffee, which some had not tasted for a year. The city is much dilapidated, and many houses are injured. The Vicksburg paper of July 2d admits the eating of mule meat, and the pilfering of soldiers.

THE SURRENDER.

They marched out of their intrenchments by regiments upon the grassy declivity immediately outside their fort ; they stacked their arms, hung their colors upon the centre, laid off their knapsacks, belts, cartridge-boxes, and cap-pouches, and, thus shorn of the accoutrements of the soldier, returned inside their works, and thence down the Jackson road into the city. The men went through the ceremony with that look so touching on a soldier's face ; not a word was spoken ; there was none of that gay badinage we are so much accustomed to hear from the ranks of regiments marching through our streets ; the few words of command necessary were given by their own officers in that low tone of voice we hear used at funerals. . . . .

At Forney's head-quarters . . . . were gathered all the notables of both armies. In a damask armed rocking-chair sat Lieut.-Gen. Pemberton, the most discontented-looking man I ever saw. Presently there appeared in the midst of the throng a man small in stature, heavily set, stoop-shouldered, a broad face, covered with a short, sandy beard, habited in a plain suit of blue flan-

nel, with the two stars upon his shoulder denoting a
Major-General in the United States army. He approached Pemberton and entered into conversation with
him ; there was no vacant chair, but neither Pemberton
nor any of his generals offered him a seat, and thus for
five minutes the conqueror stood talking to the van-
quished seated, when Grant turned away into the house
and left Pemberton to his pride or his grief, — it was
hard to tell which. — *Cincinnati Commercial.*

CHAPTER VIII.

GETTYSBURG.

AT the moment of General Lee's retreat after Antietam, General McClellan was at the very height of a new wave of popularity. But the country which was eager to see Lee's retreat followed was again disappointed. "Can you tell me why General McClellan does not advance?" said a distinguished statesman to President Lincoln. "I cannot guess," said the President, "and I do not know." In his own despatches, written long after, the boys found his reasons. He thought his army not at all prepared for a winter campaign. Meanwhile General Burnside had conducted with spirit a campaign on the coast of North Carolina, and the President was eager to give the army to some one who had the confidence of the nation; and after McClellan had at last started with the army, Burnside was appointed in his place.

This time Lee selected the line of the Rappahannock for his line of defence, and here the two armies looked at each other across the stream, till Burnside, whose force was superior, boldly crossed,

on the 10th of December, and began a series of
attacks which lasted for three days, but failed.
On the 15th, he withdrew all his men. Following
the old policy of never retaining unsuccessful
generals, the President superseded Burnside by
General Joseph Hooker, an officer so vigorous and
spirited that he had the nickname in the army of
" Fighting Joe Hooker." He attempted to dislodge
Lee's army by another attack. He crossed the
river on the 28th, and the battle known as the
battle of Chancellorsville followed. It was a series
of bloody conflicts which lasted three days. In
the end the Union army was again withdrawn, after
losing twelve thousand in killed and wounded, and
five thousand prisoners. The Rebels lost ten
thousand in killed and wounded, and three thousand prisoners.

Lee chose this opportunity for another rapid
and secret movement upon the Northern States.
Hooker's army was discouraged. Lee's, well reinforced, was in high spirits. Each army had about
seventy thousand men.

Lee's plan was to move swiftly and silently,
without Hooker's knowledge, beyond the first
range of the Alleghanies to the Shenandoah Valley.
He then could march on Philadelphia or Baltimore
before Hooker could catch up with him, and could
avoid the strong fortifications of Washington,
which would delay him too much. He was to live
on the country, keeping open his lines of connec-

tion through the Shenandoah Valley for his ammunition trains only.

If it had not been for those wretched ammunition trains, how much longer might not the war have been prolonged! But the army's present supply of powder was not large enough for Lee to rely on, and he had to depend on what they sent from Richmond, and little enough — too little indeed — it proved.

Well and quietly did Lee move to the Shenandoah, but not without alarming Hooker. Lee was gone, but where? North or west it must be, so Hooker broke camp and moved himself westward and northward till the news came of the capture by the Rebels of Winchester on the Shenandoah, and later that the rebel advance was crossing the Potomac. So Hooker crossed the Potomac too, and marched northwest still, to threaten Lee's lines of supply; for if you step on the tail of an army it will curl round its head to bite you.

It was in this march that General Hooker had some difference with General Halleck, from Washington, who commanded the armies, about the use of the troops at Harper's Ferry. Hooker asked Halleck for them, Halleck refused him, and Hooker resigned. In his place was appointed General Meade, who was in command of the Fifth Corps, and who had distinguished himself at Fredericksburg, and under General Meade our soldiers fought the battle of Gettysburg.

When Lee left the Rappahannock he left behind most of his cavalry under General Stuart, a dashing officer who had much the same reputation that our General Custer had later. Stuart was to watch the Union army, and when they crossed the Potomac Lee was to be informed. But Stuart, like other cavalry officers, was too fond of dashing excursions, and he reconnoitred to such an extent that when he found the Union army it was between him and Lee. The Union army crossed the Potomac, and so long was the detour that Stuart had to make, that, when the news arrived, Lee had already felt the pressure on his army's snake-tail, and was turning round to the east to bite his assailant. He had hoped to manœuvre so that he should be always on the defensive, but — that ammunition!

So, on the last day of June, the two armies were blindly approaching each other. Each knew that the other was north of the Potomac, but that was all. Lee was marching eastward toward Gettysburg, Meade was marching northward toward Gettysburg. They did not know it, but it was fated that at Gettysburg they should meet.

Meade's plan of action was to take up a defensive position on Pipe Creek, to the east of Gettysburg; he had given his orders for the march of July 2d, and according to his programme his left wing under Reynolds was to occupy Gettysburg. The rest of the army was to the south and east, at different towns in the neighborhood.

Reynolds led his men to Gettysburg on July 1st, and had taken possession when he was informed of the advance of the Rebels from the west. Hastily he deployed such of his men as had come up to meet the enemy, and fought successfully for a short time; but as the regiments on regiments of Lee's column came up, Reynolds's corps was outnumbered. In the sharp action which took place Reynolds was killed, and his men, under Howard, retreated beyond the town southward to the heights of Cemetery Ridge. Here they made a stand, though a large number of them had been surrounded and captured in the streets of the town.

These heights south of Gettysburg were the Union lines during the battle of the next two days. In shape they are like a fish-hook lying north and south with the point on the eastern side. The straight part is Cemetery Ridge, ending at the south in two hills easily fortified. Here was the left flank of the Union army. The lines extended northward along Cemetery Ridge, and then, as they stretched to the right, they turned to the east and south. On the night of the 1st, Meade brought up the rest of his command, and next morning he drew it up on the crest of this range of hills.

But a mistake was made in the arrangement. General Sickles, on the left, instead of taking his place on the crest of the hill, drew up his men on a lower range of hills to the front of the real line.

As he had also to occupy the two hills on the left his line was a V with the vertex turned toward the enemy, and a very thin line of men made the V, for he had none too many to fill the ground allotted him.

So when Lee made his attack on both flanks on the 2d, Longstreet's men easily drove Sickles back, though reinforced, to the ground he should have taken in the beginning. At the same time the Union right was slightly driven in, and at night the Rebels, having gained ground on both flanks, went to sleep in jubilant expectation.

The next day, the 3d of July, Lee saw that the flanks had been pushed back as far as was practicable, and he ordered an attack on the centre, — just where the fish-hook begins to bend. Before attacking with infantry he cannonaded the ridge. Our men replied; and from one o'clock till three two hundred and fifty cannon were doing their worst. Our men, however, were well intrenched, and the enemy's guns did but little harm, though one hundred and twenty rounds were fired on our side, and many more on his.

At three o'clock his main attack began. Fifteen thousand men were massed against our centre, and marched down from the ridge where they were posted, and up to our lines. It was nearly a mile for them to march under fire of our artillery, and half a mile under our rifles. The fire on our side was too tremendous, — their loss too horrible;

no soldiers could bear it. Still their broken columns rolled up the incline to our guns, but only to be thrown back.

It was enough. Lee had not enough ammunition for such another day, and sullenly he retreated back to the Shenandoah Valley whence he had come.

On the same day Vicksburg fell. It was the turning point of the Rebellion.

General Lee afterwards said that, after Gettysburg, he knew that the collapse of the Rebellion was merely a question of time.

DEATH OF REYNOLDS.

General Reynolds now rode forward to inspect the field and ascertain the most favorable line for the disposal of his troops. One or two members of his staff were with him. The enemy at that instant poured in a cruel musketry fire upon the group of officers; a bullet struck General Reynolds in the neck, wounding him mortally. Crying out, with a voice that thrilled the hearts of his soldiers, "Forward! for God's sake, forward!" he turned for an instant, beheld the order obeyed by a line of shouting infantry, and, falling into the arms of Captain Wilcox, his aid, who rode beside him, his life went out with the words, "Good God, Wilcox, I am killed!"—*N. Y. World.*

THE FIRST DAY'S REPULSE.

Cutler, having the advance, opened the attack; Meredith was at it a few minutes later. Short, sharp fighting, the enemy handsomely repulsed, three hundred Rebel prisoners taken, General Archer himself reported at their head, — such was the auspicious opening. No wonder the First determined to hold its ground.

Yet they were ill-prepared for the contest that was coming. Their guns had sounded the tocsin for the Eleventh, but so had they too for Ewell, already marching down from York to rejoin Lee. They were fighting two divisions of A. P. Hill's now, numerically stronger than their dwindled three. Their batteries were not up in sufficient number, — on Meredith's left a point that especially needed protection, there were none at all. A battery with Buford's cavalry stood near. Wadsworth cut red tape, and in an instant ordered it up. The captain, preferring red tape to red fields, refused to obey. Wadsworth ordered him under arrest, could find no officer for the battery, and finally fought it under a sergeant. Sergeant and captain there should henceforth exchange places. . . . .

Small resistance is made on our right. The Eleventh does not flee wildly from its old antagonists, as at their last meeting, when Stonewall Jackson scattered them as if they had been pygmies, foolishly venturing into the war of the Titans. It even makes stout resistance for a little while; but the advantage of position, as of numbers, is all with the Rebels, and the line is forced to retire. It is done deliberately, and without confusion, till they reach the town. Here the evil genius of the Eleventh falls upon it again. To save the troops from the terrible enfilading fire through the streets the officers wheel them by detachments into cross-streets, and attempt to march thus around one square after another, diagonally, through the town. The Germans are confused by the manœuvre; perhaps the old panic at the battle-cry of Jackson's flying corps comes over them; at any rate they break in wild confusion, some pouring through the town a rout, and are with difficulty formed again on the heights to the southward. They lose over one thousand two hundred prisoners in twenty minutes. One of their generals, Schimmelfennig, an old officer in the Russian service in the Crimean war, is cut off, but he shrewdly takes to cover, conceals himself somewhere in the town, and finally escapes.—*Cincinnati Gazette.*

AN INCIDENT.

General Schimmelfennig escaped capture by resorting to a dodge worthy of the sharpest Yankee. When he found his retreat cut off, he seized the coat of a private and buttoned it closely over his uniform; he was knocked down and run over by a gang of Rebels who were after plunder. He then stumbled away into a cellar and lay there concealed and without food for two days; but when he heard the boys playing "Yankee Doodle" in the streets, he thought it safe to come out. He is now in command of his brigade, and ready for work. — *Rebellion Record.*

SKIRMISHING ON THE SECOND DAY.

All Thursday forenoon there was lively firing between our skirmishers and those of the enemy, but nothing betokening a general engagement. Standing on Cemetery Hill, which, but for its exposed position, constituted the best point of observation on the field, I could see the long line of our skirmishers stretching around centre and left, well advanced, lying flat on the ground in the meadows or corn-fields, and firing at will as they lay. The little streak of curling smoke that rose from their guns faded away in a thin vapor, that marked the course of the lines down the left. With a glass the Rebel line could be even more distinctly seen, every man of them with his blanket strapped over his shoulder, — no foolish "stripping for the fight" with these trained soldiers. Occasionally the gray-coated fellows rose from cover, and with a yell rushed on our men, firing as they came. Once or twice in the half-hour that I watched them they did this with such impetuosity as to force our skirmishers back, and call out a shell or two from our nearest batteries, — probably the very object their officers had in view. — *Cincinnati Gazette.*

SICKLES'S MISTAKE.

About three P. M. I rode out to the extreme left to await the arrival of the Fifth Corps and post it, when I found that Major-General Sickles, commanding the Third Corps, not fully apprehending my instructions in regard to the position to be occupied, had advanced, or rather was in the act of advancing, his corps some half-mile or three quarters of a mile in the front of the line of the Second Corps, on a prolongation of which it was designed his corps should rest.

Having found Major-General Sickles I was explaining to him that he was too far in the advance, and discussing with him the propriety of withdrawing, when the enemy opened upon him with several batteries in his front and his flank, and immediately brought forward columns of infantry and made a vigorous assault. The Third Corps sustained the shock most heroically. Troops from the Second Corps were immediately sent by Major-General Hancock to cover the right flank of the Third Corps, and soon after the assault commenced.

The Fifth Corps most fortunately arrived and took a position on the left of the Third, Major-General Sykes commanding, immediately sending a force to occupy "Round Top" ridge, where a most furious contest was . maintained, the enemy making desperate but unsuccessful efforts to secure it. Notwithstanding the stubborn resistance of the Third Corps, under Major-General Birney (Major-General Sickles having been wounded early in the action), superiority in numbers of corps of the enemy enabling him to outflank its advanced position, General Birney was counselled to fall back and re-form behind the line originally desired to be held.

In the mean time, perceiving the great exertions of

the enemy, the Sixth Corps, Major-General Sedgwick, and part of the First Corps, to which I had assigned Major-General Newton, particularly Lockwood's Maryland Brigade, together with detachments from the Second Corps, were all brought up at different periods, and succeeded, together with a gallant resistance of the Fifth Corps, in checking and finally repulsing the assault of the enemy, who retired in confusion and disorder about sunset, and ceased any further efforts on our extreme left. — *Maj.-Gen. Meade.*

THE SECOND DAY'S REPULSE ON THE LEFT.

I cannot trace the movements further in detail; let me give one phase of the fight, fit type of many more. Some Massachusetts batteries, — Captain Bigelow's, Captain Phillips's, — two or three more under Captain McGilroy of Maine, were planted on the extreme left, advanced now well down to the Emmetsburgh road, with infantry in their front, — the first division, I think, of Sickles's corps. A little after five a fierce Rebel charge drove back the infantry and menaced the batteries. Orders are sent to Bigelow, on the extreme left, to hold his position at every hazard short of sheer annihilation, till a couple more batteries can be brought to his support. Reserving his fire a little, then with depressed guns opening with double charges of grape and canister, he smites and shatters, but cannot break the advancing line. His grape and canister are exhausted, and still closely, grandly up over their slain on they come. He falls back on spherical case, and pours this in at the shortest range. On, still onward comes the artillery-defying line, and still he holds his position. They are within six paces of the guns, — he fires again. Once more and he blows devoted soldiers from his very muzzles, and, still mindful of that solemn order, he holds his place. They spring upon his carriages and shoot down his horses! And then, his Yankee artillerists still about him, he seizes the guns

9

with the hand, and from the very front of that line drags two of them off. The caissons are further back,—five of out of the six are saved.

That single company, in that half-hour's fight, lost thirty-three of its men, including every sergeant it had. The Captain himself was wounded. Yet it was the first time it was ever under fire! I give it simply as a type. So they fought along that fiery line!—*Cincinnati Gazette.*

~ JOHN BURNS.

On the morning of the first day's fight at Gettysburg, he sent his wife away, telling her that he would take care of the house. The firing was near by, over Seminary Ridge. Soon a wounded soldier came into the town and stopped at an old house on the opposite corner. Burns saw the poor fellow lay down his musket, and the inspiration to go into the battle seems the first to have seized him. He went over and demanded the gun.

"What are you going to do with it?" asked the soldier.

"I'm going to shoot some of the damned Rebels," replied John.

He is not a swearing man; and the adjective is to be taken in a strictly literal, not a profane sense.

Having obtained the gun, he pushed out on the Chambersburg Pike, and was soon in the thick of the skirmish.

"I wore a high-crowned hat and a long-tailed blue, and I was seventy years old," said he.

The sight of so old a man, in such costume, rushing fearlessly forward to get a shot in the very front of the battle of course attracted attention. He fought with the Seventh Wisconsin Regiment, the colonel of which ordered him back and questioned him; and finally, seeing the old man's patriotic determination, gave him a good rifle in place of the musket he had brought with him.

"Are you a good shot?"

"Tolerable good," said John, who is an old fox-hunter.

"Do you see that Rebel riding yonder?"

"I do."

"Can you fetch him?"

"I can try."

The old man took deliberate aim, and fired. He does n't say he killed the Rebel, but simply that his shot was cheered by the Wisconsin boys, and that afterward the horse the Rebel rode was seen galloping with an empty saddle. "That's all I know about it."

He fought until our forces were driven back in the afternoon. He had already received two slight wounds, and a third one through the arm, to which he paid little attention. "Only the blood running down my hand bothered me a heap." Then, as he was slowly falling back with the rest, he received a final shot through the leg. "Down I went, and the whole Rebel army ran over me." Helpless, nearly bleeding to death from his wounds, he lay upon the field all night.

"About sun-up the next morning I crawled to a neighbor's house, and found it full of wounded Rebels." The neighbor afterwards took him to his own house, which had also been turned into a Rebel hospital. — *Atlantic Monthly.*

THE THIRD DAY'S ATTACK.

Soon from the Cemetery Hill (I did not see this, but tell it as actors in it told me) could be seen the forming columns of Hill's corps. Their batteries had already opened in almost a semicircle of fire on that scarred hill-front. Three cross-fires thus came in upon it, and to-day the tracks of shells ploughing the ground in as many directions may be seen everywhere among the graves. Howard never moved his head-quarters an inch. There was his Eleventh Corps, and there he meant to stay, and make them do their duty if he could. They did it well.

When the fierce cannonade had, as they supposed, sufficiently prepared the way, down came the Rebel lines, "dressed to the right," as if for a parade before some grand master of reviews. To the front they had a line of skirmishers, double or treble the usual strength, next the line of battle for the charge, next another equally strong in reserve, if the fierce fire they might meet should melt away the first.

Howard sent orders for his men to lie down, and for a little our batteries ceased firing. The Rebels thought they had silenced us, and charged. They were well up to our front when the whole corps of concealed Germans sprang up and poured out their sheet of flame and smoke, and swiftly flying death; the batteries opened, the solid lines broke and crisped up into little fragments, and were beaten wildly back. Our men charged, company after company, once at least a whole regiment, threw down down their arms, and rushed over to be taken prisoners and carried out of this fearful fire.

Simultaneously, similar scenes were enacting along the front of the Second, Third, and Fifth Corps. Everywhere the Rebel attack was beaten back, and the cannonade on both sides continued at its highest pitch.

When this broke out I had been coming over from the neighborhood of Pleasanton's head-quarters. Ascending the high hill to the rear of Slocum's head-quarters, I saw such a sight as few men may ever hope to see twice in a lifetime. Around our centre and left the Rebel line must have been from four to five miles long, and over that whole length there rolled up the smoke from their two hundred and fifty guns. The roar, the bursting bombs, the impression of magnificent power, "all the glory visible, all the horror of the fearful field concealed," a nation's existence trembling as the clangor of those iron monsters swayed the balance, — it was a sensation for a century!

About two the fire slackened a little, then broke out deadlier than ever, till, beaten out against our impenetrable sides, it ebbed away, and closed in broken, spasmodic dashes. — *Cincinnati Gazette.*

Then there was a lull, and we knew that the Rebel infantry was charging. And splendidly they did this work, the highest and severest test of the stuff soldiers are made of. Hill's division in the line of battle came first on the double-quick, their muskets at the "right-shoulder-shift." Longstreet's came as the support, at the usual distance, with war-cries and a savage insolence as yet untutored by defeat. They rushed in perfect order across the open field, up to the very muzzles of the guns, which tore lanes through them as they came.

But they met men who were their equals in spirit and their superiors in tenacity. There never was better fighting since Thermopylæ than was done yesterday by our infantry and artillery. The Rebels were over our defences. They had cleared cannoneers and horses from one of the guns, and were whirling it around to use upon us. The bayonet drove them back. But so hard pressed was this brave infantry, that at one time, from the exhaustion of their ammunition, every battery upon the principal crest of attack was silent except Crowen's.

His services of grape and canister were awful. It enabled our line, outnumbered two to one, first to beat back Longstreet, and then to charge upon him and take a great number of prisoners. Strange sight! So terrible was our musketry and artillery fire, that, when Armistead's brigade was checked in its charge and stood reeling, all of its men dropped their muskets and crawled on their hands and knees underneath the stream of shot, till close to our troops, where they made signs of surrendering. They passed through our ranks scarcely noticed, and slowly went down the slope to the road in the rear. — *N. Y. Times.*

FROM A SOUTHERN POINT OF VIEW.

Now the storming party was moved up. Pickett's division in advance, supported on the right by Wilcox's brigade and on the left by Heth's division, commanded by Pettigrew. The left of Pickett's division occupied the same ground over which Wright had passed the day before. I stood upon an eminence and watched this advance with great interest; I had seen brave men pass over that fated valley the day before; I had witnessed their death-struggle with the foe on the opposite heights; I had observed their return with shattered ranks, a bleeding mass, but with unstained banners. Now I saw their valiant comrades prepare for the same bloody trial, and already felt that their efforts would be vain unless their supports should be as true as steel and brave as lions. Now they move forward, with steady, measured tread they advance upon the foe. Their banners float defiantly in the breeze, as onward in beautiful order they press across the plain. I have never seen since the war began (and I have been in all the great fights of this army) troops enter a fight in such splendid order as did this splendid division of Pickett's. Now Pettigrew's command emerges from the woods upon Pickett's left, and sweeps down the slope of the hill to the valley beneath, and some two or three hundred yards in rear of Pickett. I saw by the wavering of this line as they entered the conflict that they wanted the firmness of nerve and steadiness of tread which so characterized Pickett's men, and I felt that these men would not, could not stand the tremendous ordeal to which they would be soon subjected. These were mostly raw troops, which had been recently brought from the South, and who had, perhaps, never been under fire, — who certainly had never been in any very severe fight, — and I trembled for their conduct. Just as Pickett was getting well under the enemy's fire, our batteries ceased firing. This was a fearful moment for Pickett and his brave command. Why do not our guns re-open their fire? is the inquiry that rises upon every lip. Still our batteries are silent as death! But on press Pickett's brave Virginians; and now the enemy open upon them, from more than fifty guns, a terrible fire of grape, shell, and canister. On, on they move, in unbroken line, delivering a deadly fire as they advance. Now they have reached the Emmetsburgh road, and here they meet a severe fire from the heavy masses of the enemy's infantry, posted behind the stone fence, while their artillery, now free from the annoyance of our artillery, turn their whole fire upon this devoted band. Still they remain firm. Now again they advance; they storm the stone fence; the Yankees fly. The enemy's batteries are, one by one, silenced in quick succession as Pickett's men deliver their fire at the gunners and drive them from their pieces. I see Kemper and Armistead plant their banner in the enemy's works. I hear their glad shout of victory!

Let us look after Pettigrew's division. Where are they now? While the victorious shout of the gallant Virginians is still ringing in my ears, I turn my eyes to the left, and there, all over the plain, in utmost confusion, is scattered this strong division. Their line is broken; they are flying, apparently panic-stricken, to the rear. The gallant Pettigrew is wounded; but he still retains command, and is vainly striving to rally his men. Still the moving mass rush pell-mell to the rear, and Pickett is left alone to contend with the hordes of the enemy now pouring in upon him on every side. Garnett falls, killed by a minie ball, and Kemper, the brave and chivalrous, reels under a mortal wound, and is taken to the rear. Now the enemy move around strong flanking bodies of infantry, and are rapidly gaining Pickett's rear. The order is given to fall back, and our men commence the movement, doggedly contending for every inch of ground. The enemy press heavily our retreating line, and many noble spirits who had passed safely through the fiery ordeal of the advance and charge now fall on the right and on the left. Armistead is wounded, and left in the enemy's hands. At this critical moment the shattered remnant of Wright's Georgia brigade is moved forward to cover their retreat, and the fight closes here. Our loss in this charge was very severe, and the Yankee prisoners taken acknowledge that theirs was immense. — *Richmond Enquirer.*

A REBEL CHARGE.

Reaching my post I looked up the line and there stood the brave Stuart, calmly waiting for the troops to get in position. "Fix bayonets!" was the command, quietly given, and the last act in this bloody drama was about to be enacted. It was a dreadful moment. But one brief second of life yet left! The sword of the general is raised on high! "Forward, double-quick!" rings out in clarion tones, and the race to meet death began. The fated brigade emerged from the woods into the open plain, and here, O God! what a fire greeted us, and the death-shriek rends the air on every side! But on the gallant survivors pressed, closing up the dreadful gaps as fast as they were made. At this moment I felt a violent shock, and found myself instantly stretched upon the ground. I had experienced the feeling before, and knew what it meant, but to save me I could not tell where I was struck. In the excitement I felt not the pain, and, resting upon my elbow, anxiously watched that struggling column. Column, did I say? A column no longer, but the torn and scattered fragments of one. But flesh and blood could not live in such a fire; and a handful of survivors of what had been a little more than twelve hours before the pride and boast of the army sought to reach the cover of the woods. — *Maj. Golasborough, 1st Md. C. S. A.*

THE THICK OF THE FIGHT.

Men fired in each other's faces not five feet apart. There were bayonet-thrusts, cuttings with sabres, pistol-shots, cool, deliberate movements on the part of some, — hot, passionate, despairing efforts with others, — hand-to-hand contests. There was recklessness of life, tenacity of purpose, oaths, curses, yells, hurrahs, shoutings, — men went down, some on their faces, some leaping into the air with exclamations wrung from their hearts. There were ghastly heaps of dead where the cannon tore open the ranks. —*C. C. Coffin.*

ADVANCE OF THE COLORS.

When the fight was most terrific, Colonel Hall, commanding the brigade, quietly ordered the color-bearer of the Fifteenth Massachusetts to advance upon the enemy alone. It was like an electric impulse. It thrilled the entire line. Men forgot that they were on the defensive ; and, without an order from a commanding officer, the line, as if bent on one common purpose, surged ahead. Thousands of bayonets flashed in the setting sun. Then came a wild hurrah, and the mass of Rebels melted away over the plain. —*C. C. Coffin.*

CUSTER'S CAVALRY CHARGE.

To repel their advance I ordered the Fifth Cavalry to a more advanced position, with instructions to maintain their ground at all hazards. Colonel Alger, commanding the Fifth, assisted by Majors Trowbridge and Ferry of the same regiment, made such admirable disposition of their men behind fences and other defences, as enabled them to successfully repel the repeated advance of a greatly superior force. I attributed their success in a great measure to the fact that this regiment is armed with the Spencer repeating rifle, which, in the hands of brave, determined men, like those composing the Fifth Michigan Cavalry, is, in my estimation, the most effective fire-arm that our cavalry can adopt. Colonel Alger held his ground until his men had exhausted their ammunition, when he was compelled to fall back on the main body. The beginning of this movement was the signal for the enemy to charge, which they did, with two regiments, mounted and dismounted. I at once ordered the Seventh Michigan Cavalry, Colonel Mann, to charge the advancing column of the enemy. The ground over which we had to pass was very unfavorable for the manœuvring of cavalry, but despite all obstacles this regiment advanced boldly to the assault, which was executed in splendid style, the enemy being driven from field to field until our advance reached a high and unbroken fence, behind which the enemy were strongly posted. Nothing daunted, Colonel Mann, followed by the main body of his regiment, bravely rode up to the fence and discharged their revolvers in the very face of the foe. No troops could have maintained this position; the Seventh was, therefore, compelled to retire, followed by twice the number of the enemy. By this time Colonel Alger of the Fifth Michigan Cavalry had succeeded in mounting a considerable portion of his regiment, and gallantly advanced to the assistance of the Seventh, whose further pursuit by the enemy he checked. At the same time an entire brigade of the enemy's cavalry, consisting of four regiments, appeared just over the crest in our front. They were formed in column of regiments. To meet this overwhelming force I had but one available regiment, the First Michigan Cavalry and the fire of Battery M, Second Regular Artillery. I at once ordered the First to charge, but learned at the same moment that similar orders had been given by Brigadier-General Gregg. As before stated, the First was formed in column of battalions. Upon receiving the orders to charge, Colonel Town, placing himself at the head of his command, ordered the "trot" and sabres to be drawn. In this manner this gallant body of men advanced to the attack of a force outnumbering them five to one. In addition to this numerical superiority the enemy had the advantage of position, and were exultant over the repulse of the Seventh Michigan Cavalry. All these facts considered would seem to render success on the part of the First impossible. Not so, however. Arriving within a few yards of the enemy's column, the charge was ordered, and, with a yell that spread terror before them, the First Michigan Cavalry, led by Colonel Town, rode upon the front rank of the enemy, sabring all who came within reach. For a moment, but only a moment, that long heavy column stood its ground, then, unable to withstand the impetuosity of our attack, it gave way into a disorderly rout, leaving vast numbers of their dead and wounded in our possession, while the First, being masters of the field, had the proud satisfaction of seeing the much vaunted "Chivalry" led by their favorite commander, seek safety in headlong flight. I cannot find language to express my high appreciation of the gallantry and daring displayed by the officers and men of the First Michigan Cavalry. They advanced to the charge of a vastly superior force with as much order and precision as if going upon parade; and I challenge the annals of warfare to produce a more brilliant or successful charge of cavalry than the one just recounted. — *Maj.-Gen. Custer.*

THE REPULSE.

As soon as the bullets began to whistle, a general said to the orderly who carried the color of his brigade, which he supposed would attract notice and draw the fire of the enemy upon him, "Take away that flag, go to the rear with that flag!" and the person who obeyed this direction remarked in stating it, "Faith, an' I was as willin' to run with it to the rear as he was to have me." . . . .

At sunset, at a critical time, in obedience to a universal cry among the soldiers, "Charge on them!" "Take our old ground!" the fragments of the brigade, with the colors of five regiments unfurled within the distance of one hundred feet, in the absence of its general, and against the orders of General Humphreys, the division commander, who vainly shouted, "Halt! halt! stop those men!" pursued the enemy half a mile, captured several prisoners, retook cannon that had been left upon the field, and assisted to achieve a conclusive success. . . . .

The Rebels told me that their generals and officers said that there was nothing in their front except a force of militia which would run away at the first volley; but this falsehood was detected as soon as the fighting commenced. They deceived others, who implored the National troops not to kill them. I observed one wounded youth, about sixteen years of age, who was crying, and stated as the cause of his grief that "General Lee always put the Fifth Florida in the front!" . . . .

One of the staff arrived and stated that a brigadier-general had decided to establish a new line of battle about a mile in the rear, but was unable to find his regiments, and delivered an order for the ranks to return at once to that point. The men were very indignant, because they wished to enjoy that rest which is so precious to every soldier, — a sleep upon the field which they had won by their bravery; and an officer said, "Tell the general that if he will come to the front he will find his commands with their colors, and, if he was not such a d——d coward, he would be here with them." . . . .

The Rebels were dispirited by the repulses upon the 2d and 3d; called the plain a "slaughter-pen"; declared that further fighting was useless; and some, who considered Jackson their "very heart of hope," mournfully said, "We have not got Stonewall with us now." They related the following incident regarding Amistead, who commanded a brigade, and was killed in the unsuccessful charge. He skulked behind the trunk of a poplar-tree, in one of the battles before Richmond; and, as they advanced upon the open plain, several men who disliked him shouted, "There are no poplar-trees to get behind now"; and he replied to their taunts by saying, "Before this charge is ended, you will wish that there were some poplar-trees here." — *Capt. Blake,* 11*th Mass.*

GENERAL LEE AFTER THE BATTLE. –

He was engaged in rallying and encouraging the broken troops, and was riding about, a little in front of the wood, quite alone, — the whole of his staff being engaged in a similar manner, further to the rear. His face, which is always placid and cheerful, did not show signs of the slightest disappointment, care, or annoyance; and he was addressing to every soldier he met a few words of encouragement, such as, " All this will come right in the end; we 'll talk it over afterwards; but, in the mean time, all good men must rally. We want all good and true men just now," &c. He spoke to all the wounded that passed him, and the slightly wounded he exhorted to bind up their hurts and take up a musket in this emergency. Very few failed to answer his appeal, and I saw many badly wounded men take off their hats and cheer him.

I saw General Willcox (an officer who wears a short round jacket and a battered straw hat) come up to him, and explain, almost crying, the state of his brigade. General Lee immediately shook hands with him, and said, cheerfully, " Never mind, General, *all this has been* MY *fault,* — it is *I* that have lost this fight, and you must help me out of it in the best way you can."

In this manner I saw General Lee encourage and re-animate his somewhat dispirited troops, and magnanimously take upon his own shoulders the whole weight of the repulse. — *An English Officer.*

WORK OF THE SANITARY COMMISSION.

" Have you friends in the army, madam?" a Rebel soldier, lying on the floor of the car, said to me as I gave him some milk. " Yes, my brother is on ——'s staff." " I thought so, ma'am. You can always tell; when people are good to soldiers, they are sure to have friends in the army." " We are Rebels, you know,

ma'am," another said; " do you treat Rebels *so?* "
It was strange to see the good brotherly feeling come
over the soldiers, our own and the Rebels, when, side
by side, they lay in our tents. " Hallo, boys! this is
the pleasantest way to meet, is n't it? We are better
friends when we are as close as this, than a little farther off." And then they would go over the battles
together: " we were here," and " you were there," in
the friendliest way. . . . .

Few good things can be said of the Gettysburg farm-
ers, and I only use Scripture language in calling them
"evil beasts." One of this kind came creeping into our
camp three weeks after the battle. He lived five miles
only from the town, and had " never seen a Rebel."
He heard we had some of them, and came down to see
them. " Boys, here 's a man who never saw a Rebel
in his life, and wants to look at you"; and then he
stood with his mouth wide open, and there they lay in
rows, laughing at him, stupid old Dutchman. " And
why have n't you seen a Rebel?" Mrs. —— said; " why
did n't you take your gun and help to drive them out of
your town?" — " A feller might 'er got hit!" — which
reply was quite too much for the Rebels; they roared
with laughter at him, up and down the tents. — *Miss
Woolsey.*

GENERAL MEADE'S OFFICIAL REPORT.

Major-General Reynolds immediately moved around
the town of Gettysburg, and advanced on the Cashtown road, and without a moment's hesitation deployed
his advance division and attacked the enemy, at the
same time sending orders for the Eleventh Corps
(General Howard) to advance as promptly as possible.
Soon after making his dispositions for the attack, Major-
General Reynolds fell mortally wounded, the command
of the First Corps devolving on Major-General Doubleday, and the command of the field on Major-General
Howard, who arrived about this time (11.30 A. M.),

with the Eleventh Corps, then commanded by Major-General Schurz. Major-General Howard pushed forward two divisions of the Eleventh Corps to support the First Corps, now warmly engaged with the enemy on the ridge to the north of the town, and posted his Third Division, with three batteries of artillery, on Cemetery Ridge, on the south side of the town. Up to this time the battle had been with the forces of the enemy debouching from the mountains on the Cashtown Road, known to be Hill's corps. In the early part of the action, success was on our side, — Wadsworth's division of the First Corps having driven the enemy back some distance, and capturing numerous prisoners, among them, General Archer, of the Confederate army.

The arrival of reinforcements to the enemy on the Cashtown Road, and the junction with Ewell's corps, coming on the York and Harrisburg roads, which occurred between one and two o'clock P. M., enabled the enemy to bring vastly superior forces against both the First and Eleventh Corps, outflanking our line of battle and pressing it so severely that, at about four P. M., Major-General Howard deemed it prudent to withdraw these two corps to Cemetery Ridge, on the south side of the town, which operation was successfully accomplished, — not, however, without considerable loss in prisoners, arising from the confusion incident to portions of both corps passing through the town, and the men getting confused in the streets.

About the time of the withdrawal, Major-General Hancock arrived, whom I had despatched to represent me on the field on hearing of the death of General Reynolds. In conjunction with Major-General Howard, General Hancock proceeded to post troops on Cemetery Ridge, and to repel an attack that the enemy made on our right flank. This attack was not, however, very vigorous. The enemy, seeing the strength of the position occupied, seemed to be satisfied with the success he had accomplished, desisting from any further attack this day.

About seven P. M., Major-Generals Slocum and Sickles, with the Twelfth Corps and part of the Third, reached the ground and took post on the right and left of the troops previously posted.

Being satisfied, from reports received from the field, that it was the intention of the enemy to support, with his whole army, the attack already made, and reports from Major-Generals Hancock and Howard on the character of the position being favorable, I determined to give battle at this point, and early in the evening of the 1st, issued orders to all corps to concentrate at Gettysburg, directing all trains to be sent to the rear at Westminster.

At eleven P. M. of the 1st, I broke up my head-quarters, which, till then, had been at Taneytown, and proceeded to the field, arriving there at one A. M. of the 2d. So soon as it was light I proceeded to inspect the position occupied, and to make arrangements for posting several corps as they should reach the ground. By seven A. M. the Second and Fifth Corps, with the rest of the Third, had reached the ground, and were posted as follows. The Eleventh Corps retained its position on the cemetery side, just opposite to the town. The First Corps was posted on the right of the Eleventh, on an elevated knoll, connecting with a ridge extending to the south and east, on which the Second Corps was placed. The right of the Twelfth Corps rested on a small stream at a point where it crossed the Baltimore Pike, and which formed on the right flank of the Twelfth something of an obstacle. Cemetery Ridge extended in a westerly and southerly direction, gradually diminishing in elevation till it came to a very prominent ridge, called Round Top, running east and west. The Second and Third Corps were directed to occupy the continuation of Cemetery Ridge, on the left of the Eleventh Corps. The Fifth Corps, pending the arrival of the Sixth, was held in reserve. While these dispositions were being made, the enemy was massing his troops on the exterior ridge, distant from the line occupied by us from a mile to a mile and a half.

At two P. M. the Sixth Corps arrived, after a march of thirty-two miles, accomplished from nine A. M. the day previous. On its arrival being reported, I immediately directed the Fifth Corps to move over to our extreme left, and the Sixth to occupy its place as a reserve for the right. . . . . .

Another assault was, however, made, about eight P. M., on the Eleventh Corps, from the left of the town, which was repulsed with the assistance of the troops from the Second and First Corps. During the heavy assault upon our extreme left, portions of the Twelfth Corps were sent as reinforcements. During their absence, the line on the extreme right was held by a very much reduced force. This was taken advantage of by the enemy, who, during the absence of Geary's division of the Twelfth Corps, advanced and occupied part of the line. On the morning of the 3d, General Geary, having returned during the night, was attacked at early dawn by the enemy, but succeeded in driving him back, and occupying his former position. A spirited contest was maintained all the morning along this part of the line. General Geary, reinforced by Wheaton's brigade, Sixth Corps, maintained his position, inflicting very severe losses on the enemy. With this exception, the quiet of the lines remained undisturbed till one P. M. on the 3d, when the enemy opened from over one hundred and twenty-five guns, playing upon our centre and left. This cannonade continued for over two hours, when, our guns failing to make any reply, the enemy ceased firing, and soon his masses of infantry became visible, forming for an assault on our left and left centre. The assault was made with great firmness, being directed principally against the point occupied by the Second Corps, and was repelled with equal firmness by the troops of that corps, supported by Doubleday's division and Stannard's brigade of the First Corps.

During the assault, both Major-General Hancock, commanding the left centre, and Brigadier-General

Gibbon, commanding the Second Corps, were severely wounded.

This terminated the battle, the enemy retiring to his lines leaving the field strewed with his dead and wounded, and numbers of prisoners fell into our hands.

The result of the campaign may be briefly stated in the defeat of the enemy at Gettysburg, his compulsory evacuation of Pennsylvania and Maryland, and his withdrawal from the upper valley of the Shenandoah; and in the capture of three guns, forty-one standards, and 13,621 prisoners. 24,978 small arms were collected on the battle-field. Our own losses were very severe, amounting, as will be seen by the accompanying return, to 2,834 killed, 13,709 wounded, and 6,643 missing, — in all, 23,186.

GENERAL LEE'S OFFICIAL REPORT.

The preparations for attack were not completed until the afternoon of the 2d.

The enemy held a high and commanding ridge, along which he had massed a large amount of artillery. General Ewell occupied the left of our line, General Hill the centre, and General Longstreet the right.   In front of General Longstreet the enemy held a position, from which, if he could be driven, it was thought that our army could be used to advantage in assailing the more elevated ground beyond, and thus enable us to reach the crest of the ridge.   That officer was directed to endeavor to carry this position, while General Ewell attacked directly the high ground on the enemy's right, which had already been partially fortified.   General Hill was instructed to threaten the centre of the Federal line, in order to prevent reinforcements being sent to either wing, and to avail himself of any opportunity that might present itself to attack.

After a severe struggle, Longstreet succeeded in getting possession of and holding the desired ground. Ewell also carried some of the strong positions which he assailed, and the result was such as to lead to the belief that he would ultimately be able to dislodge the enemy. The battle ceased at dark.

These partial successes determined me to continue the assault next day. Pickett, with three of his brigades, joined Longstreet the following morning, and our batteries were moved forward to the position gained by him the day before.

The general plan of attack was unchanged, except that one division and two brigades of Hill's corps were ordered to support Longstreet.

The enemy, in the mean time, had strengthened his line with earth-works. The morning was occupied in necessary preparations, and the battle recommenced in the afternoon of the 3d, and raged with great violence until sunset. Our troops succeeded in entering the advanced works of the enemy, and getting possession of some of his batteries; but our artillery having nearly expended its ammunition, the attacking columns became exposed to the heavy fire of the numerous batteries near the summit of the ridge, and, after a most determined and gallant struggle, were compelled to relinquish their advantage, and fall back to their original position, with severe loss.

The conduct of the troops was all that I could desire or expect, and they deserved success so far as it can be deserved by heroic valor and fortitude. More may have been required of them than they were able to perform, but my admiration of their noble qualities, and confidence in their ability to cope successfully with the enemy, has suffered no abatement from the issue of this protracted and sanguinary conflict.

Owing to the strength of the enemy's position and the reduction of our ammunition, a renewal of the engagement could not be hazarded, and the difficulty of procuring supplies rendered it impossible to continue longer where we were. Such of the wounded as were in condition to be removed, and part of the arms collected on the field, were ordered to Williamsport. The army remained at Gettysburg during the 4th, and at night began to retire by the road to Fairfield, carrying with it about four thousand prisoners. Nearly two thousand had previously been paroled, but the enemy's numerous wounded, that had fallen into our hands after the first and second day's engagements, were left behind.

Little progress was made that night, owing to a severe storm, which greatly embarrassed our movements. The rear of the column did not leave its position near Gettysburg until after daylight on the 5th.

The march was continued during that day without interruption by the enemy, except an unimportant demonstration upon our rear in the afternoon, when near Fairfield, which was easily checked. Part of our train moved by the road through Fairfield, and the rest by the way of Cashtown, guarded by General Imboden. In passing through the mountains, in advance of the column, the great length of the trains exposed them to attack by the enemy's cavalry, which captured a number of wagons and ambulances; but they succeeded in reaching Williamsport without serious loss.

They were attacked at that place on the 6th by the enemy's cavalry, which was gallantly repulsed by General Imboden. The attacking force was subsequently encountered and driven off by General Stuart, and pursued for several miles in the direction of Boonesboro. The army, after an arduous march, rendered more difficult by the rains, reached Hagerstown on the afternoon of the 6th and morning of the 7th of July.

The Potomac was found to be so much swollen by the rains that had fallen almost incessantly since our entrance into Maryland as to be unfordable. Our communications with the south side were thus interrupted, and it was difficult to procure either ammunition or subsistence, the latter difficulty being enhanced by the high waters impeding the working of neighboring mills. The trains with the wounded and prisoners were compelled to await at Williamsport the subsiding of the river and the construction of boats, as the pontoon bridge left at Falling Waters had been partially destroyed. The enemy had not yet made his appearance; but as he was in condition to obtain large reinforcements, and our situation, for the reasons above mentioned, was becoming daily more embarrassing, it was deemed advisable to recross the river. Part of the pontoon bridge was recovered, and new boats built, so that by the 13th a good bridge was thrown over the river at Falling Waters.

The enemy in force reached our front on the 12th. A position had been previously selected to cover the Potomac from Williamsport to Falling Waters, and an attack was awaited during that and the succeeding day. This did not take place, though the two armies were in close proximity, the enemy being occupied in fortifying his own lines. Our preparations being completed, and the river, though still deep, being pronounced fordable, the army commenced to withdraw to the south side on the night of the 13th.

Ewell's corps forded the river at Williamsport, those of Longstreet and Hill crossed upon the bridge. Owing to the condition of the roads the troops did not reach the bridge until after daylight of the 14th, and the crossing was not completed till one P. M., when the bridge was removed. The enemy offered no serious interruption, and the movement was attended with no loss of material except a few disabled wagons and two pieces of artillery, which the horses were unable to move through the deep mud. Before fresh horses could be sent back for them, the rear of the column had passed.

During the slow and tedious march to the bridge, in the midst of a violent storm of rain, some of the men lay down by the way to rest. Officers sent back for them failed to find many in the obscurity of the night, and these, with some stragglers, fell into the hands of the enemy.

CHAPTER IX.

CHICKAMAUGA AND CHATTANOOGA.

CHATTANOOGA, in Eastern Tennessee, was another of the points which were very important to each party in the war. It is the centre of a great system of railroads, which unite the Eastern and Western regions of the South. The armies in Virginia and the East received by these roads their supplies of grain and beef from Alabama, Florida, and Georgia. The inhabitants of the neighborhood were loyal to the Union; and on this account alone the National government would have been glad to take and hold Chattanooga, for their encouragement. After the fall of Vicksburg, Chattanooga was the most important point excepting Richmond for the National army to seize.

General Rosecrans took possession of it accordingly, on the 9th of September, 1863, having outgeneralled the Southern General Bragg, who was intrusted with holding it. But Bragg had no intention of leaving his enemy in possession, and, having been largely reinforced, on the 19th of September he attacked the widely extended army of Rosecrans, " demolished his right wing," and pierced his centre. But the persistency of General Thomas — who always distinguished himself by holding on — foiled Bragg in his principal object, and, though Rosecrans lost sixteen thousand men and thirty-six cannon in this battle, which is known as the battle of Chickamauga, Chattanooga was, for the moment, saved. Still, with his army so terribly reduced, Rosecrans could do little more than hold it. General Bragg considered its reduction a mere question of time.[1] He held all the high land on the south side of the city, and as the Tennessee River, not easily passed, shut it in on the north and west, the National army was virtually besieged in the city. The supply trains from Bridgeport, twenty-five miles distant by road, could not cross the mountains after the fall rains set in ; and General Rosecrans was obliged to put his whole command on half-rations. Under these circumstances General Rosecrans was removed, and General Grant appointed in his place ; and, to relieve Chattanooga, as soon as he could gather strength sufficient, he fought the battle known as " the battle of Chattanooga."

Of this battle General Badeau says : " It was the grandest one fought west of the Alleghanies. It covered an extent of thirteen miles, and Grant had over sixty thousand men engaged. . . . . At

---

[1] General Bragg says in an official report : " We held him at our mercy, and his destruction was only a question of time."

Vicksburg it had been the strategy, at Shiloh the hard fighting, but at Chattanooga it was the manœuvring in the presence of the enemy that brought about the result; aided, of course, in the highest possible degree, by the gallantry of the soldiers, without which the greatest of generals is in fact unarmed. Few battles have ever been won so strictly according to the plan laid down; certainly no battle, during the war of the Rebellion, was carried out so completely according to the programme. Grant's instructions in advance would almost serve as a history of the contest. Changes were indeed made in the orders; but before the battle began, the original plan was resumed."

That plan was simple, and any boy who will fix this in his mind, or set it down on an imaginary map, on a bit of paper, will understand well enough the more important places alluded to in the narratives of details which follow. Remember that Lookout Mountain is a high mountain which commands the view of the whole scene. The fighting at Missionary Ridge was thirteen miles northeast of Lookout Mountain. Missionary Ridge runs south from where it touches the Tennessee, and along its summit ran, for six miles, the Rebel intrenchments, shutting in Chattanooga from the east; then they turned westward and ran for four miles across the valley of Chattanooga Creek, to Lookout Mountain, which was held by a strong force to secure his left flank. Bragg had just weakened himself by sending Longstreet on an expedition into Eastern Tennessee with fifteen thousand men, so that his effective force was only forty-five thousand, scattered along his ten miles of intrenchments.

Grant had thirty thousand men under Thomas in Chattanooga, Hooker with ten thousand west of Lookout Mountain on the south side of the Tennessee, and Sherman on the north side, behind the hills, with twenty thousand.

This is his plan in his own words : " The general plan is for Sherman . . . . to effect a crossing of the Tennessee River, just below the mouth of the Chickamauga ; his crossing to be protected by artillery from the heights on the north bank of the river, and to secure the heights from the northern extremity to about the railroad tunnel, before the enemy can concentrate against him. You " (Thomas) " will co-operate with Sherman. . . . . Further movements will then depend on those of the enemy."

But on the 23d of November it seemed as if the knot was to be cut in an entirely different way. A Rebel soldier, who had seen the departure from the Rebel camp of a corps sent to reinforce Longstreet, deserted, and brought the news into the Union camp that Bragg was evacuating his position. Grant, unwilling to allow Bragg to make an orderly retreat, and anxious to learn the truth, ordered an advance to feel the Rebels' centre, although Sherman had not yet reached his position behind Chattanooga. Sherman had been for more than a month marching up from Vicksburg.

Accordingly at noon of the 23d two corps of Thomas's command formed in line of battle and advanced quickly on the Rebel line. The enemy were taken entirely by surprise, and driven a mile and a half to their second line of defences. Thomas immediately strengthened his position by earthworks, and on the morning of the 24th he had several guns in position on his new line. Here he waited all the next day.

While he was fortifying himself, Sherman was floating down pontoons from a creek above, and building a bridge across the Tennessee north of the enemy's position. The next morning, under cover of the mist, he began ferrying his troops across, and continued his work on the bridge, so that at one of the 24th all his men were on the south side of the river, and their line of communication secure. As soon as his last men were across, he advanced toward the south till he came to the main line of the enemy, who offered vigorous resistance. Sherman's immediate object was to get possession of the railroad from Chattanooga east, but the enemy were strongly fortified and kept him back till night.

Hooker on the west also made an attack on the 24th, and in the afternoon fought his " Battle among the Clouds." He had to build a bridge over the

Lookout Creek before advancing, but, once across, he drove the enemy from their superior position, and at four had gained a point which commanded the enemy's works; for two hours he had been fighting in a cloud-mist, only more darkened by the smoke of the battle.

In the night the enemy retreated from Lookout Mountain across the Chattanooga Creek, burning the bridges as they went. At the same time they evacuated some of the ground they had held so well in front of Sherman, and retreated to still stronger defences.

Next morning, the morning of the 25th, Sherman advanced over the ground given by the Rebels and attacked them again and again. So hard he struck that Bragg had again and again to reinforce his men in this position, which they must keep. Division after division was sent to the right, and the centre and left weakened by so much.

At last the time had come, and Grant gave the word to Thomas in the centre. His army, the army which had been defeated at Chickamauga, sprang forward on the double-quick. Every man knew that here was the moment to avenge that defeat. The defence of the Rebels was nothing to them, the Rebels were less; on they went, with cheers ⸱ ˙ ʰouts, over line after line of breastworks, over h.. .er line of soldiers, till the last pits on the top of the ridge were gained, the enemy's centre was crushed, the battle was won.

Thomas turned some of his men to the left, to rout the Rebels still holding out against Sherman; with others he pursued the retreat — the flight — of the enemy.

"For Chickamauga," said Uncle Fritz, "we cannot do much with the reports of our side: it is sad work. But you will find a book the Rebel government published with all their reports of that battle; perhaps you can pick out something interesting out of that."

So Horace, who knew enough not to expect picturesqueness from the report of any one higher than a brigadier, picked out these three bits.

A REBEL BRIGADE.

The attack was soon made by the whole line. It was stubbornly resisted from a very strong position just behind the crest of the hill. A portion of two of my regiments gained the crest of the hill and planted colors there, but the position was a hot one, and some breaking to the rear on the left caused the whole to give way for a time. The troops were rallied on the slope of the hill, lines reformed, and all in readiness to resume the attack, when the enemy advanced his line immediately in my front, down the hill, with some impetuosity. The line was instantly ordered forward to meet this charge, and the command quickly responded to. The enemy was met by a volley and a charge which did much execution, his line broken, and his troops fled in some confusion; but as there was no corresponding forward movement by the brigades on my right and left, and as the hill near the crest was very difficult to ascend, he had time either to re-form or to bring up a second line

before we reached the top of the hill, and another repulse was the consequence. Troops never rallied more
promptly, nor with less confusion or clamor. — *Brig.-
Gen. Patton Anderson, C. S. A.*

DEATH OF GENERAL DESHLER, C. S. A.

About twelve o'clock our supply of ammunition
began to give out, and I sent a courier to Brigadier-
General Deshler to inform him of the fact, and to ask
where we could get more. A few minutes after, I saw
him coming towards my right, some forty paces from
me, when he was struck by a shell in the chest and his
heart literally torn from his bosom. . . . . Refusing to
permit a staff-officer to endanger his life in going to ex-
amine the cartridge-boxes to see what amount of ammunition his men had, he cheerfully started himself to brave
the tempest of death that raged on the crest of the hill.
He had gone but a little way when he fell, — fell as he
would wish to fall. . . .—*Col. R. Q. Mills, commanding
Brigade C. S. A.*

A BRAVE REBEL.

Private McCann was under my own eye. He stood
upright, cheerful and self-possessed in the very hail of
deadly missiles, and cheered up his comrades around
him. After he had expended all his ammunition, he
gathered up the cartridge-boxes of the dead and wounded, and distributed them to his comrades. He bore
himself like a hero through the entire contest, and fell
mortally wounded by the last volleys of the enemy. I
promised him during the engagement that I would mention his good conduct, and, as he was borne dying from
the field, he turned his boyish face upon me, and, with
a light and pleasant smile, reminded me of my promise. —*Col. R. Q. Mills, commanding Brigade C. S. A.*

But for Chattanooga they had only too much. Uncle Fritz only let them read half of what they wanted to, and it is to be hoped they halved their book-marks wisely. Florence confesses that she only left out the shorter extracts.

SHERMAN'S ADVANCE TO CHATTANOOGA.

Another bridge was in course of construction at Chattanooga, under the immediate direction of Quartermaster-General Meigs, but at the time all the wagons, etc. had to be ferried across by a flying bridge. Men were busy and hard at work everywhere inside our lines, and boats for another pontoon bridge were being rapidly constructed under Brigadier-General W. F. Smith, familiarly known as "Baldy Smith," and this bridge was destined to be used by my troops, at a point of the river about four miles above Chattanooga, just below the mouth of the Chickamauga River. General Grant explained to me that he had reconnoitred the Rebel line from Lookout Mountain up to Chickamauga, and he believed that the northern portion of Missionary Ridge was not fortified at all; and he wanted me, as soon as my troops got up, to lay the new pontoon bridge by night, cross over, and attack Bragg's right flank on that part of the ridge abutting on Chickamauga Creek, near the tunnel; and he proposed that we should go at once to look at the ground. In company with Generals Thomas, W. F. Smith, Brannan, and others, we crossed by the flying bridge, rode back of the hills some four miles, left our horses, and got on a hill overlooking the whole ground about the mouth of the Chickamauga River, and across to the Missionary Hills near the tunnel. Smith and I crept down behind a fringe of trees that lined the river-bank, to the very point selected for the new bridge, where we sat for some time, seeing the Rebel pickets on the opposite bank, and almost hearing their words.

Having seen enough we returned to Chattanooga; and in order to hurry up my command, on which so much depended, I started back to Kelley's in hopes to catch the steamboat that same evening; but on my arrival the boat had gone. I applied to the commanding officer, got a rough boat, manned by four soldiers, and started down the river by night. I occasionally took a turn at the oars to relieve some tired man, and about midnight we reached Shell Mound, where General Whittaker, of Kentucky, furnished us a new and good crew, with which we reached Bridgeport by daylight. I started Ewing's division in advance, with orders to turn aside towards Trenton, to make the enemy believe we were going to turn Bragg's left by pretty much the same road Rosecrans had followed; but with the other three divisions I followed the main road, via the Big Trestle at Whitesides, and reached General Hooker's head-quarters, just above Wauhatchee, on the 20th; my troops strung all the way back to Bridgeport. It was on this occasion that the Fifteenth Corps gained its peculiar badge; as the men were trudging along the deeply-cut, muddy road, of a cold, drizzly day, one of our Western soldiers left his ranks and joined a party of the Twelfth Corps at their camp-fire. They got into conversation, the Twelfth Corps men asking what troops we were, etc., etc. In turn, our fellow (who had never seen a corps-badge, and noticed that everything was marked with a star) asked if they were all brigadier-generals. Of course they were not, but the star was their corps-badge, and every wagon, tent, hat, etc. had its star. Then the Twelfth Corps men inquired what corps he belonged to, and he answered, "The Fifteenth Corps." "What is your badge?" "Why," said he, (and he was an Irishman,) suiting the action to the word, "forty rounds in the cartridge-box, and twenty in the pocket!" At that time Blair commanded the corps; but Logan succeeded soon after, and, hearing the story, adopted the cartridge-box and forty rounds as the corps-badge.—*Gen. Sherman.*

THE FIRST ATTACK.

At a given signal, Granger moved forward into the plain, in front and on the right of Fort Wood. The fog that had lain in the valley all day lifted, and the rays of the sun glanced back from twenty thousand bayonets. The superb pageant went on, under the eyes of curious crowds on Missionary Ridge ; but the troops moved with such precision, that the enemy mistook their evolutions for a parade. The Rebel pickets leaned on their muskets, and quietly watched the advance of Thomas's battalions. This unmeant deception was heightened by the troops remaining nearly half an hour in position, and in full view of the Rebel army, before they received the final order to advance. At last, a dozen shots of the National skirmishers scattered the Rebel pickets, who fled in haste through a strip of timber, lying between the open ground and some secondary eminences, on which the first line of rebel rifle-pits was built. Wood followed rapidly, directly towards the front, driving not only the Rebel pickets, but their reserves. A heavy fire of musketry was poured upon the advancing troops as they entered the strip of woods ; but they fell rapidly upon the grand guards stationed on the first line of Bragg's rifle-pit, captured about two hundred men, and secured themselves in their new positions, before the enemy had sufficiently recovered from his surprise to attempt to send reinforcements from his main camp on the ridge. Sheridan now moved up rapidly on Wood's right, and in fifteen minutes the Rebels had abandoned their whole advanced line. Nothing remained to them west of the ridge but the rifle-pit at its foot.—*Brig.-Gen. Badeau.*

LOOKOUT MOUNTAIN.

Simultaneously with these operations the troops on the mountain rushed on in their advance, the right passing directly under the muzzles of the enemy's guns on the summit, climbing over ledges and bowlders, up hill and down, furiously driving the enemy from his camp and from position after position. This lasted until twelve o'clock, when Geary's advance heroically rounded the peak of the mountain. Not knowing to what extent the enemy might be reinforced, and fearing, from the rough character of the field of operations, that our lines might be disordered, directions had been given for the troops to halt on reaching this high ground; but, fired by success, with a flying panic-stricken force before them, they pressed impetuously forward. Cobham's brigade, occupying the high ground on the right, between the enemy's main line of defence on the plateau and the palisades, incessantly plied them with fire from above and behind, while Freeland's brigade was vigorously rolling them up on the flank, both being closely supported by the brigades of Whitaker and Creighton. Our success was uninterrupted and irresistible. Before losing the advantages the ground presented us, (the enemy had been reinforced meantime,) after having secured the prisoners, two of Osterhaus's regiments had been sent forward on the Chattanooga road, and the balance of his and Cruft's divisions had joined Geary. All the Rebel efforts to resist us only resulted in rendering our success more thorough. After two or three short but sharp conflicts the plateau was cleared. The enemy, with his reinforcements, driven from the walls and pits, around Craven's house, (the last point at which he could make a stand in force,) all broken and destroyed, were hurled in great numbers over the rocks and precipices into the valley.

It was now near two o'clock, and our operations were arrested by the darkness. The clouds, which had hovered over and enveloped the summit of the mountain during the morning, and to some extent favored our movements, gradually settled into the valley and completely veiled it from our view. Indeed, from the moment we rounded the peak of the mountain, it was only from the roar of battle, and the occasional glimpse our comrades

11

in the valley could catch of our lines and standards, that they knew of the strife in its progress; and when, from these evidences, our true condition was revealed to them, their painful anxiety yielded to transports of joy.—*Maj.-Gen. Hooker.*

THE ATTACK ON THE LEFT.

General Jefferson C. Davis's division was ready to take the bridge, and I ordered the columns to form in order to carry Missionary Hills. The movement had been carefully explained to all division commanders, and at one P. M. we marched from the river in three columns in echelon; the left, General Morgan L. Smith, the column of direction, following substantially Chickamauga Creek; the centre, General John E. Smith, in column, doubled on the centre, at one brigade interval to the right and rear, prepared to deploy to the right, on the supposition that we would meet an enemy in that direction. Each head of column was covered by a good line of skirmishers, with supports. A light drizzling rain prevailed, and the clouds hung low, cloaking our movements from the enemy's tower of observation on Lookout Mountain.[1] We soon gained the foot-hills; our skirmishers crept up the face of the hills, followed by their supports; at half past three P. M. we had gained, with no loss, the desired point. A brigade of each division was pushed rapidly to the top of the hill, and the enemy for the first time seemed to realize the movement, but too late, for we were in possession. He opened with artillery, but General Ewing soon got some of Captain Richardson's guns up that steep hill, and gave back artillery, and the enemy's light skirmishers made one or two ineffectual dashes at General Lightburn, who had swept round and got a farther hill, which was the real continuation of the

---

[1] Indeed, the enemy were engaged nearer home on Lookout Mountain, as the reader has seen. — HORACE.

ridge. From studying all the maps, I had inferred that Missionary Ridge was a continuous hill; but we found ourselves on two high points, with a deep depression between us and the one immediately over the tunnel, which was my chief objective point. The ground we had gained, however, was so important, that I could leave nothing to chance, and ordered it to be fortified during the night. One brigade of each division was left on the hill, one of General Morgan L. Smith's closed the gap to Chickamauga Creek, two of General John E. Smith's were drawn back to the base in reserve, and General Ewing's right was extended down into the plain, thus crossing the ridge in a general line, facing southeast.

The enemy felt our left flank about four P. M., and a pretty smart engagement with artillery and muskets ensued, when he drew off; but it cost us dear, for General Giles A. Smith was severely wounded, and had to go to the rear; and the command of the brigade devolved on Colonel Tupper (One hundred and sixteenth Illinois), who managed it with skill during the rest of the operations. At the moment of my crossing the bridge, General Howard appeared, having come with three regiments from Chattanooga, along the east bank of the Tennessee, connecting my new position with that of the main army in Chattanooga. He left the three regiments attached temporarily to General Ewing's right, and returned to his own corps at Chattanooga. As night closed in, I ordered General Jefferson C. Davis to keep one of his brigades at the bridge, one close up to my position, and one intermediate. Thus we passed the night, heavy details being kept busy at work on the intrenchments on the hill. . . . .

The sun had hardly risen before General Corse had completed his preparations, and his bugle sounded the "Forward!" The Fortieth Illinois, supported by the Forty-sixth Ohio, on our right centre, with the Thirtieth Ohio (Colonel Jones), moved down the face of our hill, and up that held by the enemy. The line advanced to within about twenty yards of the intrenched position, where General Corse found a secondary crest, which he gained and held. To this point he called his reserves, and asked for reinforcements, which were sent; but the space was narrow, and it was not well to crowd the men, as the enemy's artillery and musketry fire swept the approach to his position, giving him great advantage. As soon as General Corse had made his preparations, he assaulted, and a close, severe contest ensued, which lasted more than an hour, gaining and losing ground, but never the position first obtained, from which the enemy in vain attempted to drive him. General Morgan L. Smith kept gaining ground on the left spurs of Missionary Ridge, and Colonel Loomis got abreast of the tunnel and railroad embankment on his side, drawing the enemy's fire, and to that extent relieving the assaulting party on the hill crest. Captain Callender had four of his guns on General Ewing's hill, and Captain Woods his Napoleon battery on General Lightburn's; also, two guns of Dillon's battery were with Colonel Alexander's brigade. All directed their fire as carefully as possible, to clear the hill to our front, without endangering our own men. The fight raged furiously about ten A. M., when General Corse received a severe wound, was brought off the field, and the command of the brigade and of the assault of that key-point devolved on that fine young gallant officer, Colonel Walcutt, of the Forty-Sixth Ohio, who fulfilled his part manfully. He continued the contest, pressing forward at all points. Colonel Loomis had made good progress to the right, and about two P. M. General John E. Smith, judging the battle to be most severe on the hill, and being required to support General Ewing, ordered up Colonel Raum's and General Mathias's brigades across the field to the summit that was being fought for. They moved up under a heavy fire of cannon and musketry, and joined Colonel Walcutt; but the crest was so narrow that they necessarily occupied the west face of the hill.

The enemy, at the time, being massed in great strength in the tunnel-gorge, moved a large force under cover of the ground and the thick bushes, and suddenly appeared on the right rear of this command. The suddenness of the attack disconcerted the men, exposed as they were in the open field; they fell back in some disorder to the lower edge of the field, and re-formed. These two brigades were in the nature of supports, and did not constitute a part of the real attack. The movement, seen from Chattanooga (five miles off) with spy-glasses, gave rise to the report, which even General Meigs has repeated, that we were repulsed on the left. It was *not so.* The real attacking columns of General Corse, Colonel Loomis, and General Smith were not repulsed. They engaged in a close struggle all day, persistently, stubbornly, and well. When the two reserve brigades of General John E. Smith fell back as described, the enemy made a show of pursuit, but were in their turn caught in flank by the well-directed fire of our brigade on the wooded crest, and hastily sought cover behind the hill.

Thus matters stood about three P. M. The day was bright and clear, and the amphitheatre of Chattanooga lay in beauty at our feet. I had watched for the attack of General Thomas " *early in the day.*"

Column after column of the enemy was streaming toward me; gun after gun poured its concentric shot on us, from every hill and open that gave a view of any part of the ground held by us. An occasional shot from Fort Wood and Orchard Knoll, and some musketry fire and artillery over about Lookout Mountain, was all I could detect on our side; but about three P. M. I noticed the white line of musketry fire in front of Orchard Knoll extending farther and farther right and left and on. We could only hear a faint echo of sound, but enough was seen to satisfy me that General Thomas was at last moving on the *centre.* I knew that our attack had drawn vast masses of the enemy to our flank, and felt sure of the result. Some guns which had been firing on us all day were silent, or were turned in a different direction.

The advancing line of musketry fire from Orchard Knoll disappeared to us behind a spur of the hill, and could no longer be seen; and it was not until night closed in that I knew that the troops in Chattanooga had swept across Missionary Ridge and broken the enemy's centre. Of course, the victory was won and pursuit was the next step.—*Gen. Sherman.*

THE STORMING OF THE RIDGE.

Twenty minutes to four, and from a battery at which the gunners have been waiting with ill-concealed impatience, the signal-guns agreed upon are fired, — a regular salute, — one — two — three — four — five — six !

Number six has hardly sounded his brazen note, before the inert mass is instinct with life. The skirmishers of Wood and Sheridan are away, followed by the fiery lines. All the forts and batteries bellow their harsh thunder over the heads of our men. . . . . They charge the rifle-pits at the foot of the ridge. . . . . They have no orders to go farther than the foot of the ridge, but when they see the enemy swarming like bees out of the rifle-pits, and flying before them, they do not stop for orders. They halt but a moment to re-form, and then, in spite of a terrible storm of soughing shot, screaming shell, pattering canister, and whizzing bullets, they dash forward to storm the height. An aidde-camp follows them, crying out, " Take the ridge, if you can "; but it was an order to sanction what they were already doing.[1]

[1] " I asked General Sheridan how he accounted for the ease with which the first line of rifle-pits was carried. He said that he happened to be in advance of his own line as it charged, and, looking back, was impressed with the terrible sight presented by the mass of approaching bayonets. The men were on a run and the line had become almost a crowd, and the Rebels appeared unable to resist the effect upon their imagination or their nerves of this waving, glittering mass of steel.

The lines ascend the hill in many wedge-forms,[1] the advancing colors in the forward angle of each. The artillery, from our positions, fires furiously over the heads of our men. A gun from Orchard Knoll, sighted by General Granger in person, explodes a Rebel caisson on the ridge. The enemy, in surprise and confusion, fire too high, and do less damage to our men than might have been expected.

It is now evident to the excited beholders that the color-bearers are running a race. The men partake of the enthusiasm, until all are at a white heat. Each regiment strains forward to place its colors first upon the rebel battlements. Let all win ! . . . .

Just as the sun is sinking in the west, the great sea of Union soldiers bursts upon the Rebel ridge, and the day is ours. To the searcher among military pictu-resques, there is no more splendid scene than this in any war ; — the wild mountain scenery ; the crests gilded by the slanting light ; the ravines and valleys in shadow ; the thunder of battle, the shouts of victory, and the great sun, seeming to pause for a moment to take in the story which he was to tell as he journeyed to the Western lands, and which the whole world was to learn and never forget.— *Col. Coppee.*

"When they had got a third of the way up, an aid of Granger's ordered one of Sheridan's brigades down the hill, in conformity with the original plan ; but Sheridan soon came up, and saw that the flags were advancing steadily, and that two of his brigades were still mounting the hill. He at once ordered back the troops which had begun to descend. 'When I saw those flags going up,' he said, 'I knew we should carry the ridge, and I took the responsibility.'"— *Brig.-Gen. Coppee.*

[1] Compare this with the account of the battle of Preston Pans in Waverley : "Both lines were now moving forward, the first prepared for instant combat. The clans of which it was composed formed each a sort of separate phalanx, narrow in front, and in depth ten, twelve, or fifteen files, according to the strength of the following. The best-armed and best-born, for the words were synonymous, were placed in front of each of these irregular subdivisions. The others in the rear shouldered forward the front, and by their pressure added both physical impulse and additional ardor and confidence to those who were first to encounter the danger."— FLORENCE.

CHAPTER X.

WITH the spring of 1864 there came the feeling through the whole country that the end
must come now. I cannot say what this feeling was
at the South. But I know that General Lee said,
that after Gettysburg the fall of the Confederacy
was only a matter of time. At the North there was
a determination to put the matter through, and that
thoroughly. Abraham Lincoln, the President, had
full confidence in General Grant. This confidence
was shared by Stanton, his Secretary of War, and
Halleck, who had great power at Washington, as
director of the army at that centre, either to make
or ruin generals, as he liked them or disliked them.
With the accord of everybody who had to be consulted, Mr. Washburne of Illinois, the same who
afterwards distinguished himself in France, introduced a bill in Congress reviving the office of
Lieutenant-General. This office had existed only
twice in the history of the country. It was created for Washington in 1798, a little before he
died, that he might take the oversight of the

impending war with France and Spain. As a post
of honor, it had been revived for General Scott
in his last days. It was now revived for a third
time, both for honor and for efficiency, that the
whole gripe of affairs might be in one hand, and
that, from the Potomac to the Rio Grande, one will
might direct all the effort to crush the enemy.

Napoleon the Great once said that there was
only one thing worse than a bad general, and that
this was " two good generals."

You see the value and the humor of the statement. But it was not known, or it was not acted
upon, at the beginning of this war. There was a
"Department of the Potomac," and a " Department of the Shenandoah," and a " Department of
West Virginia," and a " Department of the Ohio,"
and a " Department of the Mississippi," each with
a general almost independent, and so on without
end. Of course, as one says after all this was
over, there was endless misunderstanding; and
even where the mutual understanding was cordial,
there was no end of lost time and opportunity,
because in war two heads are worse than one.

All this was to be ended now. The moment
the new law passed General Grant was appointed
Lieutenant-General. He was the one man of
importance who had not been consulted regarding
the matter.

In one of his vivid conversational epigrams at
this time, General Butler described the campaign

before the army thus : " We go at the heart now. If you cut out a man's heart, his fingers and toes do not live long." It had early been General Grant's policy to seek the armies of the enemy and beat them. In such a war he considered the capture of one city or another as of less importance than the end of war itself by the breaking up of an organized army.

The country received the news of his appointment with enthusiasm. Every one felt that the end had now come.

His own narrative of the year which followed is one of the best pieces of history which has been written in the last fifty years, and stands a better chance of being read in America in the year 2500 than any other bit of the history of our time. He became Lieutenant-General on the 2d of March, 1864. General Lee in person surrendered to him at Appomattox on the 9th of April, 1865. The year between divides itself into the campaign of the Wilderness, so called ; the siege of Richmond and Petersburg ; and the pursuit of the broken army. Of the Wilderness campaign General Grant's own story is short and clear.

By " the Wilderness" is meant a region, mostly of forest, extending through Northeastern Virginia, from the Pamunky River to the Rappahannock. It was perhaps never before the fortune of the capital of a nation to be defended from invaders by the forests which careless agriculture, penury, and laziness had permitted to grow up within a hundred miles of the seat of government. But the blight of slavery was ruining Virginia first of all. Such is the divine law of compensation. The lands which had been corn-lands and tobacco-lands were now covered by the forest growth, and you have no epigram which better describes the Southern "Confederacy" than this fact of history, which tells you that its metropolis was guarded by a "Wilderness."

GENERAL GRANT'S NARRATIVE.—THE BEGINNING.

The movement of the army of the Potomac commenced early on the morning of the 4th of May, 1864, under the immediate direction and orders of Major-General Meade, pursuant to instructions. Before night the whole army was across the Rapidan, (the Fifth and Sixth Corps crossing at Germania Ford, and the Second in advance,) with the greater part of its trains, numbering about four thousand wagons, meeting with but slight opposition. The average distance travelled by the troops that day was about twelve miles. This I regarded as a great success, and it removed from my mind the most serious apprehensions I had entertained, that of crossing the river in the face of an active, large, well-appointed and ably-commanded army, and how so large a train was to be carried through a hostile country and protected. Early on the 5th, the advance corps (the Fifth, Major-Gen. G. K. Warren commanding) met and engaged the enemy outside his intrenchments near Mine Run. The battle raged furiously all day, the whole army being brought into the fight as fast as the corps could be got upon the field, which, considering the density of the forest and narrowness of the roads, was done with commendable promptness.

General Burnside, with the Ninth Corps, was, at the time the Army of the Potomac moved, left with the bulk of his corps at the crossing of the Rappahannock River and Alexandria Railroad, holding the road back to Bull Run, with instructions not to move until he received notice that a crossing of the Rapidan was secured, but to move promptly as soon as such notice was received. This crossing he was apprised of on the afternoon of the 4th. By six o'clock of the morning of the 6th he was leading his corps into action near the Wilderness Tavern, some of his troops having marched a distance of over thirty miles, crossing both the Rappahannock and Rapidan Rivers. Considering that a large proportion, probably two thirds, of his command was composed of new troops, unaccustomed to marches and carrying the accoutrements of a soldier, this was a remarkable march.

THE SECOND AND THIRD DAYS.

The battle of the Wilderness was renewed by us at five o'clock on the morning of the 6th, and continued with unabated fury until darkness set in, each army holding substantially the same position that they had on the evening of the 5th. After dark the enemy made a feeble attempt to turn our right flank, capturing several hundred prisoners and creating considerable confusion. But the promptness of General Sedgwick, who was personally present and commanded that part of our line, soon re-formed it and restored order. On the morning of the 7th, reconnoissances showed that the enemy had fallen behind his intrenched lines, with pickets to the front, covering a part of the battle-field. From this it was evident to my mind that the two days' fighting had satisfied him of his inability to further maintain the contest in the open field, notwithstanding his advantage of position, and that he would await an attack behind his works. I therefore determined to push on and put my whole force between him and Richmond; and orders were at once issued for a movement by his right flank.

THE MARCH AFTERWARD.

On the night of the 7th, the march was commenced toward Spottsylvania Court-House, the Fifth Corps moving on the most direct road. But the enemy having become apprised of our movement, and having the shorter line, was enabled to reach there first. On the 8th, General Warren met a force of the enemy which had been sent out to oppose and delay his advance, to gain time to fortify the line taken up at Spottsylvania. This force was steadily driven back on the main force, within the recently constructed works, after considerable fighting, resulting in severe loss to both sides. On the morning of the 9th, General Sheridan started on a raid against the enemy's lines of communication with Richmond. The 9th, 10th, and 11th were spent in manœuvring and fighting without decisive results. Among the killed on the 9th was that able and distinguished soldier, Major-Gen. John Sedgwick, commanding the Sixth Army Corps. Major-Gen. H. G. Wright succeeded him in command. Early on the morning of the 12th, a general attack was made on the enemy in position. The Second Corps, Major-General Hancock commanding, carried a salient of his line, capturing most of Johnston's division of Ewell's corps and twenty pieces of artillery. But the resistance was so obstinate that the advantage gained did not prove decisive. The 13th, 14th, 15th, 16th, 17th, and 18th were consumed in manœuvring and awaiting the arrival of reinforcements from Washington. Deeming it impracticable to make any further attack upon the enemy at Spottsylvania Court-House, orders were issued on the 18th with a view to a movement to the North Anna, to commence at twelve o'clock on the night of the 19th. Late in the afternoon of the 19th, Ewell's corps came out of its works on our extreme right flank; but the attack was promptly repulsed, with heavy loss. This delayed the movement to the North Anna until the night of the 21st, when it was commenced. But the enemy, again having the shorter line, and being in possession of the main roads, was enabled to reach the North Anna in advance of us, and took position behind it. The Fifth Corps reached the North Anna on the afternoon of the 22d, closely followed by the Sixth Corps. The Second and Ninth Corps got up about the same time, the Second holding the railroad bridge, and the Ninth lying between that and Jericho Ford. General Warren effected a crossing the same afternoon, and got a position without much opposition. Soon after getting into position he was violently attacked, but repulsed the enemy with great slaughter. On the 25th General Sheridan rejoined the Army of the Potomac from the raid on which he started from Spottsylvania, having destroyed the depots at Beaver Dam and Ashland Stations, four trains of cars, large supplies of rations, and many miles of railroad track; recaptured about four hundred of our men, on their way to Richmond as prisoners of war; met and defeated the enemy's cavalry at Yellow Tavern; carried the first line of works around Richmond; but, finding the second line too strong to be carried by assault, recrossed to the north bank of the Chickahominy at Meadow's Bridge, under heavy fire, and moved by a detour to Haxall's Landing, on the James River, where he communicated with General Butler. This raid had the effect of drawing off the whole of the enemy's cavalry force, and making it comparatively easy to guard our trains. . . . .

Finding the enemy's position on the North Anna stronger than either of his previous ones, I withdrew on the night of the 26th to the north bank of the North Anna, and moved via Hanovertown to turn the enemy's position by his right.

Generals Torbert's and Merritt's divisions of cavalry, under Sheridan, and the Sixth Corps, led the advance; crossed the Pamunky River at Hanovertown after considerable fighting, and on the 28th the two divisions of cavalry had a severe but successful engagement with the enemy at Haw's shop. On the 29th and 30th we advanced, with heavy skirmishing, to the Hanover Court-House and Cold Harbor road, and developed the enemy's position north of the Chickahominy. Late on the evening of the last day the enemy came out and attacked our left, but was repulsed with very considerable loss. An attack was immediately ordered by General Meade along his whole line, which resulted in driving the enemy from a part of his intrenched skirmish line.

On the 31st, General Wilson's division of cavalry destroyed the railroad bridges over the South Anna River, after defeating the enemy's cavalry. General Sheridan on the same day reached Cold Harbor, and held it until relieved by the Sixth Corps and General Smith's command, which had just arrived, via White House, from General Butler's army.

On the 1st day of June an attack was made at five P. M. by the Sixth Corps and the troops under General Smith, the other corps being held in readiness to advance on the receipt of orders. This resulted in our carrying and holding the enemy's first line of works in front of the right of the Sixth Corps and in front of General Smith. During the attack the enemy made repeated assaults on each of the corps not engaged in the main attack, but were repulsed with heavy loss in every instance. That night he made several assaults to regain what he had lost in the day, but failed. The 2d was spent in getting troops into position for an attack on the 3d. On the 3d of June we again assaulted the enemy's works, in the hope of driving him from his position. In this attempt our loss was heavy, while that of the enemy, I have reason to believe, was comparatively light. It was the only general attack made from the Rapidan to the James which did not inflict upon the enemy losses to compensate for our own losses. I would not be understood as saying that all previous attacks resulted in victories to our arms, or accomplished as much as I had hoped from them; but they inflicted upon the enemy severe losses, which tended, in the end, to the complete overthrow of the Rebellion.

GRANT'S PLANS.

From the proximity of the enemy to his defences around Richmond, it was impossible by any flank movement to interpose between him and the city. I was still in a condition to either move by his left flank and invest Richmond from the north side, or continue my move by his right flank to the south side of the James. While the former might have been better as a covering for Washington, yet a full survey of all the ground satisfied me that it would be impracticable to hold a line north and east of Richmond that would protect the Fredericksburg Railroad, — a long, vulnerable line, which would exhaust much of our strength to guard, and that would have to be protected to supply the army, and would leave open to the enemy all his lines of communication on the south side of the James. My idea, from the start, had been to beat Lee's army north of Richmond, if possible. Then, after destroying his lines of communication north of the James River, to transfer the army to the south side, and besiege Lee in Richmond, or follow him south if he should retreat. After the battle of the Wilderness it was evident that the enemy deemed it of the first importance to run no risks with the army he then had. He acted purely on the defensive behind breastworks, or feebly on the offensive immediately in front of them, and where, in case of repulse, he could easily retire behind them. Without a greater sacrifice of life than I was willing to make, all could not be accomplished that I had designed north of Richmond. I therefore determined to continue to hold substantially the ground we then occupied, taking advantage of any favorable circumstances that might present themselves, until the cavalry could be sent to

Charlottesville and Gordonsville, to effectually break up the railroad connection between Richmond and the Shenandoah Valley and Lynchburg; and, when the cavalry got well off, to move the army to the south side of the James River, by the enemy's right flank, where I felt I could cut off all his sources of supply except by the canal.

CAUSE AND EFFECT.

During three long years the armies of the Potomac and Northern Virginia had been confronting each other. In that time they had fought more desperate battles than it probably ever before fell to the lot of two armies to fight, without materially changing the vantage-ground of either. The Southern press and people, with more shrewdness than was displayed in the North, finding that they had failed to capture Washington and march on to New York, as they had boasted they would do, assumed that they only defended their capital and Southern territory. Hence, Antietam, Gettysburg, and all the other battles that had been fought, were by them set down as failures on our part, and victories for them. Their army believed this. It produced a morale which could only be overcome by desperate and continuous hard fighting. The battles of the Wilderness, Spottsylvania, North Anna, and Cold Harbor, bloody and terrible as they were on our side, were even more damaging to the enemy, and so crippled him as to make him wary ever after of taking the offensive. His losses in men were probably not so great, owing to the fact that we were, save in the Wilderness, almost invariably the attacking party; and when he did attack it was in the open field. The details of these battles, which for endurance and bravery on the part of the soldiery have rarely been surpassed, are given in the report of Major-General Meade, and the subordinate reports accompanying it. — *Gen. Grant.*

12

We cannot copy from General Meade's reports, though the boys read them with eager interest. Here are some little details of that slow advance through the Wilderness.

ONE OF THE ATTACKS.

As soon as the troops were in readiness, general orders were read to them, detailing the brilliant operations of General Sherman in the West, and General Butler south of Richmond. This news fired the ardor of the troops, and each man seemed to be determined not to be outdone by those belonging to the other commands. A wild enthusiasm was apparent in their eyes, and for a moment the men appeared to be ungovernable. But the word of command restored order and silence. General Grant, surrounded by his staff, took up a prominent and elevated position, and the corps commanders also occupied eminences within view of the General-in-chief and of each other. They were thus enabled to watch the movements of the vast columns of the mighty army as they advanced to the respective positions whence they were to make the attack. . . . .

The hour for the assault was fixed at half past six, and once more the time-pieces were compared. The generals separated, to take up their assigned positions and to direct their troops to victory. The signal guns boomed aloud, and twelve reports declared that the moment had arrived for the attack. A wild cheer rang along the whole line, and the mass advanced with a steady front, — column after column, line after line, the whole moving together. In the face of a murderous fire our troops pushed on determinedly, each corps fighting its own battle, until the army was master of the field. Two thousand prisoners were taken, and, when night closed, the Union forces were the conquerors. — *N. Y. Herald.*

CHARGE OF THE VERMONT BRIGADE.

Too much cannot be said in praise of the gallant charge of the Vermont Brigade, commanded by Colonel Grant. On the 10th of May, after the line of Rebel works was carried, and their expected support did not come up, the division of General Russell not being able to remain, owing to the galling fire poured into their serried ranks by the second line of the enemy's rifle-pits, and being in imminent danger of being cut off from the main line, on account of their advanced position, had to fall back, and along with them their prisoners, nearly two thousand in number. Twelve pieces of cannon were in the works. These had to be left, as they could not be removed, and they had not with them the necessary implements for spiking them. The Vermont Brigade utterly refused to fall back upon the main line, even after the position had been occupied two hours, and they had given up all hopes of being reinforced. Colonel Upton rode down to them and told them how dangerous it was to attempt to hold the works they were in, since their last round of cartridge had been discharged at the enemy, and they were rapidly being flanked. But the blood of the Green Mountain Boys was up, and they absolutely refused to budge a single hair from the field they had wrested from the enemy, and from the spot where their comrades had fallen. Colonel Upton, assisted by some of their own officers, by promising them another charge when they had supplied themselves with ammunition, at last induced them sullenly to retire. — *Mr. Long, N. Y. Herald.*

PICKET FIRING AND THE REASON.

All last evening and night there was a constant musketry-firing in our immediate front. Thinking it unusually incessant, I inquired the cause, and it seems that between our two skirmish lines are fifteen of our

captured cannon, which we had been unable to take
from the field. The enemy was determined that we
should not get them, and our men were as determined
that they should not go back again into the possession
of the enemy. Hence the constant mutual firing. The
possession of these guns promises to become a hotly
contested point before it is decided. — *Mr. Hendrick,
N. Y. Herald.*

FIGHT WITH FIRE.

Unfortunately the dry logs of which the breastwork
was formed were but partially covered with earth ; and
the flames ignited by the burning wadding during the
conflict — an enemy that could not be resisted as easily
as the myrmidons of Longstreet — destroyed them, and
every second of time widened the breaches. The un-
daunted men crowded together until they formed fourteen
or sixteen ranks ; and those who were in the front discharged the guns which were constantly passed to them
by their comrades who were in the rear and could not
aim with accuracy or safety. The fire triumphed when
it flashed along the entire barrier of wood, reduced it to
ashes, and forced the defenders, who had withstood to
the last its intolerable heat, to retire to the rifle-pits
which were a short distance in the rear. — *Capt. Blake,
11th Mass.*

BACK AND FORTH.

Both armies had protected their main columns by felling trees and forming almost impassable abatis, and the
fighting was done principally by divisions sent out from
these lines. The movements during the entire battle
were of a remarkable character, most expressively described as seesaw, — the Rebels making frantic efforts
to pierce our lines, first at one point and then another, to be driven back by our troops, who charged
impetuously up to the Rebel barricades. It is impossi-

ble now to particularize the individual achievements of divisions, as these were frequently taken from one corps to support another, and at times one corps commander would have under his direction nearly one half the army. Occasionally there was considerable disorder, but nothing serious, as troops that broke and ran in the wildest manner afterwards made some of the most brilliant charges of the day. — *N. Y. Herald.*

After the Wilderness fighting the armies of the Potomac and of the James were united. The James River was so bridged that communication could be readily kept up between North and South. From this time till Richmond fell, in the next spring, the united armies were surrounding the two cities of Richmond and Petersburg more and more closely, and compelling them to draw all supplies from the west and northwest exclusively.

Lee and his generals were eager at every possible moment to try the old strategy, of dashing down the valley of the Shenandoah to alarm Washington or the Northern States. But this time they had General Phil Sheridan before them. After the raid which Grant describes in the despatch you have read, he was in command in the Valley of Virginia.

There is hardly a boy or a girl who has not read the ballad of Sheridan's Ride. Here is his own description of that day, and what led to it.

He is speaking of a plan which he did not approve of, — for which the consultations called him away.

SHERIDAN'S RIDE.

This plan I would not indorse, but in order to settle
it definitely, I was called to Washington by the following telegram : —

                                    Washington, October 13, 1864.

MAJOR-GENERAL SHERIDAN [*through General Augur*] : —
    If you can come here a consultation on several points is
extremely desirable.   I propose to visit General Grant, and would
like to see you first.
        (Signed,)   E. M. STANTON, *Secretary of War.*

On the evening of the 15th, I determined to go,
believing that the enemy at Fisher's Hill could not
accomplish much, and as I had concluded not to attack
him at present, I ordered the whole of the cavalry force
under General Torbert to accompany me to Front
Royal, from whence I intended to push it through
Chester Gap to the Virginia Central Railroad at
Charlottesville, while I passed through Manassas Gap
to Piedmont, thence by rail to Washington.   Upon my
arrival with the cavalry at Front Royal, on the night
of the 16th, I received the following despatch from General Wright, who was left at Cedar Creek in command
of the army : —

                        Head-quarters, Middle Military Division,
                                    October 16, 1864.

MAJOR-GENERAL P. H. SHERIDAN, *commanding Middle Military
    Division :* —
    GENERAL : — I enclose you despatch which explains itself.   [See
copy following]
    If the enemy should be strongly reinforced in cavalry, he
might, by turning our right, give us a great deal of trouble.   .I
shall hold on here until the enemy's movements are developed,
and shall only fear an attack on my right, which I shall make
every preparation for guarding against and resisting.
            Very respectfully, your obedient servant,
        (Signed,)   H. G. WRIGHT, *Major-General Commanding.*

To LIEUTENANT-GENERAL EARLY : —
    *Be ready to move as soon as my forces join you, and we will crush
Sheridan.*
        (Signed,)   LONGSTREET, *Lieutenant-General.*

This message was taken off the Rebel signal flag, on Threetop Mountain.

My first thought was that it was a *ruse*, but, on reflection, deemed it best to abandon the cavalry raid, and give to General Wright the entire strength of the army. I therefore ordered the cavalry to return and report to him, and addressed the following note on the subject: —

Head-quarters Middle Military Division,
Front Royal, October 16, 1854.

Major-Gen. H. G. Wright, *commanding Sixth Army Corps :* —

General : — The cavalry is all ordered back to you; make your position strong. If Longstreet's despatch is true, he is under the impression that we have largely detached. I will go over to Augur, and may get additional news.

Close in Colonel Powell, who will be at this point. If the enemy should make an advance, I know you will defeat him. Look well to your ground and be well prepared. Get up everything that can be spared. I will bring up all I can, and will be up on Tuesday, if not sooner.

(Signed,)　　　　　P. H. Sheridan, *Major-General.*

After sending this note, I continued through Manassas Gap and on to Piedmont, and from thence by rail to Washington, arriving on the morning of the 17th. At 12 o'clock M., I returned by special train to Martinsburg, arriving on the evening of the 18th at Winchester, in company with Colonels Thom and Alexander, of the Engineer Corps, sent with me by General Halleck. During my absence the enemy had gathered all his strength, and, in the night of the 18th, and early on the 19th, moved silently from Fisher's Hill, through Strasburg, pushed a heavy turning column across the Shenandoah, on the road from Strasburg to Front Royal, and again recrossed the river at Bowman's Ford, striking Crook, who held the left of our line, in flank and rear, so unexpectedly and forcibly as to drive in his outposts, invade his camp, and turn his position. This surprise was owing, probably, to not closing in Powell, or to the cavalry divisions of Merritt and Custer being placed on the right of our line, where it had always occurred to me there was but little danger of attack.

This was followed by a direct attack upon our front, and the result was, that the whole army was driven back in confusion, to a point about one and a half miles north of Middletown, a very large portion of the infantry not even preserving a company organization.

At about seven o'clock on the morning of the 19th of October, an officer on picket at Winchester reported artillery firing; but, supposing it resulted from a reconnoissance which had been ordered for this morning, I paid no attention to it, and was unconscious of the true condition of affairs until about nine o'clock, when, having ridden through the town of Winchester, the sound of the artillery made a battle unmistakable, and, on reaching Mill Creek, half a mile south of Winchester, the head of the fugitives appeared in sight, trains and men coming to the rear with appalling rapidity.

I immediately gave directions to halt and park the trains at Mill Creek, and ordered the brigade at Winchester to stretch across the country and stop all stragglers. Taking twenty men from my escort, I pushed on to the front, leaving the balance, under General Forsyth and Colonels Thom and Alexander, to do what they could in stemming the torrent of fugitives.

I am happy to say that hundreds of the men, who, on reflection, found they had not done themselves justice, came back with cheers.

On arriving at the front, I found Merritt's and Custer's divisions of cavalry, under Torbert, and General Getty's division of the Sixth Corps, opposing the enemy. I suggested to General Wright that we would fight on Getty's line, and to transfer Custer to the right at once, as he (Custer) and Merritt, from being on the right in the morning, had been transferred to the left, — that the remaining two divisions of the Sixth Corps, which were to the right and rear of Getty about two miles, should be ordered up, and also that the Nineteenth Corps, which was on the right and rear of these two divisions, should be hastened up before the enemy attacked Getty.

I then started out all my staff officers to bring up these troops, and was so convinced that we would soon be attacked, that I went back myself to urge them on.

Immediately after, I returned and assumed command, General Wright returning to his corps, Getty to his division, and the line of battle was formed on the prolongation of General Getty's line, and a temporary breastwork of rails, logs, &c. thrown up hastily.

Shortly after this was done, the enemy advanced, and, from a point on the left of our line of battle, I could see his columns moving to the attack, and at once notified corps commanders to be prepared.

This assault fell principally on the Nineteenth Corps, and was repulsed.

I am pleased to be able to state that the strength of the Sixth and Nineteenth Corps, and Crook's command, was now being rapidly augmented by the return of those who had gone to the rear early in the day.

Reports coming in from the Front Royal pike, on which Powell's division of cavalry was posted, to the effect that a heavy column of infantry was moving on that pike in the direction of Winchester, and that he (Powell) was retiring, and would come in at Newtown, caused me great anxiety for the time, and, although I could not fully believe that such a movement would be undertaken, still it delayed my general attack.

At four o'clock P. M. I ordered the advance.

This attack was brilliantly made, and, as the enemy was protected by rail breastworks, and at some portions of his line by stone fences, his resistance was very determined. His line of battle overlapped the right of mine, and, by turning with this portion of it on the flank of the Nineteenth Corps, caused a slight momentary confusion. This movement was checked, however, by a counter-charge of General McMillan's brigade upon the re-entering angle thus formed by the enemy, and his flanking party cut off.

It was at this stage of the battle that Custer was ordered to charge with his entire division: but, al-

though the order was promptly obeyed, it was not in
time to capture the whole of the force thus cut off,
and many escaped across Cedar Creek.

Simultaneously with this charge, a combined movement of the whole line drove the enemy in confusion
to the Creek, where, owing to the difficulties of crossing, his army became routed.

Custer, finding a ford on Cedar Creek west of the
Pike, and Devens, of Merritt's division, one to the east
of it, they each made the crossing just after dark,
and pursued the routed mass of the enemy to Fisher's
Hill, where this strong position gave him some protection against our cavalry, but the most of his transportation had been captured, the road from Cedar
Creek to Fisher's Hill, a distance of over three miles,
being literally blocked by wagons, ambulances, artillery, caissons, &c.

The enemy did not halt his *main* force at Fisher's
Hill, but continued the retreat during the night to
New Market, where his army had, on a similar previous occasion, come together by means of the numerous roads that converge to this point.

This battle practically ended the campaign in the
Shenandoah Valley. When it opened, we found our
enemy boastful and confident, unwilling to acknowledge
that the soldiers of the Union were their equal in courage and manliness; when it closed with Cedar Creek,
this impression had been removed from his mind, and
gave place to good sense and a strong desire to quit
fighting.

The very best troops of the Confederacy had not
only been defeated, but had been routed in successive
engagements, until their spirit and esprit was destroyed; in obtaining these results, however, our loss
in officers and men was severe. Practically, all territory north of the James River now belonged to me, and
the holding of the lines about Petersburg and Richmond by the enemy must have been embarrassing,
and invited the question of good military judgment.

On entering the Valley, it was not my object, by flank movements, to make the enemy change his base, nor to move as far up as the James River, and thus give him the opportunity of making me change my base, therefore converting it into a race-course as heretofore, but to destroy, to the best of my ability, that which was truly the Confederacy, — its armies; in doing this, so far as the opposing army was concerned, our success was such that there was no one connected with the army of the Shenandoah who did not so fully realize it as to render the issuing of congratulatory orders unnecessary; every officer and man was made to understand that, when a victory was gained, it was not more than their duty, nor less than their country expected from her gallant sons!

" Uncle Fritz," said Horace, " Phil Sheridan never read your book about writing."

" How do you know that, boy?"

" Oh! he writes such awful long sentences."

" Well, my boy, I do not care how long your sentences are, if you will do your work as well as he."

CHAPTER XI.

SHERMAN'S GREAT MARCH.

IN March, 1864, when Grant was appointed Lieutenant-General and Commander-in-Chief, he left Chattanooga and Nashville for the East. General Sherman was then put in his place, with Johnson in front of him, commanding what was left of the army which had been defeated at Chattanooga.

Sherman took the offensive as soon as the spring came, and began driving the enemy back on Atlanta. By a series of tactical manœuvres, in several instances by flanking his opponent, Sherman forced him farther and farther back without any serious battle, until, on the night of the 1st of September, Atlanta was abandoned. The whole campaign was a moving siege. Johnson would evacuate the lines which Sherman had rendered untenable, and the next day he would be found, ten miles back, behind another line of intrenchments.

Had this mode of offensive defence been continued, the famous "March to the Sea" would never have been made, though the Union army was much the superior; but the Rebel government was not satisfied with these slow measures, and superseded General Johnson by General Hood, a rash soldier, who did not possess the confidence of the army. He was not satisfied with looking on while Sherman was establishing himself in Atlanta, and with cutting his connections once in a while. He looked with longing eyes to Tennessee, and finally, early in October, he turned Sherman's right, and attacked Allatoona, a fortified place commanding the railroad north from Atlanta. If he had taken it, he could, with a small number of men, have kept Sherman south, while he marched on Nashville.

But Allatoona was bravely defended by General Corse,[1] and held against vastly superior numbers, till it was relieved. Hood "caromed off," as Sherman says, to the west, and then made himself busy in equipping his army for a march north, whether Sherman followed or no.

On this, Sherman sent two corps to General Thomas, at Nashville, with orders to check Hood's advance, or to follow him, as the case might require. He stripped Atlanta, and the northern posts as far as Chattanooga, and, reserving for himself sixty-five guns, with thirty days' rations and two hundred rounds of ammunition for each of his sixty thousand men, he sent the rest to Union ground.

---

[1] Sherman's order, signalled to Corse, was the celebrated message upon which the song " Hold the Fort " is based.

Then he turned to the southeast, and set out for the sea.

Savannah is three hundred miles from Atlanta. In marching these three hundred miles, Sherman meant to destroy the railroad system of Georgia, to disgust the inhabitants of the State with war, and so to cut the Rebellion through in a second place, as Grant had cut it before when he took Vicksburg. The capture of Savannah was a secondary point.

This has all been done now. The new departure in war has been taken. But then it was another matter. To give up one base of supplies, and to strike so far for another, through an enemy's country, was almost unheard of. Whatever else generals abandoned, they kept open their lines of connection. We have seen how, at a slight pressure on his line of communication, before the battle of Gettysburg, Lee totally changed his line of march in order to save them. In this he was following the usual practice, and for a general to attempt to feed sixty thousand men from what he could carry and collect in a hostile country, was unknown. The authorities in Washington gave only a reluctant consent, and there were too many so-called authorities elsewhere who pronounced Sherman crazy. For almost a month, no word came to the North from him, except by the Southern newspapers, which insisted that he was retreating in disorder and on the point of destruction.

Great were the rejoicings in the North when they learned that he had taken Fort McAllister, had joined our fleet, and captured Savannah!

Sherman met with but little resistance till he reached Savannah; his total loss in the campaign was fourteen hundred, so that he was quite ready to march north again through the Carolinas, and receive the sword of his old rival, Johnson, when the end came.

"HOLD THE FORT, FOR I AM COMING."

I inferred that Allatoona was their objective point,—and on the 4th of October I signalled from Vining's Station to Kenesaw, and from Kenesaw to Allatoona, over the heads of the enemy, a message for General Corse, at Rome, to hurry back to the assistance of the garrison at Allatoona.

Reaching Kenesaw Mountain about eight A. M. of October 5th (a beautiful day), I had a superb view of the vast panorama to the north and west. To the southwest, about Dallas, could be seen the smoke of camp-fires, indicating the presence of a large force of the enemy, and the whole line of railroad from Big Shanty up to Allatoona (full fifteen miles) was marked by the fires of the burning railroad. We could plainly see the smoke of battle about Allatoona, and hear the faint reverberation of the cannon.

From Kenesaw I ordered the Twenty-third Corps (General Cox) to march due west on the Burnt Hickory road, and to burn houses or piles of brush as it progressed, to indicate the head of column, hoping to interpose this corps between Hood's main army at Dallas and the detachment then assailing Allatoona. The rest of the army was directed straight for Allatoona, northwest, distant eighteen miles. The signal officer on Kenesaw reported that since daylight he had failed to obtain any answer to his call for Allatoona; but, while I was with him, he caught a faint glimpse of the tell-tale flag through an embrasure, and after much time he made out these letters, — "C.," "R.," "S.," "E.," "H.," "E.," "R.," — and translated the message, "Corse is here." It was a source of great relief, for it gave me the first assurance that General Corse had received his orders, and that the place was adequately garrisoned.

I watched with painful suspense the indications of the battle raging there, and was dreadfully impatient at the slow progress of the relieving column, whose advance was marked by the smokes which were made according to orders, but about two P. M. I noticed with satisfaction that the smoke of battle about Allatoona grew less and less, and ceased altogether about four P. M. For a time I attributed this result to the effect of General Cox's march, but later in the afternoon the signal flag announced the welcome tidings that the attack had been fairly repulsed, but that General Corse was wounded.

Inasmuch as the enemy had retreated southwest, and would probably next appear at Rome, I answered General Corse with orders to get back to Rome with his troops as quickly as possible.

General Corse's report of this fight at Allatoona is very full and graphic. It is dated Rome, October 27, 1864; recites the fact that he received his orders by signal to go to the assistance of Allatoona on the 4th, when he telegraphed to Kingston for cars, and a train of thirty empty cars was started for him, but about ten of them got off the track and caused delay. By seven P. M. he had at Rome a train of twenty cars, which he loaded up with Colonel Rowett's brigade, and part of the Twelfth Illinois Infantry; started at eight P. M., reached Allatoona (distant thirty-five miles) at one A. M. of the 5th, and sent the train back for more men; but the road was in bad order, and no more men came in time. He found Colonel Tourtellotte's garrison composed of eight hundred and ninety men; his reinforcement was one thousand and fifty-four: total for the defence, nineteen hundred and forty-four. The outposts were already engaged, and as soon as daylight came he drew back the men from the village to the ridge on which the redoubts were built.

ALLATOONA FIGHT.

The enemy was composed of French's division of three brigades, variously reported from four to five thousand strong. This force gradually surrounded the place by eight A. M., when General French sent in by flag of truce this note: —

Around Allatoona, October 5, 1864.

COMMANDING OFFICER, UNITED STATES FORCES, *Allatoona :* —

I have placed the forces under my command in such positions that you are surrounded, and to avoid a needless effusion of blood I call on you to surrender your forces at once, and unconditionally.

Five minutes will be allowed you to decide. Should you accede to this, you will be treated in the most honorable manner as prisoners of war.

I have the honor to be, very respectfully, yours,
S. G. FRENCH,
Major General commanding forces Confederate States.

General Corse answered immediately: —

Headquarters, Fourth Division, Fifteenth Corps,
Allatoona, Georgia, 8 30 A M., Oct. 5, 1864.

MAJOR GENERAL S. G. FRENCH, *Confederate States, &c.:* —

Your communication demanding surrender of my command I acknowledge receipt of, and respectfully reply that we are prepared for the "needless effusion of blood" whenever it is agreeable to you.

I am, very respectfully, your obedient servant,
JOHN M. CORSE,
Brigadier-General commanding forces United States.

Of course the attack began at once, coming from front, flank, and rear. There were two small redoubts, with slight parapets and ditches, one on each side of the deep railroad-cut. These redoubts had been located by Colonel Poe, United States Engineers, at the time of our advance on Kenesaw, the previous June. Each redoubt overlooked the storehouses close by the railroad, and each could aid the other defensively by catching in flank the attacking force of the other. Our troops at first endeavored to hold some ground outside the redoubts, but were soon driven inside, when the enemy made repeated assaults, but were always driven back.. About eleven A. M., Colonel Redfield, of the Thirty-ninth Iowa, was killed, and Colonel Rowett was wounded, but never ceased to fight and encourage his men. Colonel Tourtellotte was shot through the hips, but continued to command. General Corse was, at one P. M., shot across the face, the ball cutting his ear, which stunned him, but he continued to encourage his men and to give orders. The enemy (about 1.30 P. M.) made a last and desperate effort to carry one of the redoubts, but was badly cut to pieces by the artillery and infantry fire from the other, when he began to draw off, leaving his dead and wounded on the ground.

Before finally withdrawing, General French converged a heavy fire of his cannon on the block-house at Alla-toona Creek, about two miles from the depot, set it on fire, and captured its garrison, consisting of four officers and eighty-five men. By four P. M. he was in full retreat south, on the Dallas road, and got by before the head of General Cox's column had reached it; still, several ambulances and stragglers were picked up by this command on that road. General Corse reported two hundred and thirty-one Rebel dead, four hundred and eleven prisoners, three regimental colors, and eight hundred muskets captured.

Among the prisoners was a Brigadier-General Young, who thought that French's aggregate loss would reach two thousand. Colonel Tourtellotte says that, for days after General Corse had returned to Rome, his men found and buried at least a hundred more dead Rebels, who had doubtless been wounded, and died in the woods, near Allatoona. I know that when I reached Allatoona, on the 9th, I saw a good many dead men, which had been collected for burial.

Corse's entire loss, officially reported, was: —

	Killed.	Wounded.	Missing.	Total.
Officers	6	23	6	35
Men	136	330	206	672
Total . . .	142	353	212	707

I esteemed this defence of Allatoona so handsome and important, that I made it the subject of a general order, viz. No. 86, of October 7, 1864 : —

The general commanding avails himself of the opportunity, in the handsome defence made of Allatoona, to illustrate the most important principle in war, that fortified posts should be defended to the last, regardless of the relative numbers of the party attacking and attacked. . . . . The thanks of this army are due and are hereby accorded to General Corse, Colonel Tourtellotte, Colonel Rowett, officers, and men, for their determined and gallant defence of Allatoona, and it is made an example to illustrate the importance of preparing in time, and meeting the danger when present, boldly, manfully, and well.

Commanders and garrisons of the posts along our railroad are hereby instructed that they must hold their posts to the last minute, sure that the time gained is valuable and necessary to their comrades at the front.

By order of Major-General W. T. Sherman.

L. M. DAYTON, *Aid-de-Camp.*

A PART OF THE FIELD ORDERS FOR THE MARCH.

4. The army will forage liberally on the country during the march. To this end, each brigade commander will organize a good and sufficient foraging party, under the command of one or more discreet officers, who will gather, near the route travelled, corn or forage of any ·kind, meat of any kind, vegetables, corn-meal, or whatever is needed by the command, aiming at all times to keep in the wagons at least ten days' provisions for his

command, and three days' forage. Soldiers must not enter the dwellings of the inhabitants, or commit any trespass; but, during a halt or camp, they may be permitted to gather turnips, potatoes, and other vegetables, and to drive in stock in sight of their camp. To regular foraging-parties must be intrusted the gathering of provisions and forage, at any distance from the road travelled.

5. To corps commanders alone is intrusted the power to destroy mills, houses, cotton-gins, &c.; and for them this general principle is laid down: in districts and neighborhoods where the army is unmolested, no destruction of such property should be permitted; but should guerillas or bushwhackers molest our march, or should the inhabitants burn bridges, obstruct roads, or otherwise manifest local hostility, then army commanders should order and enforce a devastation more or less relentless, according to the measure of such hostility.

6. As for horses, mules, wagons, &c., belonging to the inhabitants, the cavalry and artillery may appropriate freely and without limit; discriminating, however, between the rich, who are usually hostile, and the poor and industrious, usually neutral or friendly. Foraging-parties may also take mules or horses, to replace the jaded animals of their trains, or to serve as pack-mules for the regiments or brigades. In all foraging of whatever kind, the parties engaged will refrain from abusive or threatening language, and may, where the officer in command thinks proper, give written certificates of the facts, but no receipts; and they will endeavor to leave with each family a reasonable portion for their maintenance.

7. Negroes who are able-bodied and can be of service to the several columns may be taken along; but each army commander will bear in mind that the question of supplies is a very important one, and that his first duty is to see to those who bear arms.

8. The organization, at once, of a good pioneer battalion for each army corps, composed if possible of

negroes, should be attended to. This battalion should follow the advance-guard, repair roads and double them if possible, so that the columns will not be delayed after reaching bad places. Also army commanders should practise the habit of giving the artillery and wagons the road, marching their troops on one side, and instruct their troops to assist wagons at steep hills or bad crossings of streams. — *Gen. Sherman.*

THE MARCH BEGINS.

About seven A. M. of November 16th we rode out of Atlanta by the Decatur road, filled by the marching troops and wagons of the Fourteenth Corps; and reaching the hill, just outside of the old Rebel works, we naturally paused to look back upon the scenes of our past battles. We stood upon the very ground whereon was fought the bloody battle of July 22d, and could see the copse of wood where McPherson fell. Behind us lay Atlanta, smouldering and in ruins, the black smoke rising high in air, and hanging like a pall over the ruined city. Away off in the distance, on the McDonough road, was the rear of Howard's column, the gun-barrels glistening in the sun, the white-topped wagons stretching away to the south; and right before us the Fourteenth Corps, marching steadily and rapidly, with a cheery look and swinging pace, that made light of the thousand miles that lay between us and Richmond. Some band, by accident, struck up the anthem of " John Brown's soul goes marching on"; the men caught up the strain, and never before or since have I heard the chorus of " Glory, glory, hallelujah!" done with more spirit, or in better harmony of time and place.

Then we turned our horses' heads to the east; Atlanta was soon lost behind the screen of trees, and became a thing of the past. Around it clings many a thought of desperate battle, of hope and fear, that now seem like the memory of a dream; and I have never seen the place since. The day was extremely beautiful, clear sunlight, with bracing air, and an unusual feeling of exhilaration seemed to pervade all minds, — a feeling of something to come, vague and undefined, still full of venture and intense interest. Even the common soldiers caught the inspiration, and many a group called out to me as I worked my way past them, "Uncle Billy, I guess Grant is waiting for us at Richmond!" Indeed, the general sentiment was that we were marching for Richmond, and that there we should end the war, but how and when they seemed to care not; nor did they measure the distance, or count the cost in life, or bother their brains about the great rivers to be crossed, and the food required for man and beast, that had to be gathered by the way. There was a "devil-may-care" feeling pervading officers and men, that made me feel the full load of responsibility, for success would be accepted as a matter of course, whereas, should we fail, this "march" would be adjudged the wild adventure of a crazy fool. I had no purpose to march direct for Richmond by way of Augusta and Charlotte, but always designed to reach the sea-coast first at Savannah or Port Royal, South Carolina, and even kept in mind the alternative of Pensacola.

The first night out we camped by the road-side near Lithonia. Stone Mountain, a mass of granite, was in plain view, cut out in clear outline against the blue sky; the whole horizon was lurid with the bonfires of rail-ties, and groups of men all night were carrying the heated rails to the nearest trees, and bending them around the trunks. Colonel Poe had provided tools for ripping up the rails and twisting them when hot; but the best and easiest way is the one I have described, of heating the middle of the iron-rails on bonfires made of the cross-ties, and then winding them around a tele-graph-pole or the trunk of some convenient sapling. I attached much importance to this destruction of the railroad, gave it my own personal attention, and made reiterated orders to others on the subject.

The next day we passed through the handsome town of Covington, the soldiers closing up their ranks, the color-bearers unfurling their flags, and the bands striking up patriotic airs. The white people came out of their houses to behold the sight, spite of their deep hatred of the invaders, and the negroes were simply frantic with joy. Whenever they heard my name, they clustered about my horse, shouted and prayed in their peculiar style, which had a natural eloquence that would have moved a stone. I have witnessed hundreds, if not thousands, of such scenes; and can now see a poor girl, in the very ecstasy of the Methodist "shout," hugging the banner of one of the regiments, and jumping up to the " feet of Jesus."

I remember, when riding around by a by-street in Covington, to avoid the crowd that followed the marching column, that some one brought me an invitation to dine with a sister of Sam. Anderson, who was a cadet at West Point with me; but the messenger reached me after we had passed the main part of the town. I asked to be excused, and rode on to a place designated for camp, at the crossing of the Ulcofauhachee River, about four miles to the east of the town. Here we made our bivouac, and I walked up to a plantation-house close by, where were assembled many negroes, among them an old, gray-haired man. of as fine a head as I ever saw. I asked him if he understood about the war and its progress. He said he did; that he had been looking for the "angel of the Lord" ever since he was knee-high, and, though we professed to be fighting for the Union, he supposed that slavery was the cause, and that our success was to be his freedom. I asked him if all the negro slaves comprehended this fact, and he said they surely did. I then explained to him that we wanted the slaves to remain where they were, and not to load us down with useless mouths, which would eat up the food needed for our fighting-men ; that our success was their assured freedom ; that we could receive a few of their young, hearty men as

pioneers; but that, if they followed us in swarms of
old and young, feeble and helpless, it would simply load
us down and cripple us in our great task. I think
Major Henry Hitchcock was with me on that occasion,
and made a note of the conversation, and I believe that
old man spread this message to the slaves, which was
carried from mouth to mouth, to the very end of our
journey, and that it in part saved us from the great
danger we incurred of swelling our numbers so that
famine would have attended our progress. It was at
this very plantation that a soldier passed me with a
ham on his musket, a jug of sorghum-molasses under
his arm, and a big piece of honey in his hand, from
which he was eating, and, catching my eye, he remarked
sotto voce and carelessly to a comrade, " Forage liberally
on the country," quoting from my general orders. On
this occasion, as on many others that fell under my
personal observation, I reproved the man, explained
that foraging must be limited to the regular parties
properly detailed, and that all provisions thus obtained
must be delivered to the regular commissaries, to be
fairly distributed to the men who kept their ranks.

The skill and success of the men in collecting forage
was one of the features of this march. Each brigade
commander had authority to detail a company of
foragers, usually about fifty men, with one or two com-
missioned officers selected for their boldness and enterprise. This party would be despatched before daylight,
with a knowledge of the intended day's march and
camp; would proceed on foot five or six miles from the
route travelled by their brigade, and then visit every
plantation and farm within range. They would usually
procure a wagon or family carriage, load it with bacon,
corn-meal, turkeys, chickens, ducks, and everything
that could be used as food or forage, and would then
regain the main road, usually in advance of their train.
When this came up, they would deliver to the brigade
commissary the supplies thus gathered by the way.
Often would I pass these foraging-parties at the road-

side, waiting for their wagons to come up, and was amused at their strange collections, — mules, horses, even cattle, packed with old saddles and loaded with hams, bacon, bags of corn-meal, and poultry of every character and description. Although this foraging was attended with great danger and hard work, there seemed to be a charm about it that attracted the soldiers, and it was a privilege to be detailed on such a party. Daily they returned mounted on all sorts of beasts, which were at once taken from them and appropriated to the general use; but the next day they would start out again on foot, only to repeat the experience of the day before. No doubt, many acts of pillage, robbery, and violence, were committed by these parties of foragers, usually called "bummers"; for I have since heard of jewelry taken from women, and the plunder of articles that never reached the commissary; but these acts were exceptional and incidental.

I have seen much skill and industry displayed by these quartermasters on the march, in trying to load their wagons with corn and fodder by the way without losing their place in column. They would, while marching, shift the loads of wagons, so as to have six or ten of them empty. Then, riding well ahead, they would secure possession of certain stacks of fodder near the road, or cribs of corn, leave some men in charge, then open fences and a road back for a couple of miles, return to their trains, divert the empty wagons out of column, and conduct them rapidly to their forage, load up, and regain their place in column without losing distance. On one occasion I remember to have seen ten or a dozen wagons thus loaded with corn from two or three full cribs, almost without halting. These cribs were built of logs, and roofed. The train-guard, by a lever, had raised the whole side of the crib a foot or two; the wagons drove close alongside, and the men in the cribs, lying on their backs, kicked out a wagon-load of corn in the time I have taken to describe it.

In a well-ordered and well-disciplined army, these

things might be deemed irregular, but I am convinced
that the ingenuity of these younger officers accomplished
many things far better than I could have ordered, and
the marches were thus made, and the distances were
accomplished, in the most admirable way. | Habitually
we started from camp at the earliest break of dawn, and
usually reached camp soon after noon. The marches
varied from ten to fifteen miles a day, though sometimes
on extreme flanks it was necessary to make as much as
twenty, but the rate of travel was regulated by the
wagons; and, considering the nature of the roads,
fifteen miles per day was deemed the limit.

The pontoon trains were in like manner distributed
in about equal proportions to the four corps, giving
each a section of about nine hundred feet. The pontoons were of the skeleton pattern, with cotton-canvas
covers, each boat, with its proportion of balks and
chesses, constituting a load for one wagon. By uniting
two such sections together, we could make a bridge of
eighteen hundred feet, enough for any river we had to
traverse; but habitually the leading brigade would, out
of the abundant timber, improvise a bridge before the
pontoon train could come up, unless in the cases of
rivers of considerable magnitude. — *Gen. Sherman.*

CUTTING LOOSE.

November 13th. — Yesterday the last train of cars
whirled rapidly past the troops moving south, speeding
over bridges and into the woods as if they feared they
might be left helpless in the deserted land. At Car-
tersville the last communications with the North were
severed with the telegraph-wire. It bore the message
to General Thomas, "All is well." And so we have
cut adrift from our base of operations, from our line of
communications, launching out into uncertainty at the
best, on a journey whose projected end only a few in
the command know. Its real fate and destination they
do not know, since that rests with the goodness of God

and the brave hearts and strong limbs of our soldiers. The history of war bears no similar example, except that of Cortés burning his ships. It is a bold, hazardous undertaking. There is no backward step possible here. Thirty days' rations and a new base : that time and those supplies will be exhausted in the most rapid march ere we can arrive at the nearest sea-coast ; arrived there, what then? I never heard that manna grew on the sand-beaches or in the marshes, though we are sure that we can obtain forage on our way ; and I have reason to know that General Sherman is in the highest degree sanguine and cheerful, — sure even of success.

As for the soldiers, they do not stop to ask questions. Sherman says "Come," and that is the entire vocabulary to them. A most cheerful feature of the situation is the fact that the men are healthful and jolly as men can be ; hoping for the best, willing to dare the worst.

Behind us we leave a track of smoke and flame. Half of Marietta was burned up, — not by orders, however ; for the command is that proper details shall be made to destroy all property which can ever be of use to the Rebel armies. Stragglers will get into these places, and dwelling-houses are levelled to the ground. In nearly all cases these are the deserted habitations formerly owned by Rebels who are now refugees.

Yesterday, as some of our men were marching toward the Chattahoochee River, they saw in the distance pillars of smoke rising along its banks, — the bridges were in flames. Said one, hitching his musket on his shoulder in a free and easy way, " I say, Charley, I believe Sherman has set the river on fire." " Reckon not," replied the other, with the same indifference ; " if he has, it's all right." And so they pass along ; obeying orders, not knowing what is before them, but believing in their leader.

From Kingston to Atlanta the rails have been taken up on the road, fires built about them, and the iron twisted into all sorts of curves ; thus they are left, never to be straightened again. The Rebel inhabitants are in agony of wonder at all this queer manœuvring. It appears as if we intended evacuating Atlanta; but our troops are taking the wrong direction for the hopes and purposes of these people.

Atlanta is entirely deserted by human beings, excepting a few soldiers here and there. The houses are vacant; there is no trade or traffic of any kind; the streets are empty. Beautiful roses bloom in the gardens of fine houses, but a terrible stillness and solitude cover all, depressing the hearts even of those who are glad to destroy it. In the peaceful homes at the North there can be no conception how these people have suffered for their crimes. — *Capt. Nichols.*

BREAKING CAMP.

The order of march is issued by the army commanders the preceding night, from them to the corps commanders, and then pass along until every soldier, teamster, and camp-follower knows that an early start is to be made. "The second division will be on the Milledgeville road promptly at five o'clock," reads an order, by way of instance.

At three o'clock the watch-fires are burning dimly, and, but for the occasional neighing of horses, all is so silent that it is difficult to imagine that twenty thousand men are within a radius of a few miles. The ripple of the brook can be distinctly heard as it breaks over the pebbles, or winds petulantly about the gnarled roots. The wind sweeping gently through the tall pines overhead only serves to lull to deeper repose the slumbering soldier, who in his tent is dreaming of his far-off Northern home.

But in an instant all is changed. From some commanding elevation the clear-toned bugle sounds out the *reveillé,* and another and another responds, until the startled echoes double and treble the clarion calls. Intermingled with this comes the beating of drums, often rattling and jarring on unwilling ears. In a few moments the peaceful quiet is replaced by noise and tumult, arising from hill and dale, from field and forest. Camp-fires, hitherto extinct or smouldering in dull gray ashes, awaken to new life and brilliancy, and send forth their sparks high into the morning air. Although no gleam of sunrise blushes in the east, the harmless flames on every side light up the scene, so that there is no disorder or confusion.

The æsthetic aspects of this sudden change do not, however, occupy much of the soldier's time. He is more practically engaged in getting his breakfast ready. The potatoes are frying nicely in the well-larded pan, the chicken is roasting delicately on the red-hot coals, and grateful fumes from steaming coffee-pots delight the nostrils. The animals are not less busy. An ample supply of corn and huge piles of fodder are greedily devoured by these faithful friends of the boys in blue, and any neglect is quickly made known by the pawing of neighing horses and the fearful braying of the mules. Amid all is the busy clatter of tongues and tools, — a Babel of sound, forming a contrast to the quiet of the previous hour as marked as that between peace and war.

Then the animals are hitched into the traces, and the droves of cattle relieved from the night's confinement in the corral. Knapsacks are strapped, men seize their trusty weapons, and as again the bugles sound the note of command, the soldiers fall into line and file out upon the road, to make another stage of their journey, — it may be to win fresh laurels in another victory, or perhaps to find a rest which shall only be broken by the *reveillé* of the last trump).

A day's march varies according to the country to be traversed or the opposition encountered. If the map indicates a stream crossing the path, probably the strong party of mounted infantry or of cavalry which has been sent forward the day before has found the bridges burned, and then the pontoons are pushed on to the front. If a battle is anticipated, the trains are shifted to the rear of the centre. Under any circumstances, the divisions having the lead move unencumbered by wagons, and in close fighting trim. The ambulances following in the rear of the division are in such close proximity as to be available if needed. In the rear of each regiment follow the pack-mules, laden with every kind of camp baggage, including blankets, pots, pans, kettles, and all the kitchen-ware needed for cooking. Here will be found the led horses, and with them the negro servants, who form an important feature of the *ménage*.

Having placed the column upon the road, let us now follow that long line of muskets gleaming in the rays of the morning sunlight, and ride, heedless of the crack of the rifles, to the head of the column. The advance are driving a squad of Rebel cavalry before them so fast that the march is not in the least impeded. The flankers spread out, on a line parallel to the leading troops, for several hundred yards, more or less, as the occasion may require. They search through the swamps and forests, ready for any concealed foe, and anxiously looking out for any line of works which may have been thrown up by the enemy to check our progress. Here the general of the division, if a fighting man, is most likely to be found; his experienced eye noting that there is no serious opposition, he orders up a brigade or another regiment, who, in soldier's phraseology, send the Rebel rascals "kiting," and the column moves on. A large plantation appears by the road-side. If the "bummers" have been ahead, the chances are that it has been visited, in which event the interior is apt to show evidences of confusion; but the barns are full of corn and fodder, and parties are at once detailed to secure and convey the prize to the road-side. As the wagons pass along, they are not allowed to halt, but the grain or fodder is stuffed into the front and rear of the vehicles as they pass, the unhandy operation affording much amusement to the soldiers, and not unfrequently giving them a poor excuse for swearing as well as laughing.

When 'he treasure-trove of grain and poultry and vegetables has been secured, one man is detailed to guard it until the proper wagon comes along. Numbers of these details will be met, who, with proper authority, have started off early in the morning, and have struck out miles away from the flank of the column. They sit upon some cross-road, surrounded with their spoils, — chickens, turkeys, geese, ducks, pigs, hogs, sheep, calves, nicely-dressed hams, buckets full of honey, and pots of fresh white lard.

A Roman consul, returning with victorious eagles, could not wear a more triumphant air than this solitary guard. The soldiers see it, and gibe him as they pass.

" Say, you thar! where did you steal them pigs?"

" Steal!" is the indignant response; " steal! — perhaps you would like to have one of ' *them* ' pigs yourself."

An officer who is riding along gazes upon the appetizing show. He has recently joined, never has been on one of Sherman's raids, and does not know that a soldier will not sell his chickens for any price.

" Ah! a nice pair of ducks you have there, soldier; what will you take for them?"

Firmly, but respectfully, the forager makes answer, touching his cap the while, " They are not in the market. We *never* sell our stuff, sir, — couldn't think of it." — *Capt. Nichols.*

TORPEDOES.

General Hardee was ahead, between us and Savannah, with McLaw's division, and other irregular troops, that could not, I felt assured, exceed ten thousand men. I caused the fine depot at Millen to be destroyed, and other damage done, and then resumed the march directly on Savannah, by the four main roads. The Seventeenth

Corps (General Blair) followed substantially the railroad, and, along with it, on the 5th of December, I reached Ogeechee Church, about fifty miles from Savannah, and found there fresh earth-works, which had been thrown up by McLaw's division; but he must have seen that both his flanks were being turned, and prudently retreated to Savannah without a fight. All the columns then pursued leisurely their march toward Savannah, corn and forage becoming more and more scarce, but rice-fields beginning to occur along the Savannah and Ogeechee Rivers, which proved a good substitute, both as food and forage. The weather was fine, the roads good, and everything seemed to favor us. Never do I recall a more agreeable sensation than the sight of our camps by night, lit up by the fires of fragrant pine-knots. The trains were all in good order, and the men seemed to march their fifteen miles a day as though it were nothing. No enemy opposed us, and we could only occasionally hear the faint reverberation of a gun to our left rear, where we knew that General Kilpatrick was skirmishing with Wheeler's cavalry, which persistently followed him. But the infantry columns had met with no opposition whatsoever. McLaw's division was falling back before us, and we occasionally picked up a few of his men as prisoners, who insisted that we would meet with strong opposition at Savannah.

On the 8th, as I rode along, I found the column turned out of the main road, marching through the fields. Close by, in the corner of a fence, was a group of men standing around a handsome young officer, whose foot had been blown to pieces by a torpedo planted in the road. He was waiting for a surgeon to amputate his leg, and told me that he was riding along with the rest of his brigade staff of the Seventeenth Corps, when a torpedo trodden on by his horse had exploded, killing the horse and literally blowing off all the flesh from one of his legs. I saw the terrible wound, and made full inquiry into the facts. There had been no resistance at that point, nothing to give warning of danger, and the Rebels had planted eight-inch shells in the road, with friction matches to explode them by being trodden on. This was not war, but murder, and it made me very angry. I immediately ordered a lot of Rebel prisoners to be brought from the provost-guard, armed with picks and spades, and made them march in close order along the road, so as to explode their own torpedoes, or to discover and dig them up. They begged hard, but I reiterated the order, and could hardly help laughing at their stepping so gingerly along the road, where it was supposed sunken torpedoes might explode at each step, but they found no other torpedoes till near Fort McAllister. — *Gen. Sherman.*

"SET FIRE TO THE WELL."

At Sandersville I halted the left wing until I heard that the right wing was abreast of us on the railroad. During the evening a negro was brought to me, who had that day been to the station (Tenille), about six miles south of the town. I inquired of him if there were any Yankees there, and he answered, " Yes." He described in his own way what he had seen. " First, there come along some cavalry-men, and they burned the depot ; then come along some infantry-men, and they tore up the track, and burned it " ; and just before he left they had " sot fire to the well" !

The next morning, viz. the 27th, I rode down to the station, and found General Corse's division (of the Fifteenth Corps) engaged in destroying the railroad, and saw the well which my negro informant had seen " burnt." It was a square pit about twenty-five feet deep, boarded up, with wooden steps leading to the bottom, wherein was a fine copper pump, to lift the water to a tank above. The soldiers had broken up the pump, heaved in the steps and lining, and set fire to the mass of lumber in the bottom of the well, which corroborated the negro's description. — *Gen. Sherman.*

MARCH THROUGH THE PINES.

All day long the army has been moving through magnificent pine woods. I have never seen, and I cannot conceive, a more picturesque sight. The pines, destitute of branches, rise to a height of eighty or ninety feet, their tops being crowned with tufts of pure green. They are widely apart, so that frequently two trains of wagons and troops in double column are marching abreast. In the distance may be seen a troop of horsemen, — some general and his staff, — turning about here and there, their gay uniforms and red and white flags contrasting harmoniously with the bright yellow grass underneath and the deep evergreen. War has its romance and its pleasures, and nothing could be more delightful, nor can there be more beautiful subjects for the artist's pencil, than a thousand sights which have met my eye for days past, and which can never be seen outside the army. There is, by the way, a most excellent artist accompanying the expedition, who is working for the Harpers. His sketches are artistically executed, and he has the genuine spirit of an artist in his choice of subject; but I would have wished that Johnson, Hennessey, or Kensett might have been here also, to give us in enduring colors scenes now passing away, which belong to the history of the great day in which we live.

The most pathetic scenes occur upon our line of march daily and hourly. Thousands of negro women join the column, some carrying household goods, and many of them carrying children in their arms, while older boys and girls plod by their side. All these women and children are ordered back, heart-rending though it may be to refuse them liberty. One begs that she may go to see her husband and children at Savannah. Long years ago she was forced from him and sold. Another has heard that her boy was in Macon, and she is " done gone with grief goin' on four years."

But the majority accept the advent of the Yankees as the fulfilment of the millennial prophecies. The " day of jubilee," the hope and prayer of a lifetime, has come. They cannot be made to understand that they must remain behind, and they are satisfied only when General Sherman tells them, as he does every day, that we shall come back for them some time, and that they must be patient until the proper hour of deliverance arrives.

The other day a woman with a child in her arms was working her way along among the teams and crowds of cattle and horsemen. An officer called to her kindly, " Where are you going, aunty? "

She looked up into his face with a hopeful, beseeching look, and replied, " I'se gwine whar you'se gwine, massa." — *Capt. Nichols.*

FORT McALLISTER.

About two P. M. we observed signs of commotion in the fort, and noticed one or two guns fired inland, and some musket-skirmishing in the woods close by.

This betokened the approach of Hazen's division, which had been anxiously expected, and soon thereafter the signal officer discovered, about three miles above the fort, a signal flag, with which he conversed, and found it to belong to General Hazen, who was preparing to assault the fort, and wanted to know if I were there. On being assured of this fact, and that I expected the fort to be carried before night, I received by signal the assurance of General Hazen that he was making his preparations, and would soon attempt the assault. The sun was rapidly declining, and I was dreadfully impatient.

At that very moment some one discovered a faint cloud of smoke, and an object gliding, as it were, along the horizon above the tops of the sedge toward the sea, which, little by little, grew till it was pronounced to be the smoke-stack of a steamer coming up the river. " It

must be one of our squadron!" Soon the flag of the
United States was plainly visible, and our attention
was divided between this approaching steamer and the
expected assault. When the sun was about an hour
high, another signal message came from General Hazen
that he was all ready, and I replied to go ahead, as a
friendly steamer was approaching from below. Soon
we made out a group of officers on the deck of this vessel, signalling with a flag, " Who are you?" The answer went back promptly, " General Sherman." Then
followed the question, " Is Fort McAllister taken?"
" Not yet, but it will be in a minute!" Almost at that
instant of time, we saw Hazen's troops come out of the
dark fringe of woods that encompassed the fort, the
lines dressed as on parade, with colors flying, and
moving forward with a quick steady pace. Fort Mc-
Allister was then all alive, its big guns belching forth
dense clouds of smoke, which soon enveloped our assaulting lines. One color went down, but was up in a
moment. On the lines advanced, faintly seen in the
white, sulphurous smoke; there was a pause, a cessation of fire; the smoke cleared away, and the parapets
were blue with our men, who fired their muskets in the
air, and shouted so that we actually heard them, or
felt that we did. Fort McAllister was taken, and the
good news was instantly sent by the signal officer to
our navy friends on the approaching gun-boat, for a
point of timber had shut out Fort McAllister from their
view, and they had not seen the action at all, but must
have heard the cannonading. . . . .

The fort was an enclosed work, and its land front was
in the nature of a bastion and curtains, with good parapet, ditch, *fraise*, and *cheraux-de-frise*, made out of
the large branches of live-oaks. Luckily, the Rebels
had left the larger and unwieldy trunks on the ground,
which served as a good cover for the skirmish line,
which crept behind these logs, and from them kept the
artillerists from loading and firing their guns accu-
rately.

The assault had been made by three parties in line, one from below, one from above the fort, and the third directly in rear, along the capital. All were simultaneous, and had to pass a good abatis and line of torpedoes, which actually killed more of the assailants than the heavy guns of the fort, which generally overshot the mark. Hazen's entire loss was reported, killed and wounded, ninety-two. Each party reached the parapet about the same time, and the garrison inside, of about two hundred and fifty men (about fifty of them killed or wounded), were in his power. — *Gen. Sherman.*

December 13th. — Fort McAllister is ours. It has been gallantly and bravely won. I saw the heroic assault from the point of observation selected by General Sherman at the adjacent rice-mill.

During the greater part of to-day the General gazed anxiously toward the sea, watching for the appearance of the fleet. About the middle of the afternoon he descried a light column of smoke creeping lazily along over the flat marshes, and soon the spars of a steamer were visible, and then the flag of our Union floated out. What a thrilling, joyful sight! How the blood bounded, when, answering the signal waved above us, we saw that the brave tars had recognized us, and knew that our General was here with his army!

The sun was now fast going down behind a grove of water-oaks, and as his last rays gilded the earth, all eyes once more turned toward the Rebel fort. Suddenly white puffs of smoke shot out from the thick woods surrounding the line of works. Hazen was closing in, ready for the final rush of his column directly upon the fort. A warning answer came from the enemy in the roar of heavy artillery, — and so the battle opened.

General Sherman walked nervously to and fro, turning quickly now and then from viewing the scene of conflict to observe the sun sinking slowly behind the tree-tops. No longer willing to bear the suspense, he said, " Signal General Hazen that he must carry the fort by assault, to-night, if possible."

The little flag waved and fluttered in the evening air, and the answer came, " I am ready, and will assault at once!"

The words had hardly passed when from out the encircling woods there came a long line of blue coats and bright bayonets, and the dear old flag was there, waving proudly in the breeze. Then the fort seemed alive with flame; quick, thick jets of fire shooting out from all its sides, while the white smoke first covered the place and then rolled away over the glacis. The line of blue moved steadily on; too slowly, as it seemed to us, for we exclaimed, " Why don't they dash forward?" but their measured step was unfaltering. Now the flag goes down, but the line does not halt. A moment longer, and the banner gleams again in the front. We, the lookers-on, clutched one another's arms convulsively, and scarcely breathed in the eager intensity of our gaze. Sherman stood watching with anxious air, awaiting the decisive moment. Then the enemy's fire redoubled in rapidity and violence. The darting streams of fire alone told the position of the fort. The line of blue entered the enshrouding folds of smoke. The flag was at last dimly seen, and then it went out of sight altogether.

" They have been repulsed!" said one of the group of officers who watched the fight.

" No, by heaven!" said another; " there is not a man in retreat, — not a straggler in all the glorious line!"

The firing ceased. The wind lifted the smoke. Crowds of men were visible on the parapets, fiercely fighting, — but our flag was planted there. There were a few scattering musket-shots, and then the sounds of battle ceased. Then the bomb-proofs and parapets were alive with crowding swarms of our gallant men, who fired their pieces in the air for a *feu de joie.* — *Capt. Nichols.*

SAVANNAH.

An incident connected with our occupation of Savannah illustrates the watchfulness and daring of our officers and soldiers. Colonel Barnum, of New York, commanding a brigade in the Twentieth Corps, a brave soldier, who bears scars and unhealed wounds from many a battle-field, was in command in the immediate front upon our extreme left, and near midnight crept out beyond his picket lines, which were only three hundred yards from the Rebel works. Not hearing the voices of the enemy, and not seeing their forms passing before their camp-fires, he suspected that they had evacuated their lines, notwithstanding he could hear the boom of their guns, which echoed through the dark forests away off to the right. He selected ten of his best men, and cautiously scaled the parapets of the outside Rebel line; passing rapidly and silently from these to the fortifications from whose bastions frowned the black muzzles of ponderous sixty-four-pounders. Although their camp-fires still burned brightly, no Rebels were to be seen. Sending back for reinforcements, he marched from earth-work to earth-work, and finally entered the city just as the early morning light appeared in the eastern horizon; while the forms of the retreating enemy could be seen flying into the gray mist across the marshes on the other side of the river. —*Capt. Nichols.*

CHAPTER XII.

NASHVILLE.

YOU remember how it tells, in the last chapter, that Sherman sent a couple of corps up to Thomas, at Nashville, and how he trusted to Thomas to keep Hood away from his own rear. This chapter is to show how Thomas attacked Hood in his lines before Nashville, and drove him, broken and defeated, beyond the Tennessee.

GEN. GRANT DESCRIBES THE CAMPAIGN IN BRIEF.

Hood, instead of following Sherman, continued his move northward, which seemed to me to be leading to his certain doom. At all events, had I had the power to command both armies, I should not have changed the orders under which he seemed to be acting. On the 24th of October, the advance of Hood's army attacked the garrison at Decatur, Ala., but, failing to carry the place, withdrew toward Courtland, and succeeded, in the face of our cavalry, in effecting a lodgment on the north side of the Tennessee River, near Florence. On the 28th, Forrest reached the Tennessee, at Fort Hieman, and captured a gun-boat and three transports. On the 2d of November, he planted batteries above and below Johnsonville, on the opposite side of the river, isolating three gun-boats and eight transports. On the 4th, the enemy opened his batteries upon the place, and was replied to from the gun-boats and the garrison. The gun-boats, becoming disabled, were set on fire, as also were the transports, to prevent their falling into the hands of the enemy. About a million and a half dollars' worth of stores and property, on the levee and in storehouses, was consumed by fire. On the 5th, the enemy disappeared and crossed to the north side of the Tennessee River, above Johnsonville, moving toward Clifton, and subsequently joined Hood. On the night of the 5th, General Schofield, with the advance of the Twenty-third Corps, reached Johnsonville, but, finding the enemy gone, was ordered to Pulaski, and put in command of all the troops there, with instructions to watch the movements of Hood, and retard his advance, but not to risk a general engagement until the arrival of General A. J. Smith's command from Missouri, and until General Wilson could get his cavalry remounted.

On the 19th, General Hood continued his advance. General Thomas, retarding him as much as possible, fell back toward Nashville for the purpose of concentrating his command, and gaining time for the arrival of reinforcements. The enemy coming up with our main force, commanded by General Schofield, at Franklin, on the 30th, assaulted our works repeatedly during the afternoon until late at night, but were in every instance repulsed. His loss in this battle was 1,750 killed, 702 prisoners, and 3,800 wounded. Among his losses were six general officers killed, six wounded, and one captured. Our entire loss was 2,300. This was the first serious opposition the enemy met with, and, I am satisfied, was the fatal blow to all his expectations. During the night, General Schofield fell back toward Nashville. This left the field to the enemy, — not lost by the battle, but voluntarily abandoned, — so that General Thomas's whole force might be brought together. The enemy followed up, and commenced the establishment of his line in front of Nashville on the 2d of December.

As soon as it was ascertained that Hood was crossing the Tennessee River, and that Price was going out
of Missouri. General Rosecrans was ordered to send
to General Thomas the troops of General A. J. Smith's
command and such other troops as he could spare.
The advance of this reinforcement reached Nashville
on the 30th of November.

On the morning of the 15th of December General
Thomas attacked Hood in position, and, in a battle
lasting two days, defeated and drove him from the field
in the utmost confusion, leaving in our hands most of
his artillery and many thousand prisoners, including
four general officers.

Before the battle of Nashville, I grew very impatient
over, as it appeared to me, the unnecessary delay.
This impatience was increased upon learning that the
enemy had sent a force of cavalry across the Cumberland into Kentucky. I feared Hood would cross his
whole army and give us great trouble there. After
urging upon General Thomas the necessity of immediately assuming the offensive, I started West to super-
intend matters there in person. Reaching Washington
City, I received General Thomas's despatch announcing
his attack upon the enemy, and the result as far as the
battle had progressed. I was delighted. All fears and
apprehensions were dispelled. I am not yet satisfied
but that General Thomas, immediately upon the appearance of Hood before Nashville, and before he had time
to fortify, should have moved out with his whole force
and given him battle, instead of waiting to remount his
cavalry, which delayed him until the inclemency of the
weather made it impracticable to attack earlier than he
did. But his final defeat of Hood was so complete,
that it will be accepted as a vindication of that distinguished officer's judgment. — *Gen. Grant.*

As Hood was marching north from Florence,
Schofield was also marching from Pulaski, and

there was some question which would first reach Franklin, where their roads converged. At one time, Hood was ahead, and would have cut Schofield off from Nashville, had not Schofield, by a brilliant night march, with all his trains and his whole army, passed within half a mile of Hood's camp without arousing him. The next morning he woke to find Schofield intrenched in front of him, ready to repulse his whole army in the battle of Franklin.

THE BATTLE OF NASHVILLE.

On the morning of the 15th of December, the weather being favorable, the army was formed and ready at an early hour to carry out the plan of battle promulgated in the Special Field Order of the 14th. The formation of the troops was partially concealed from the enemy by the broken nature of the ground, as also by a dense fog, which only lifted toward noon. The enemy was apparently totally unaware of any intention on our part to attack his position, and more especially did he seem not to expect any movement against his left flank. To divert his attention still further from our real intentions, Major-General Steedman had, on the evening of the 14th, received orders to make a heavy demonstration with his command against the enemy's right, east of the Nolensville pike, which he accomplished with great success, and some loss, succeeding, however, in attracting the enemy's attention to that part of his line and inducing him to draw reinforcements from toward his centre and left.

THE MAIN ATTACK BY OUR LEFT.

As soon as General Steedman had completed his movement, the commands of Generals Smith and Wilson moved out along the Harding pike, and commenced the grand movement of the day by wheeling to the left and advancing against the enemy's position across the Harding and Hillsboro' pikes. A division of cavalry (Johnson's) was sent at the same time to look after a battery of the enemy's on the Cumberland River at Bell's Landing, eight miles below Nashville. General Johnson did not get into position until late in the afternoon, when, in conjunction with the gun-boats under Lieut.-Commander Le Roy Fitch, the enemy's battery was engaged until after nightfall, and the place was found evacuated in the morning. The remainder of General Wilson's command, Hatch's division leading and Knipe in reserve, moving on the right of General A. J. Smith's troops, first struck the enemy along Richland Creek, near Harding's house, and drove him back rapidly, capturing a number of prisoners, wagons, &c., and, continuing to advance, while slightly swinging to the left, came upon a redoubt containing four guns, which was splendidly carried by assault, at one P. M., by a portion of Hatch's division, dismounted, and the captured guns turned upon the enemy. A second redoubt, stronger than the first, was next assailed and carried by the same troops that captured the first position, taking four more guns and about three hundred prisoners. The infantry, McArthur's division of General A. J. Smith's command, on the left of the cavalry, participated in both of the above assaults, and indeed the dismounted cavalry seemed to vie with the infantry who should first gain the works; as they reached the position nearly simultaneously, both lay claim to the artillery and prisoners captured.

Finding General Smith had not taken as much distance to the right as I expected he would have done, I directed General Schofield to move his command (the Twenty-third Corps) from the position in reserve to which it had been assigned over to the right of General Smith, enabling the cavalry thereby to operate more freely in the enemy's rear. This was rapidly accomplished by General Schofield, and his troops participated in the closing operations of the day.

THE CENTRE.

The Fourth Corps, Brig.-Gen. T. J. Wood commanding, formed on the left of General A. J. Smith's command, and, as soon as the latter had struck the enemy's flank, assaulted the Montgomery Hill, Hood's most advanced position, at one P. M. The assault was most gallantly executed by the Third Brigade, Second Division, Colonel P. Sidney Post, Fifty-ninth Illinois, commanding, capturing a considerable number of prisoners. Connecting with the left of Smith's troops (Brigadier-General Garrard's division), the Fourth Corps continued to advance, and carried the enemy's entire line in its front by assault, and captured several pieces of artillery, about five hundred prisoners, some stands of colors, and other material. The enemy was driven out of his original line of works and forced back to a new position along the base of Harpeth Hills, still holding his line of retreat to Franklin by the main pike through Brentwood and by the Granny White pike. Our line at nightfall was re-adjusted, running parallel to and east of the Hillsboro' pike, — Schofield's command on the right, Smith's in the centre, and Wood's on the left, with the cavalry on the right of Schofield, — Steedman holding the position he had gained early in the morning.

The total result of the day's operations was the capture of sixteen pieces of artillery and 1,200 prisoners, besides several hundred stand of small arms and about forty wagons. The enemy had been forced back at all points with heavy loss, and our casualties were unusually light. The behavior of the troops was unsurpassed for steadiness and alacrity in every movement, and the original plan of battle, with but few alterations, strictly adhered to.

The whole command bivouacked in line of battle during the night on the ground occupied at dark, while preparations were made to renew the battle at an early hour on the morrow.

THE NEXT DAY'S BATTLE.

At six A. M., on the 16th, Wood's corps pressed back the enemy's skirmishers across the Franklin pike to the eastward of it, and then, swinging slightly to the right, advanced due south from Nashville, driving the enemy before him until he came upon his new main line of works, constructed during the night, on what is called Overton's Hill, about five miles south of the city and east of the Franklin pike. General Steedman moved out from Nashville by the Nolensville pike, and formed his command on the left of General Wood, effectually securing the latter's left flank, and made preparations to co-operate in the operations of the day. General A. J. Smith's command moved on the right of the Fourth Corps (Wood's), and, establishing connection with General Wood's right, completed the new line of battle. General Schofield's troops remained in the position taken up by them at dark on the day previous, facing eastward and toward the enemy's left flank, the line of the corps running perpendicular to General Smith's troops. General Wilson's cavalry, which had rested for the night at the six-mile post on the Hillsboro' pike, was dismounted and formed on the right of Schofield's command, and by noon of the 16th had succeeded in gaining the enemy's rear, and stretched across the Granny White pike, one of his two outlets toward Franklin.

As soon as the above dispositions were completed, and having visited the different commands, I gave directions that the movement against the enemy's left flank should be continued. Our entire line approached to within six hundred yards of the enemy's at all points. His centre was weak as compared with either his right, at Overton's Hill, or his left, on the hills bordering the Granny White pike; still I had hopes of gaining his rear and cutting off his retreat from Franklin.

About three P. M. Post's brigade of Wood's Corps, supported by Streight's brigade of the same command, was ordered by General Wood to assault Overton's Hill. This intention was communicated to General Steedman, who ordered the brigade of colored troops commanded by Colonel Morgan (Fourteenth United States colored troops) to co-operate in the movement. The ground on which the two assaulting columns formed being open and exposed to the enemy's view, he, readily perceiving our intention, drew reinforcements from his left and centre to the threatened point. This movement of troops on the part of the enemy was communicated along the line from left to right.

The assault was made, and received by the enemy with a tremendous fire of grape, canister, and musketry, our men moving steadily onward up the hill until near the crest, when the reserves of the enemy rose and poured into the assaulting column a most destructive fire, causing the men first to waver and then to fall back, leaving their dead and wounded — black and white indiscriminately mingled — lying amid the abatis, the gallant Colonel Post among the wounded. General Wood readily re-formed his command in the position it had previously occupied, preparatory to a renewal of the assault.

THE THIRD SUCCESS.

Immediately following the effort of the Fourth Corps, Generals Smith's and Schofield's commands moved against the enemy's works in their respective fronts, carrying all before them, irreparably breaking his lines in a dozen places, and capturing all of his artillery and thousands of prisoners, among the latter four general officers. Our loss was remarkably small, scarcely mentionable. All of the enemy that did escape were pursued over the tops of Brentwood or Harpeth Hills.

General Wilson's cavalry, dismounted, attacked the enemy simultaneously with Schofield and Smith, striking him in reverse, and, gaining firm possession of the Granny White pike, cut off his retreat by that route.

THE ROUT.

Wood's and Steedman's troops hearing the shouts of victory coming from the right, rushed impetuously forward, renewing the assault on Overton's Hill, and, although meeting a very heavy fire, the onset was irresistible, artillery and innumerable prisoners falling into our hands. The enemy, hopelessly broken, fled in confusion through the Brentwood pass, the Fourth Corps in a close pursuit, which was continued for several miles, when darkness closed the scene and the troops rested from their labors.

As the Fourth Corps pursued the enemy on the Franklin pike, General Wilson hastily mounted Knipe's and Hatch's division of his command, and directed them to pursue along the Granny White pike and endeavor to reach Franklin in advance of the enemy. After proceeding about a mile they came upon the enemy's cavalry under Chalmers, posted across the road and behind barricades. The position was charged by the Twelfth Tennessee Cavalry, Colonel Spalding commanding, and the enemy's lines broken, scattering him in all directions, and capturing quite a number of prisoners, among them Brig.-Gen. E. W. Rucker.

During the two days' operations there were 4,462 prisoners captured, including 287 officers of all grades from that of major-general, fifty-three pieces of artillery, and thousands of small arms. The enemy abandoned on the field all of his dead and wounded.

Leaving directions for the collection of the captured property, and for the care of the wounded left on the battle-field, the pursuit was continued at daylight on the 17th. The Fourth Corps pushed on toward Franklin by the direct pike, while the cavalry moved by the Granny White Pike to its intersection with the Franklin pike, and then took the advance.

THE PURSUIT.

Johnson's division of cavalry was sent by General Wilson direct to Harpeth River, on the Hillsboro' pike, with directions to cross and move rapidly toward Franklin. The main cavalry column, with Knipe's division in advance, came up with the enemy's rear-guard strongly posted at Hollow Tree Gap, four miles north of Franklin; the position was charged in front and in flank simultaneously, and handsomely carried, capturing four hundred and thirteen prisoners and three colors. The enemy then fell back rapidly to Franklin, and endeavored to defend the crossing of Harpeth River at that place; but Johnson's division, coming up from below on the south side of the stream, forced him to retire from the river bank, and our cavalry took possession of the town, capturing the enemy's hospitals, containing over two thousand wounded, of whom about two hundred were our own men. — *Maj.- Gen. Thomas.*

15

CHAPTER XIII.

SIEGE OF RICHMOND. — THE LAST WEEK.

AFTER General Grant had crossed the James River and united his army with General Butler's, in the summer of 1864, he spent the rest of that year and the months of winter in closer and closer approaches upon Richmond and Petersburg. These two cities were united by a railroad, so that they supported each other; and the hardest fighting done was, in fact, before Petersburg. The whole effort, however, was popularly called "the Siege of Richmond," though Richmond was never besieged. It always drew provisions from the west by the Southside Railroad, and other roads through the valley of James River.

The lines of the Union army and those of the Rebels at Petersburg came closer and closer. In many bloody battles, Grant pushed his left wing farther and farther to the west, cutting off the line of the Weldon Railroad. The deep quagmires which are called roads in Virginia, as in so many years before, defended her capital so long as winter lasted. But with the opening of spring the end came. It was all like the arrangement by which a great player finishes a game at chess.

On the 24th of March, General Grant issued his orders, without any "ifs" or "perhapses," for the "general movement." They were addressed to General Meade, General Ord, and General Sheridan. They began, — "Generals, on the 29th instant, the armies operating against Richmond will be moved by our left, for the double purpose of turning the enemy out of his present position around Petersburg, and to insure the success of the cavalry, under General Sheridan, which will start at the same time in its efforts to reach and destroy the Southside and Danville railroads."

These are just such rules as a head of a family might give about a "moving," — that this cart should come at this time, that cart at another, and such and such a boy be ready at the new house to tell where the furniture should go. There is just that confidence that what is ordered will be done.

General Grant's report of the result shall be copied first.

THE ARMY MARCHES.

I had spent days of anxiety lest each morning should bring the report that the enemy had retreated the night before. I was firmly convinced that Sherman's crossing the Roanoke would be the signal for Lee to leave. With Johnston and him combined, a long, tedious and expensive campaign, consuming most of the summer, might become necessary. By moving out I would put the army in better condition for pursuit, and would at least, by the destruction of the Danville road, retard the concentration of the two armies of Lee and Johnston, and cause the enemy to abandon much material that he might otherwise save. I therefore determined not to delay the movement ordered.

On the night of the 27th, Major-General Ord, with two divisions of the Twenty-fourth Corps, Major-General Gibbon commanding, and one division of the Twenty-fifth Corps, Brigadier-General Birney commanding, and McKenzie's cavalry, took up his line of march in pursuance of the foregoing instructions, and reached the position assigned him near Hatcher's Run on the morning of the 29th. On the 28th, the following instructions were given to General Sheridan : —

City Point, Va., March 28, 1865.

GENERAL : — The Fifth Army Corps will move by the Vaughn road at 3 A. M. to-morrow morning. The Second moves at about 9 A M. having but about three miles to march to reach the point designated for it to take on the right of the Fifth Corps, after the latter reaching Dinwiddie Court-House. Move your cavalry at as early an hour as you can, and without being confined to any particular road or roads. You may go out by the nearest roads in rear of the Fifth Corps, pass by its left, and, passing near to or through Dinwiddie, reach the right and rear of the enemy as soon as you can. It is not the intention to attack the enemy in his intrenched position, but to force him out, if possible. Should he come out and attack us, or get himself where he can be attacked, move in with your entire force in your own way, and with the full reliance that the army will engage or follow, as circumstances will dictate. I shall be on the field, and will probably be able to communicate with you. Should I not do so, and you find that the enemy keeps within his main intrenched line, you may cut loose and push for the Danville road. If you find it practicable, I would like you to cross the Southside road, between Petersburg and Burkesville, and destroy it to some extent. I would not advise much detention, however, until you reach the Danville road, which I would like you to strike as near to the Appomattox as possible. Make your destruction on that road as complete as possible. You can then pass on to the Southside road, west of Burkesville, and destroy that, in like manner.

After having accomplished the destruction of the two railroads, which are now the only avenues of supply to Lee's army, you may return to this army, selecting your road further south, or you may go on into North Carolina and join General Sherman. Should you select the latter course, get the information to me as early as possible, so that I may send orders to meet you at Goldsboro'.

U. S. Grant, *Lieut.-Gen.*

Maj.-Gen. P. H. Sheridan.

On the morning of the 29th, the movement commenced. At night the cavalry was at Dinwiddie Court-House, and the left of our infantry line extended to the Quaker road, near its intersection with the Boydton plank-road. The position of the troops from left to right was as follows : Sheridan, Warren, Humphreys, Ord, Wright, Parke.

Everything looked favorable to the defeat of the enemy and the capture of Petersburg and Richmond, if the proper effort was made. I therefore addressed the following communication to General Sheridan, having previously informed him verbally not to cut loose for the raid contemplated in his orders until he received notice from me to do so :

Gravelly Creek, March 29, 1865.

General : — Our line is now unbroken from the Appomattox to Dinwiddie. We are all ready, however, to give up all, from the Jerusalem plank-road to Hatcher's Run, whenever the forces can be used advantageously. After getting into line south of Hatcher's we push forward to find the enemy's position. General Griffin was attacked near where the Quaker road intersects the Boydton road, but repulsed it easily, capturing about one hundred men. Humphreys reached Dabney's Mill, and was pushing on when last heard from.

I now feel like ending the matter, if it is possible to do so, before going back. I do not want you, therefore, to cut loose and go after the enemy's roads at present. In the morning push around the enemy, if you can, and get on to his right rear. The movements of the enemy's cavalry may, of course, modify your action. We will act all together as one army here until it is seen what can be done with the enemy. The signal officer at Cobb's Hill reported, at 11.30 A. M., that a cavalry column had passed that point from Richmond towards Petersburg, taking forty minutes to pass.

U. S. Grant, *Lieut.-Gen.*

Maj.-Gen. P. H. Sheridan.

From the night of the 29th to the morning of the 31st the rain fell in such torrents as to make it impossible to move a wheeled vehicle, except as corduroy roads were laid in front of them. During the 30th, Sheridan advanced from Dinwiddie Court-House toward Five Forks, where he found the enemy in force. General Warren advanced and extended his line across the Boydton plank-road to near the White Oak road, with a view of getting across the latter; but finding the enemy strong in his front, and extending beyond his left, was directed to hold on where he was and fortify. General Humphreys drove the enemy from his front into his main line on the Hatcher, near Burgess's mills. Generals Ord, Wright, and Parke made examinations in their fronts to determine the feasibility of an assault on the enemy's lines. The two latter reported favorably. The enemy confronting us, as he did at every point from Richmond to our extreme left, I conceived his lines must be weakly held, and could be penetrated if my estimate of his forces was correct. I determined, therefore, to extend my line no further, but to reinforce General Sheridan with a corps of infantry, and thus enable him to cut loose and turn the enemy's right flank, and with the other corps assault the enemy's lines. The result of the offensive effort of the enemy the week before, when he assaulted Fort Steadman, particularly favored this. The enemy's intrenched picket line, captured by us at that time, threw the lines occupied by the belligerents so close together at some points, that it was but a moment's run from one to the other. Preparations were at once made to relieve General Humphreys's corps, to report to General Sheridan; but the condition of the roads prevented immediate movement. On the morning of the 31st General Warren reported favorably to getting possession of the White Oak road, and was directed to do so. To accomplish this he moved with one division, instead of his whole corps, which was attacked by the enemy in superior force, and driven back on the second division, before it had time to form, and it, in turn, forced back upon the third division, when the enemy was checked. A division of the Second Corps was immediately sent to his support, the enemy driven back with heavy loss, and possession of White Oak road gained. Sheridan advanced, and with a portion of his cavalry got possession of the Five Forks, but the enemy, after the affair with the Fifth Corps, reinforced the Rebel cavalry, defending that point with infantry, and forced him back toward Dinwiddie Court-House. Here General Sheridan displayed great generalship. Instead of retreating with his whole command on the main army, to tell the story of superior forces encountered, he deployed his cavalry on foot, leaving only mounted men enough to take charge of the horses. This compelled the enemy to deploy over a vast extent of woods and broken country, and made his progress slow. At this juncture he despatched to me what had taken place, and that he was dropping back slowly on Dinwiddie Court-House. General McKenzie's cavalry and one division of the Fifth Corps were immediately ordered to his assistance. Soon after, receiving a report from General Meade that Humphreys could hold our position on the Boydton road, and that the other two divisions of the Fifth Corps could go to Sheridan, they were so ordered at once. Thus the operations of the day necessitated the sending of Warren because of his accessibility, instead of Humphreys, as was intended, and precipitated intended movements. On the morning of the 1st of April, General Sheridan, reinforced by General Warren, drove the enemy back on Five Forks, where, late in the evening, he assaulted and carried his strongly fortified position, capturing all his artillery and between five and six thousand prisoners. About the close of this battle, Brevet Major-General Charles Griffin relieved Major-General Warren in command of the Fifth Corps. The report of this reached me after nightfall. Some apprehensions filled my mind lest the enemy might desert his lines during the night, and, by falling upon General Sheridan before assistance could reach him, drive him from his position, and open the way for retreat. To guard against this, General Miles's division of Humphreys's Corps was sent to reinforce him, and a bombardment was commenced and kept

up until four o'clock in the morning (April 2), when
an assault was ordered on the enemy's lines. General
Wright penetrated the lines with his whole corps, sweeping everything before him and to his left toward Hatcher's Run, capturing many guns and several thousand
prisoners. He was closely followed by two divisions of
General Ord's command, until he met the other division
of General Ord's that had succeeded in forcing the enemy's lines near Hatcher's Run. Generals Wright and
Ord immediately swung to the right, and closed all the
enemy on that side of them in Petersburg, while General Humphreys pushed forward with two divisions and
joined General Wright on the left. General Parke succeeded in carrying the enemy's main line, capturing guns
and prisoners, but was unable to carry his inner line.
General Sheridan, being advised of the condition of
affairs, returned General Miles to his proper command.
On reaching the enemy's lines immediately surrounding
Petersburg, a portion of General Gibbon's corps, by
a most gallant charge, captured two strong, enclosed
works, — the most salient and commanding south of
Petersburg, — thus materially shortening the line of investment necessary for taking the city. The enemy
south of Hatcher's Run retreated westward to Suther-
land's Station, where they were overtaken by Miles's division. A severe engagement ensued, and lasted until
both his right and left flanks were threatened by the
approach of General Sheridan, who was moving from
Ford's Station toward Petersburg, and a division sent
by General Meade from the front of Petersburg, when
he broke in the utmost confusion, leaving in our hands
his guns and many prisoners. This force retreated by
the main road along the Appomattox River.

THE FLIGHT OF LEE FROM RICHMOND.

During the night of the 2d the enemy evacuated
Petersburg and Richmond, and retreated toward Danville. On the morning of the 3d, pursuit was com-

menced.   General Sheridan pushed for the Danville road, keeping near the Appomattox, followed by General Meade with the Second and Sixth Corps, while General Ord moved from Burkesville along the Southside road; the Ninth Corps stretched along that road behind him.   On the 4th, General Sheridan struck the Danville road near Jettersville, where he learned that Lee was at Amelia Court-House.   He immediately intrenched himself and awaited the arrival of General Meade, who reached there the next day.   General Ord reached Burkesville on the evening of the 5th.

On the morning of the 5th I addressed Major-Gen. Sherman the following communication : —

Wilson's Station, April 5, 1865.

GENERAL : — All indications now are that Lee will attempt to reach Danville with the remnant of his force. Sheridan, who was up with him last night, reports all that is left — horse, foot, and dragoons — at twenty thousand, much demoralized. We hope to reduce this number one half. I shall push on to Burkesville, and, if a stand is made at Danville, will in a very few days go there. If you can possibly do so, push on from where you are, and let us see if we cannot finish the job with Lee's and Johnston's armies. Whether it will be better for you to strike for Greensboro' or nearer to Danville, you will be better able to judge when you receive this. Rebel armies now are the only strategic points to strike at.

U. S. GRANT, *Lieutenant-General.*

MAJ.-GEN. W. T. SHERMAN.

On the morning of the 6th, it was found that General Lee was moving west of Jettersville, toward Danville. General Sheridan moved with his cavalry, (the Fifth Corps having been returned to General Meade on his reaching Jettersville,) to strike his flank, followed by the Sixth Corps, while the Second and Fifth Corps pressed hard after, forcing him to abandon several hundred wagons and several pieces of artillery. General Ord advanced from Burkesville toward Farmville, sending two regiments of infantry and a squadron of cavalry, under Brevet Brig.-Gen. Theodore Read, to reach and destroy the bridges. This advance met the head of Lee's column near Farmville, which it heroically attacked and detained until General Read was killed and his small force overpowered. This caused a delay in the enemy's movements, and enabled General Ord to get well up with the remainder of his force, on meeting which the enemy immediately intrenched himself. In the afternoon General Sheridan struck the enemy south of Sailor's Creek, captured sixteen pieces of artillery, and about four hundred wagons, and detained him until the Sixth Corps got up, when a general attack of infantry and cavalry was made, which resulted in the capture of six or seven thousand prisoners, among whom were many general officers. The movements of the Second Corps and General Ord's command contributed greatly to the day's success.

On the morning of the 7th, the pursuit was renewed, the cavalry, except one division, and the Fifth Corps moving by Prince Edward Court-House; the Sixth Corps, General Ord's command, and one division of cavalry, on Farmville; and the Second Corps by the High Bridge road. It was soon found that the enemy had crossed to the north side of the Appomattox; but so close was the pursuit that the Second Corps got possession of the common bridge at High Bridge before the enemy could destroy it, and immediately crossed over. The Sixth Corps and a division of cavalry crossed at Farmville to its support. — *Gen. Grant.*

At this point it was so sure that the Rebel chief was checkmated, that Grant addressed to him a note, which resulted in the surrender at Appomattox Court-House.

It was on the last day of this pursuit that Sheridan telegraphed to Grant this despatch, which at the time excited great attention : —

LIEUTENANT-GENERAL GRANT : —

I have the honor to report that the enemy made a stand at the intersection of the Burke's Station road, in the road upon which they were retreating.

I attacked them with two divisions of the Sixth Army Corps, and routed them handsomely, making a connection with the cavalry. I am still pressing on with both cavalry and infantry. Up to the present time we have captured General Ewell, Kershaw, Button, Corse, De Barre, and Custis Lee, several thousand prisoners, fourteen pieces of artillery, with caissons and a large number of prisoners. If the thing is pressed, I think Lee will surrender.

P. H. SHERIDAN, *Major-General commanding.*
City Point, April 7, — 9 A. M.

It was always said, and probably truly, that the answer was, "Press them."

Now that you have seen how the leader of the whole host ordered the array, you shall read how one of the accomplished men who make a part of it sees the whole. The first extract describes the assault on one of the forts at Petersburg, on the 2d of April. The description which follows is from one of the surgeons who go everywhere with an army, and even remain on the field of defeat, if need be, and are taken prisoners with the men for whom they care.

STORMING A BATTERY.

"Battery Gregg," a strong earth-work, was immediately in front. It was *ours* to assault. Could we take it, the Rebel line was untenable.

Our formation was in column by brigade, our own brigade in advance. The order reached us at about eleven o'clock on the 2d of April. Moving directly against the work, a terrific fire of musketry and grape and canister struck us in front, while shells from all the neighboring works were directed against our flanks. "When within one hundred yards of the work," writes Captain Leach, *our gallant leader on that day,* "we were obliged to lie down, *and crawl upon our hands and knees;* the enemy all the time pouring grape and canister into our ranks at a furious rate." But not a man flinched, although dead and dying comrades were lying stretched upon the ground. The ditch around the fort was reached at last, and although the water in it stood waist-deep, the brave fellows hesitated not to jump in, and scramble up the bank of the fort, vainly attempting to rush in *en masse*, and end the bloody struggle. Soon the stars and stripes could be seen floating by the side of the Rebel flag ; cheer after cheer rent the air, — the Rebels fighting with the desperation of madmen, and shouting to each other, " Never surrender! never surrender!" For twenty-seven minutes we hung upon the works, knowing we could not retreat if we wished to. One more rush and we were inside the fort, and for a minute or two there was a hand-to-hand contest. The works were ours ; and the garrison, — dead and alive. — *Gen. Lincoln, Col. 34th Mass.*

THE LAST WEEK.

As I overheard one enlisted man saying to another, down on the James, in '62, " When a man tells me all about a battle, — what was done here, and what was done there, — I know that he was n't in it. I have been in a good many fights ; and I 've always had enough to do to take care of myself, without looking around at what other people were doing." It is a piece of practical wisdom, that the war experience of every one below a certain grade will confirm. But, if every one should faithfully describe his own square, how the checker-board of a campaign might be reconstructed! One difficulty in ordinary description lies in the too general impression, that one's own little block is the whole board. At Chickamauga, a high-spirited son of a prominent Confederate general, although a mere boy, held a nominal position on his father's staff. He was given charge of a little mountain-howitzer during the action, chiefly to keep him out of worse mischief. When the day was decided, he rode up exultant: "Did you hear the howitzer, father? Did you hear the howitzer, father?" We all are apt to believe that our own little howitzers are, or ought to be, heard above the roar of the battle. Most of us look upon our personal zenith as the celestial pole, around whose axis the natural world revolves; but by an aggregation of observations, true astronomical problems are wrought out. A stereoscopic view is not to be seen with a single eye; a fraction is not the whole; but the spatter of the little piece is sometimes an epitome of the greater volleys. If barely one man in ten, in any battle, should, at its close, faithfully note down his own experience, what a magnificent mosaic might be put together! We shall never know the views of the subalterns in the retreat of the Ten Thousand; nor are there any Commentaries but the commander's on the war in Gaul. But what would not the world give for a gossipy journal by the chief of some syntagma under Xenophon, or by some lively legionary of Cæsar's? Suppose that only the generals wrote of the Rebellion: we should have abundance of grand strategy, but very little of the wayside bivouac. The prominent colors would be staring enough; but we should lose the delicate shadings.

There are many incidents of a march that are interesting without being vital, — little touches that neither make nor mar the picture. This fragment of mosaic is contributed as such.

How glorious was that last week! The Rebs may have enjoyed it slenderly; but we were filled with new life then. The cruel suspense that, mist-like, had enshrouded us during the final movement to the left, was torn aside by Five Forks and the storming of Petersburg. Lee was in retreat; and we were in full cry after him. It was a new and agreeable sensation. More than once in former days we had retired from before the Rebels. Now, it was a wilder chase than ever; and we were not in front.

As everybody knows, the national forces marched in two main columns. The Army of the Potomac, under Meade, and the ubiquitous Sheridan with his centaurs, were directly on the Rebel trail and right; while Ord, with the Army of the James, marched on their left flank along the Lynchburg Railroad, — a moving wall to resist their turning southward. Ord's first objective was Burkesville Junction, to cut off the use of the Danville Railroad, upon which the enemy expected supplies, and whose line he intended to follow south, possibly hoping to unite with Johnston in the Carolinas. Grant started with this column; and we knew that affairs on the northerly line were in the full tide of success, by little waifs borne to us from time to time, almost meaningless singly, but of most excellent omen united. How triumphant we felt! The assault and capture of the Cockade City rekindled all the flame that the ashes of a ten months' siege had covered but not extinguished. A march through its battered streets and its beautiful outskirts had deepened the sense of victory. The balmy air and invigoration of sun and cheerful fields of the Virginia spring stirred the physical man; and the very beasts of burden, escaped from plodding through the winter's mud, seemed to catch the contagion of the march. We were like so many school-boys on a holiday. Sick of the restraints of the earth-works' narrow limits, of the monotonous routine of camp, of shelling and being shelled, — an occupation that was irksome and not edifying, — of the addition of perverse columns, whose frequent resultant was disastrous subtraction, we started off with perhaps more than usual glee, because directed against no fixed point, but liable to wander over half the State before entering a permanent camp. We were very jolly. We expected one sharp fight; but the spirit of prophecy within us announced that the day of retribution for the wicked Rebels was at hand, — that we were surely crushing the Rebellion. The mother of States and of presidents had presided over many solemn marches and stately minuets, in which we had been unwilling participants during the past four years. We had danced sometimes, when the desire was not in us; we had frequently paid the piper when it was inconvenient; but now we were instituting a veritable Virginia Reel, into which we entered heart and soul. But no form of words can describe our exultation, partly physical from pure animal excitement, but chiefly moral from the consciousness of the speedy triumph of the good cause for which we had fought so desperately and so long.

The pride and pomp and all that sort of thing of war are seldom displayed — or should one say deployed? — in campaign. The pursuit of an enemy, the life-and-death business of an active army, are not favorable to stage effects, certainly not to designed effects. But little gems often sparkle in the setting of bayonets that owe their value quite as much to what they mean as to what they are. During a mid-day rest at Nottoway Court-House, a group was gathered on the stoop or porch of the deserted tavern, which, except for the dusty undress uniforms, might well have been taken for a simple party of travellers. There was no parade, no display. The main road on which the troops were marching was not in immediate view. A few orderlies held the horses and attended to their wants.

Some of the dozen men walked hither and thither, evidently unemployed. One or two were half asleep. One or two more were jotting down, or referring to, notes in little books. A sturdy, thoughtful, but cheerful-looking man, who seemed the head of the party, talked occasionally with others, who listened respectfully, or replied, as the case might be. His voice, as caught, was low, but clear and gentle. There appeared in his manner, or in that of his companions, nothing to excite remark, certainly nothing to inspire awe; and, above all, there was not the least token of parade, — no " fuss and feathers," no glitter and dash, such as the heroes of the books are often invested with. The most timid child would not have hesitated to ask a favor of that cigar-smoking, tawny-bearded, kindly-looking man, who was General Grant with his staff. A good share of the brains engaged in antagonizing the Rebellion spent an hour or two on that rusty old tavern porch; but no sign of tinsel was hung out, and no nerve-power was wasted in attitudes.

The march that day was long; but, about the middle of the afternoon, glad tidings came over from the other line; and the despatch was read to the troops while in motion. The particulars are not vital now; but many men, so many generals, so many guns, were captured. As the head of each brigade reached a certain point, the despatch was read; and it moved along with still livelier stride. Each command in turn gave the cheer of thanksgiving; and it was propagated by contagion front and rear. Those ahead renewed it, glad that others were sharing in the joy they just had felt. Those behind took it up, full of faith that there was good cause for the outburst. After a while, they seemed only to fear lest there would be no Rebels left for them to capture.

A few hours later the western sun looked full in the face of the moving column. The road, which there ran by the side of a forest, was filled with troops, who swung along with the free, full stride of men whose legs kept time to the quick-step of earnest hearts. The well-closed ranks, the accoutrements in good condition, the square shoulders, and serious but hopeful faces beneath the forage-caps, marked them veterans; and the fairly-reflecting steel of the arms shone like a glory over the entire array. That magnificent mass of infantry, apparently without end, but presenting the same effectiveness, wherever viewed, looked the incarnation of resistless power. As far as the eye could reach, the curving country road was vivid with the lively, but not boisterous, blue and steel. On the left were green fields, cultivated and refreshing to the sight. On the right, the road was bordered by a forest, whose trees

were full-grown and old. Through this forest, and by
the side of this magnificent body, Generals Grant and
Ord had been riding together; and their well-mounted
staffs and escorts' formed a large and sprightly caval-
cade, winding in and out between the trees, here comparatively free from undergrowth. Their rattling sabres,
and their greater vivacity, the more quickly-moving
horses, and the occasional change of pace or direction, gave more of the notion of mobility than the
monotonous tramp, tramp, of the infantry. The swiftly-
falling sun in the clear heavens threw shadows that
magnified the originals into an army of giants; while
its direct rays glorified all they touched. Ord had just
fallen back, and Grant was beginning to move ahead
at a livelier gait; the mingled staffs had said good-by,
and were again gathered into their proper groups; the
escorts had closed up in their respective places, — when
from the right and rear, two troopers in the Rebel uniform dashed out of the wood on literally foam-flecked
horses. They were only two; but to the outward eye
their dusty gray clothes, their long hair and wild aspect,
and their general appearance, indescribable, but typical
of the Southern cavalry, marked them as unquestionably
Rebels. But their bold and rapid advance directly up
to the column declared them, although personally un-
recognized, as scouts. Inquiring for General Grant,
they fairly pushed their horses to a run, in their eagerness to overtake him when the squadron that followed
him was pointed out. Just as our party again came up,
Grant, who had halted and read their despatch, imper-
turbable as ever, turned to two of his staff: "Colonel
—— and Colonel ——, I wish you to go with me."
While a led horse was being prepared, he spoke a few
words to his adjutant-general, and, before remounting,
wrote a line or two, using a saddled horse as a desk.
Meanwhile, the ceaseless stream of infantry was rolling
by his side; the lower and lower sun cast greater shadows from the huge trees, and still brighter beams from
the polished barrels; the great clusters of horsemen

16

again coalesced, full of chat and conjecture; the hard-riding scouts at first loosened and then tightened their horses' girths and their own belts; and then, just as the sun went down, the lieutenant-general and the two aids, with an orderly or two and the mysterious strangers, started off on a long trot directly through the darkening forest, at right angles to our line of march, and into a country which, if it held anything, held Rebels. They were going to the column; for Grant had news from Sheridan. We had had a glimpse of the romance of war.

On Friday we reached Farmville, whose inhabitants, if not overjoyed to see us, at least were not openly hostile. Lee had been foiled in his effort to escape southward, and was exerting all his energy to gain Lynchburg. We, still in pursuit, were correspondingly elated; and it was a matter of small moment who fell in love with us *en route*. Farmville very closely resembled those finished towns so common in some sections. One could almost see surrounding it the mythical fence that is said to enclose and denote such completed villages. A church was occupied for the night by the staff of General Ord, the general himself resting, by invitation, in the house of a citizen. Among the cherished traditions of Revolutionary horrors in my birthplace is the story of the desecration by the British of the village church where my ancestors preached. Circumstances so altered the relation of things, that no qualm of conscience disturbed my repose that night on the Farmville cushions. True, the red-coats used the one as permanent barracks, and introduced horses as well as men. We were heathen but for a single night; and our sacrilege was less physical than spiritual. Our horses were not admitted; the building was opened by one of its own dignitaries; and we were scrupulous to inflict no unnecessary mischief.

Diagonally opposite to the church, which was on a corner, was a young ladies' seminary, then in the midst of cultivation; but the surly shutters remained imper-

vious to the levelled field-glasses, although a sanguine
few fancied they saw signs of vitality, if not of hostility, through an occasional crevice.

Strangely enough, we were invited to tea by a gentleman, who, if memory serves, made no profession of
Union sentiments, but seemed actuated by pure, ab-
stract hospitality. It may be that he looked upon it as
a gentle species of bribery in the interest of his property
against possible destruction; for the Yankee name in-
spired much awe among the untravelled natives. Be
that as it may, he gave us a most capital supper, that
was heartily enjoyed; for we had eaten nothing since
morning, and our wagons were in the unknown rear.

All the troops passed through and beyond Farmville rapidly enough; but, notwithstanding their absence, the place was abundantly lively the next day.
Both Grant and Ord had made head-quarters there;
Meade was not far off; Sheridan halted there for a while;
and the aids and escorts, the officers and orderlies,
filled the streets with much clatter and bustle. There
was no more parade than at Nottoway; but there was
all that martial stir and tremor that necessarily marks
the head-quarters of a great army at a critical time.
Perhaps the most pronounced feature was a troop of
Sheridan's scouts, two of whom have been previously
mentioned. These, clad in gray, rode through the
streets in the most approved frontier fashion; and no
horde of Texans ever looked wilder than these pseudo-
Rebels, who did such good service for the National
cause. And, while acknowledging their usefulness, it
must be confessed that they were as cut-throat-*looking*
a gang as ever wore spurs.

But Farmville is pre-eminently remembered by a com-
ical incident, after this fashion. Falling into conversation with the wife of a civil functionary (for the citizens
were talkative enough), she finally said something to
this effect : —

"I do n't see what you Yankees want to come down
here and take away all our negroes for."

" My dear madam, that is not our object. They will go off after the army, in many cases, I know ; but we are not here for that purpose."

" What do you suppose we are going to do without our servants."

" Indeed, I hope you will not lose all your servants."

" Yes, we will; I know we will! I know they'll all go off. And what do you suppose I will do then?"

" I 'm sure that I hope they'll not all desert you; but, if they should, you can easily supply their places."

" No. They'll all go, I know they will. And what do you think will become of me? Do you think I will work?"

" I can't imagine you to be so unfortunate as not to be able to get any servants whatever."

" We won't, — I know we won't; they'll all go. And I? — do you suppose I will work? Indeed, I won't. Indeed, I *won't* work!"

" I can't believe that you will be so reduced; for there must be some servants to be had at all times."

" I tell you there won't be : they'll all go off. And do you think I'll work? I 've always had servants. Indeed, I won't work. Do you think I 'll do what I 've always had servants to do? Do you think I will cook? I shall do nothing of the sort. You come down here, and take all our servants away, and then expect me to work : indeed, I sha'n't."

" As I 've said before, madam, I sincerely hope you will be able to obtain servants, if your own should leave ; and I can scarcely conceive that you should not. But suppose it should happen so that your own servants should all go, and that you could get no assistance whatever, — that your picture should be realized, — under such circumstances, if you could get literally no one to help you, I presume you would really be obliged to make your own bed, and to cook your own food."

" Indeed, I won't. I don't care if they all go. What! Do you suppose I will work? I have always had servants. You may take them all away. Do you think I will work? Indeed, I shall do nothing of the kind."

"But just imagine the case, madam. If you have no one, and can't possibly get any one, the question becomes very simple. It is either to do it one's self, or to go without; and we know the consequences of going without. I am sure I hope you may not be so compelled; but, since that would be the only alternative, I am afraid you might have to do your own cooking."

"Indeed, I won't. I've always had servants, and I 'won't work: and I do n't see what you Yankees want to come down here for, and take our servants away."

To that style of argument, what could a man reply?

We did not overtake the column that had pushed ahead at an early hour, and with which Griffin's Fifth Corps was also marching, until after mid-day on Saturday. Even then, a long journey had been made; and the men began to feel it, notwithstanding their elation of spirits; but they persisted manfully. Towards nightfall, however, they naturally began to droop, for an all-day's march is no light thing. Then, riding along the ranks, Ord addressed them in pithy little sentences: "Legs will win this battle, men." "It rests with us to head them off." "This march will save all others." "Whichever army marches best wins." "The campaign is in your legs, men." "Good marching will carry it." "They can't escape, if you will keep up to it." "One good steady march, and the campaign is ended." And, strenuously impressing upon the troops that, by getting ahead of them, they would corral the Rebels, that the termination of certainly the campaign, perhaps the war, was virtually vested in the endurance of their legs, — in other words, by conjoined appeals to their good sense and manly pride, —their flagging strength was stimulated; and the weary troops were kept in motion. Presently, messages came from Sheridan, ahead, begging us to march to the utmost; that if we could make a certain distance, the problem would be solved. Harris's brigade of Turner's division was in the lead, — magnificent athletes, who had been trained in the mountains of West Virginia and in the Valley; and better marching infantry never did. It was ten o'clock that night before the troops went into bivouac; but, just as we lay down, a fresh despatch from Sheridan announced that Custer had captured a park of artillery and innumerable stores, and begged Ord to advance a little further, so that next morning might end it. The " assembly " rang out, the men fell in, and, weary almost to exhaustion, they staggered along up the road until past midnight. Another bivouac was made, with strict orders for the column to be stretched out at 3.30 A. M. But nature has a limit, and it was only by the strenuous personal exertions of the various general officers that we got in motion after daylight. About seven o'clock, a half-hour's halt was allowed for coffee, in the midst of which there was sharp firing ahead, and an urgent request for the immediate support of the infantry.

It was worth the fatigue of the march to watch Sheridan explaining the situation to Ord. The " battle-light" is not a myth nor a figure of speech; on that morning, it fairly transfigured Sheridan. His face in repose is impassive and not striking; but, on the edge of the fight, he grew all aflame; the transformation was absolute. It is no exaggeration to say, that, in its glow, one would scarcely recognize him as the same man; but he did not lose his head. Excited, and quivering with enthusiasm, his mind grew keener, not tremulous; his sentences were graphic, not confused. Although surrounded by woods, so that the eye rendered no aid, two minutes' conversation portrayed the situation as clearly as if mapped before us. General Ord gave his orders for the disposition of the troops; and we rode forward to witness what had been so graphically depicted. Emerging from the woods, on the crest of a little bluff, a cleared basin lay before us, ont of which, and towards us, an immense number of dismounted cavalry-men, leading their horses, were falling back. A strong Confederate skirmish-line, whose wings stretched well on each side of the main road, was in full view; two brass guns in action were conspicuous in the sunlight; and distant trains, waiting to move on, revealed that at last we had come up with the swift-footed foe. The Confederates seemed in high glee; and well they might be, for they appeared to have forced back the terrible cavalry, and to have a way to the mountains open before them. As we sat there, Sheridan, in a burst of personal daring and display, like the solitary flash of lightning before the storm, dashed off down the right to reconnoitre, directly in the face of the Rebels, and within their easy range. An orderly, bearing his crimson and white standard, making him so much the more conspicuous, followed; and his career seemed that of some storied knight, offering adventurous personal challenge, rather than a modern general, whose presumed province was the cool and comprehensive oversight of an army. But he knew his position; and his apparent recklessness was not folly.

We rode farther to the right; and, again emerging from the screen of woods, the full field was displayed. The last of our cavalry had disappeared from its first position; the Rebel guns were far down the opposite declivity; the strong skirmish-line was thrown well forward and advancing; the mass of the enemy was known to be but a little in its rear; and the view presented was that of a Confederate field-day. Just then, a loud report announced one of our own guns as opening. At the same instant, a return crackle was heard from the woods just before them; and the Rebel skirmishers halted. The legs had done their part, and our own infantry was at last engaged. Our skirmishers advanced, and the Rebels retired; but their retiring was a master-piece of discipline. They fired "at will," fell back a few paces, fired again, made a momentary ad-

vance, again fired, and again fell back, as orderly and
methodically as if on parade. The brass guns likewise
began to withdraw, then fired, then were run back, and
so on, until finally the crest of the hill was reached.
By this time, our full lines of battle had emerged from
the timber. The Fifth Corps and the Army of the
James held the right and left respectively, with the
centre between them, in common; and the remounted
cavalry massed on Griffin's right. Our artillery fired
more rapidly, our skirmishers pressed forward with
greater speed, the Rebel riflemen retired in haste, and
the guns lingered for an instant on the ridge, as we
began a general advance.

The long lines swept silently forward, to possess the
victory they were conscious awaited them. Many
events prove historic, of the importance of which the
participants are at the time ignorant; but, on that Sunday morning, not a bayonet or a sabre but knew that
the vitality of the Rebellion awaited its thrust. As we
afterwards learned, the North had gone wild over the
fall of Richmond; but in the army, although the direct
prize for which so many had fought so long, that was
regarded as but an omen of ultimate success. While
Lee and his forces were in the field, the real work was
incomplete. Every man appreciated the consequences
of the approaching action; and there was not a soldier
who had raced in the pursuit but realized that the crisis
was at hand. The advance was magnificent. The immense wave of infantry, capped and sparkling with steel
and colors, and preceded by its skirmish spray, rolled
forward as steadily as the resistless sea, and with only
the seething hiss of its own motion before the billow
breaks. The great cloud of cavalry hung ready to pour
its storm; the catastrophe was imminent, — but, just
as the culmination was at hand, a shout ran down the
line, and men's hearts beat wilder yet. A white flag
rode out. Legs had won!

The flag bore a note from General Gordon, in our
immediate front, asking a truce. General Ord, as the

senior present, granted it, until General Grant could be consulted. The lines were ordered to stand fast, the skirmishers serving as pickets. Presently, the ranking generals, on invitation, rode down to the Court-House near by; but, as Sheridan approached the Rebel lines, their pickets fired on him at short range. One explanation was, that, by an oversight, they had not been instructed as to the truce; another, that they avowed themselves South Carolinians, and would therefore "never surrender." Had one bullet struck, how that avalanche of cavalry on the neighboring ridge would have desolated the insurgents! About noon, it was officially announced that the Army of Northern Virginia would surrender. The pickets fraternized; and, were it not for the restraints of discipline, the armies themselves, to all appearance, would have coalesced.

By a curious coincidence, the articles of the surrender were drawn up in the house of a gentleman whose former home was on the field of Bull Run, and who had moved to this locality to avoid the region of active hostilities. How could he anticipate that the head-waters of the Appomattox would be the "last ditch," or that his new farm would witness the virtual close, as his old one had seen the first actual battle, of the war!

The hosts dispersed almost as rapidly as they had assembled. Promptly the next morning, Sheridan led the cavalry to Danville, and the Sixth Corps followed. Grant and Ord returned to tide-water immediately, and much the larger part of the troops were quickly marched away. Only enough remained to attend to the necessary formalities of the capitulation. Very few of those whose genius and valor accomplished it witnessed the actual surrender of the Rebels. When defeat is assured, the combatant victors are not the ones who exult in the humiliation of brave enemies.

Excepting by those to whom the afflictions directly came, there appears to have been no proper appreciation, at the North, of the daily casualties that blotted the calendar of that final week; while, in fact, at Appomattox itself, the seals of the surrender were moistened with the blood of two hundred brave fellows, contemplation of the result diverted popular attention from the road that led to it.

Two incidents, ordinarily not noteworthy, seemed of special hardship on that ultimate day. One was, a Confederate gun still in position, on the Lynchburg highway, with a dead cannoneer lying by its trail. Constant to the last, the misguided but faithful Rebel clung to his post, sacrificed himself in his effort to secure for his comrades the one avenue of escape, and died just as resistance became hopeless, — a noble but unavailing victim for the cause he loved. The thought of Appomattox always brings before me that poor dead gunner, ashen and gray, lying alone and stark in the dusty road.

The other was the case of a soldier of the Fifth New York, mortally wounded by almost the last, if not actually the last, Rebel fire. As he was borne off the field, the message of submission came in sight; the cause he died for achieved its crowning triumph; but he fell, another martyr, an apparently superfluous martyr, to the infernal Rebellion. He died in the arms of victory, ignorant that it was victory. The ranks closed up, — one man is not missed in a regiment. But all that he had he had given. He had given, as so many thousands gave, life, — had given it in faith and love. The sadness is not that he died, — we all were willing to die if need be, — but that he died when the victory was won.—*Dr. Alfred A. Woodhull.*

SHERIDAN DESCRIBES THE END.

The resistance growing stubborn, a halt was called to get up Wheaton's division of the Sixth Corps, which went into position on the left of the road, Seymour being on the right. Wheaton was ordered to guide right, with his right connecting with Seymour's left and resting on the road. I still felt the great importance of pushing the enemy, and was unwilling to wait for Getty's division of the Sixth Corps to get up. I therefore ordered an advance, sending word to General Humphreys, who was on the road to our right, and requesting him to push on, as I felt confident we could break up the enemy. It was apparent from the absence of artillery fire, and the manner in which they gave way, when pressed. that the force of the enemy opposed to us was a heavy rearguard. The enemy was driven until our lines reached Sailor's Creek ; and, from the north bank, I could see our cavalry on the high bank above the creek, and south of it, and the long line of smoke from the burning wagons. A cavalry-man, who, in a charge, cleared the enemy's works and came through their lines, reported to me what was in front. I regret that I have forgotten the name of this gallant young soldier.

As soon as General Wright could get his artillery into position I ordered the attack to be made on the left, and sent Colonel Stagg's brigade of cavalry to strike and flank the extreme right of the enemy's line.

The attack by the infantry was not executed exactly as I had directed, and a portion of our line in the open ground was broken by the terrible fire of the enemy, who were in position on commanding ground south of the creek.

This attack by Wheaton's and Seymour's divisions was splendid, but no more than I had reason to think from the gallant Sixth Corps. The cavalry in rear of the enemy attacked simultaneously, and the enemy, after a gallant resistance, were completely surrounded, and nearly all threw down their arms and surrendered.

General Ewell, commanding the enemy's forces, and a number of other general officers, fell into our hands, and a very large number of prisoners. . . . .

On the 7th instant the pursuit was continued early in the morning by the cavalry, General Couch in the advance. It was discovered that the enemy had not been cut off by the Army of the James, and under the belief that he would attempt to escape on the Danville road through Prince Edward Court-House, General Merritt was ordered to move his two divisions to that point, passing around the left of the Army of the James. General Crook continued the direct pursuit, encountering the main body of the enemy at Farmville, and again on the north side of the Appomattox, where the enemy's trains were attacked by General Gregg, and a sharp fight with the enemy's infantry ensued, in which General Gregg was unfortunately captured.

On arriving at Prince Edward Court-House I found General McKenzie, with his division of cavalry from the Army of the James, and ordered him to cross the bridge on the Buffalo River and make a reconnoissance to Prospect Station on the Lynchburg Railroad, and ascertain if the enemy were moving past that point. Meantime I heard from General Crook that the enemy had crossed to the north side of the Appomattox, and General Merritt was then moved on and encamped at Buffalo Creek, and General Crook was ordered to re-cross the Appomattox and encamp at Prospect Station. On the morning of the 8th Merritt and McKenzie continued the march to Prospect Station, and Merritt's and Crook's commands then moved on to Appomattox Court-House. Shortly after the march commenced, Sergeant White, one of my scouts, notified me that there were four trains of cars at Appomattox depot loaded with supplies for General Lee's army; Generals Merritt and Crook were at once notified, and the command pushed on briskly for twenty-eight miles. General Custer had the advance, and on nearing the depot skilfully threw a force in rear of the trains and captured them. Without halting a moment he pushed on, driving the enemy (who had reached the depot about the same time as our cavalry) in the direction of Appomattox Court-House, capturing many prisoners and twenty-five pieces of artillery, a hospital train, and a large park of wagons. General Devin coming up, went in on the right of Custer. The fighting continued till after dark, and, the enemy being driven to Appomattox Court-House, I at once notified the Lieutenant-General, and sent word to Generals Ord and Gibbon of the Army of the James, and General Griffin commanding the Fifth Corps, who were in rear, that, if they pressed on, there was now no means of escape for the enemy, who had reached "the last ditch." During the night, although we knew that the remnant of Lee's army was in our front, we held fast with the cavalry to what we had gained, and ran the captured trains back along the railroad to a point where they would be protected by our infantry that was coming up. The Twenty-fourth and Fifth Corps and one division of the Twenty-fifth Corps arrived about daylight on the 9th at Appomattox depot.

After consulting with General Ord, who was in command of these corps, I rode to the front, near Appomattox Court-House, and just as the enemy in heavy force was attacking the cavalry with the intention of breaking through our lines, I directed the cavalry, which was dismounted, to fall back, gradually resisting the enemy, so as to give time for the infantry to form its lines and march to the attack, and, when this was done, to move off to the right flank and mount. This was done, and the enemy discontinued his attack as soon as he caught sight of our infantry. I moved briskly around the left of the enemy's line of battle, and was about to charge the trains and the confused mass of the enemy, when a white flag was presented to General Custer, who had the advance, and who sent the information to me at once that the enemy desired to surrender. — *Gen. Phil. Sheridan.*

THE FIGHT OF APRIL 6TH.

The night of the 1st of April, 1865, was occupied by the Sixth Corps in preparation for a general assault on the enemy's lines below Petersburg. The brigades were formed in columns of attack, preceded by a band of pioneers and a heavy skirmish line. In our brigade, the pioneers were under the direction of Sergeant Tracy, and the skirmish line was commanded by Captain J. C. Robinson. Both these officers were of the Thirty-seventh. The skirmish line was composed entirely of men detailed from the Thirty-seventh. The Thirty-seventh itself occupying the front line of battle in the brigade. While cutting away the abatis in front of the enemy's forts, the pioneers suffered severely. Sergeant Tracy was early disabled by a ball passing through his leg. He did not leave the field, but, lying on his side, he still directed the movements of his men. While thus engaged, a second ball shattered his knee-joint. Captain Robinson charged, at the head of his skirmishers, through the abatis, when he was wounded and had to be borne back. The colors of the Thirty-seventh were the first in the division to wave over the Rebel works. The Rebels fired their last volley as the regiment climbed from the ditch to the parapet. Many personal encounters ensued. Captain Champney was foremost in entering the fort, and was indefatigable in preventing the escape of any Rebels. Sergeant Boston, of Company F, rushed on a brawny gray-back, and disarmed him at a single pass of his weapon. Corporal Welch, of Company E, succeeded in wresting a battle-flag from a Rebel color-bearer, and was rewarded with a medal. From the fort, we pushed on towards the left until we met the troops of the other brigade, and then forward to the Southside Railroad. We alone, of the Sixth Corps, entered Petersburg the next morning. Colonel Edwards received the surrender of the place. In this engagement, we lost three killed and thirty-three wounded. Among the latter were Captain Robinson, and Lieutenants Waterman and Sheldon.

Constant marching and countermarching for four days carried us over seventy miles of country, and found us again in front of the enemy in the neighborhood of Sailor's Creek. The morning of the 6th we were at Amelia Court-House. At noon we had made a march of twenty-five miles, double-quicking nearly eight miles of the way, and were confronting the enemy, with a deep stream between us. Our brigade was on the extreme right of the line, and the Thirty-seventh occupied the left of the brigade. Rushing like an avalanche across Sailor's Creek, where the water was up to our arm-pits, we dislodged the enemy from the opposite bank, and drove them over the crest of the hill.

Beyond the stream for a quarter of a mile, we advanced through a thick growth of underbrush, fighting as we went. The firing waxed hotter and hotter, until suddenly we found, to our dismay, that the regiment on our right had given way, and the brigade on our left had broken the connection, and halted some distance back. We were lost to our friends. Our nearest neighbor was our foe. The Rebels came pouring down upon us, and within a few seconds had attacked and enveloped both flanks of the regiment. A hand-to-hand conflict ensued. Many men were wounded with the bayonet, and pistol-shots were freely exchanged. Adjutant Bradley, in endeavoring to stem the torrent of their attack upon the right flank, closed with a Rebel captain, received a shot from the captain's pistol through the shoulder, wrested the pistol from his hand, was shot through both legs by a Rebel soldier, who thought it time to interfere, while one of our men in a like spirit, and with a surer aim, plunged a ball through the body of the captain, killing him instantly. Corporal Walker, of Company H, had a bayonet tilt with a stalwart Rebel. The latter had the advantage in possessing the longer weapon (Spencer rifles are hardly equal to Springfields in crossing bayonets), still, in spite of this disadvantage, the corporal succeeded in disarming his antagonist, and compelled him to surrender. Captain Chandley was the centre of a bloody struggle. Two of the Rebels and two of our own men fell fighting around his person. One of our sergeants rushed to the front and endeavored to seize a stand of colors. He was instantly shot dead. Private Taggert, of

Company B, saw him fall, darted from the line, and bore away the prize through the smoke of battle. Meanwhile, the Spencer rifle was working the havoc for which it was intended. All down the front of our regiment, the gaps that our fire opened in the enemy's ranks were fearful. They had started to attack us massed in heavy columns. Scattered fragments only reached us. They came, throwing down their guns, raising their hands, and imploring the cessation of the fire. After the battle, more than seventy corpses were counted on the ground in our immediate front. And when we consider that the proportion of the slain to the disabled on the field of battle is usually only as one to six, it will be seen that the carnage was terrific. Among the prisoners who fell into our hands was Major-General Custis Lee, the son of the commander-in-chief of the Rebel armies. We lost in this engagement eight men killed and thirty-one wounded. Among the latter, Captain Smith, Adjutant Bradley, and Lieutenant Cushman. Among the killed were Ezra D. Cowles, First Sergeant of Company D, and Sergeant Bolton, of Company C. Sergeant Cowles excited the admiration of all who saw him by his heroism. He was mortally wounded early in the engagement, but, instead of caring for himself, or allowing others to minister to him, he encouraged all around him " to fight," and, with his life-blood flowing away, shamed those who would give over the battle for lost. — *Col. Edwards in Gen. Schouler's Report.*

THE BATTLE OF HIGH BRIDGE.

Early in the 6th of April, in compliance with orders received the night previous, Colonel Washburn, with two regiments of infantry, each about four hundred strong, and a part of his own force of cavalry, numbering thirteen officers and sixty-seven men, started to destroy High Bridge, eighteen miles distant, and of great importance to the retreating Rebel army. The

bridge was reached about noon, the enemy offering
feeble resistance to his advance. The infantry were
halted in the vicinity of the bridge, while the cavalry
pushed on two miles further, meeting a superior force
of the enemy's cavalry, with artillery. A short time
before the bridge was reached, Brevet Brig.-Gen.
Theodore Read arrived, with orders to hold, and not
destroy, the bridge. He took command. The cavalry
retired to the bridge, and found the infantry warmly
engaged with another force of the enemy's cavalry, and
showing signs of breaking. It was soon evident that
the enemy was superior in numbers, and that a fight at
long range could not be maintained until General Ord
should be apprised of their situation and should send
infantry — the only troops he had — to their relief.

Thus situated between two forces of the enemy, —
the larger between him and the Army of the James, —
to charge and break through the enemy, if possible,
seemed the only honorable course for General Read to
take ; no other was suggested.

Twice the cavalry charged, breaking through and
dispersing one line of the enemy, re-forming and charging a second, which was formed in a wood too dense to
admit of free use of the sabre. In vain, however ; eight
of twelve officers engaged were put *hors du combat,* —
three killed and five severely wounded. The little
band was hemmed in and overpowered by two divisions
of cavalry. — Rosser's and Fitz Hugh Lee's, — the
advance of General Lee's army.

Colonel Washburn, whose intrepid bravery in this
fight endears his name to his associates, and adds the
crowning glory to a life elevated by the purest patriot-
ism, died a few weeks afterwards from the effect of his
wounds. Because of the influence of the affair upon
the results of the campaign I have dwelt upon it.

"To the sharpness of that fight," said a Rebel colonel, inspector-general on Lee's staff, to General Ord,
"the cutting off of Lee's army at Appomattox Court-
House was probably owing." So fierce were the charges

17

of Colonel Washburn and his men, and so determined their fighting, that General Lee received the impression that they must be supported by a large part of the army, gave what the inspector-general called " stampeding orders," and began to throw up the line of breastworks which were found there the next day. Three trains of provisions, forage, and clothing, which had been sent down from Lynchburg on the Southside road, were sent back to prevent their falling into our hands, and his army, which was on third rations, and those of corn only, was thus deprived of the provisions the want of which exhausted them so much.

Moreover, by the delay occasioned by this halt, General Sheridan was enabled to come up with Ewell's division at Sailor's Creek. When Lee discovered his mistake, and that the fighting force in his front was only a small detachment of cavalry and infantry, General Ord, with the Army of the James, had already profited by the delay, and so closed up with him that a retreat directly south was no longer practicable ; he was obliged to make the detour by way of Appomattox Court-House. General Rosser concurs in this opinion, and states that the importance of the fight has never been appreciated. — *General Schouler.*

THE REBEL ARMY.

When at last the beginning of the end came, in the evacuation of Richmond and the effort to retreat, everything seemed to go to pieces at once. The best disciplinarians in the army relaxed their reins. The best troops became disorganized, and hardly any command marched in a body. Companies were mixed together, parts of each being separated by detachments of others. Flying citizens, in vehicles of every conceivable sort, accompanied and embarrassed the columns. Many commands marched heedlessly on without orders, and seemingly without a thought of whither they were going. Others mistook the meaning of their instructions, which

it was impossible to obey in any case. At Amelia Court-
House we should have found provisions. General Lee
had ordered a train load to meet him there, but the interests of the starving army had been sacrificed to the
convenience or the cowardice of the President and his
personal following. The train had been hurried on to
Richmond and its precious cargo of food thrown out
there, in order that Mr. Davis and his people might
retreat rapidly and comfortably from the abandoned
capital. Then began the desertion of which we have
heard so much. Up to that time, as far as I can learn,
if desertions had occurred at all, they had not become
general; but now that the government, in flying from
the foe. had cut off our supply of provisions, what were
the men to do? Many others followed the example of
the government, and fled; but a singularly large proportion of the little whole stayed and starved to the last.
And it was no technical or metaphorical starvation
which we had to endure, either, as a brief statement of
my own experience will show. The battery to which I
was attached was captured near Amelia Court-House,
and within a mile or two of my home. Seven men only
escaped, and, as I knew intimately everybody in the
neighborhood, I had no trouble in getting horses for
these to ride. Applying to General Lee in person for
instructions, I was ordered to march on, using my own
judgment, and rendering what service I could in the
event of a battle. In this independent fashion I marched,
with much better chances than most of the men had to
get food, and yet during three days and nights our total
supply consisted of one ear of corn to the man, and we
divided that with our horses. — *Capt. G. C. Eggleston of
the Confederate Army.*

SHERIDAN AT FIVE FORKS.

A colonel with a shattered regiment came down upon
us in a charge. The bayonets were fixed, the men came
on with a yell. Their gray uniform seemed black amid

the smoke. Their preserved colors, torn by grape and ball, waved defiantly. Twice they halted, and poured in volleys, but came on again like the surge from the fog, depleted, but determined. Yet in the hot faces of the carabineers they read a purpose as resolute, but more calm; and while they pressed along, swept all the while by scathing volleys, a group of horsemen took them in the flank.

It was an awful instant. The horses recoiled; the charging column trembled like a single thing: but at once the Rebels, with rare organization, fell into a hollow square, and with solid sheets of steel defied our centaurs. The horsemen rode around them in vain: no charge could break the shining squares till our dismounted carabineers poured in their volleys afresh, making gaps in their spent ranks; and then in their waving line the cavalry thundered down. The Rebels could stand no more; they reeled and swayed, and fell back, broken and beaten; and on the ground their colonel lay sealing his devotion with his life. — *N. Y. World.*

JEFFERSON DAVIS'S FLIGHT.

He was at church on Sunday morning. The minister was preaching, when an orderly entered, and handed a note to the President of the Confederacy. It was a despatch from Lee, that his lines were broken in three places, and that Richmond must be evacuated. It was as if a hand had written once more, "Mene, mene, tekel .... Thou art weighed and found wanting; thy kingdom is divided." He turned pale; but, taking his hat, he hurriedly left the church. The hour of twelve came. The people, as they passed the Capitol on their way home from church, saw men hurriedly bringing out the state papers, piling them upon the ground, and setting them on fire. It was the first intimation they had that the city was to be evacuated. — *Mrs. Hanaford.*

CHAPTER XIV.

THE END.

AND so the war was done. And may the good God grant that it shall be ten million billion years before anybody proposes another like it. As for the Rebel soldiers they went home. They were soured and disappointed, but at the bottom of their hearts they were glad the fighting was over. Some one asked if they were to give up their horses. "No," said General Grant, "they will want their horses to plough the land. Let them take their horses." There is a great deal of philosophy in this word of the great soldier, and there is a vein of humor in it too, as there is in most philosophy. So they took their horses and went home.

As for the Union army, it was determined that both the great divisions, that of Meade and that of Sherman, should pass through the city of Washington, and, in a grand review, should receive a sort of farewell from the President before they were dismissed to their homes.

This review is thus described by General Sherman. Nor could I find a better last "Story of the War" than that which is told so well by this great soldier.

During the afternoon and night of the 23d, the Fifteenth, Seventeenth, and Twentieth Corps crossed Long Bridge, bivouacked in the streets about the Capitol, and the Fourteenth Corps closed up to the bridge. The morning of the 24th was extremely beautiful, and the ground was in splendid order for our review. The streets were filled with people to see the pageant, armed with bouquets of flowers for their favorite regiments or heroes, and everything was propitious. Punctually at nine A. M. the signal gun was fired, when in person, attended by General Howard and all my staff, I rode slowly down Pennsylvania Avenue, the crowds of men, women, and children densely lining the sidewalks, and almost obstructing the way. We were followed close by General Logan and the head of the Fifteenth Corps. When I reached the Treasury-building, and looked back, the sight was simply magnificent. The column was compact, and the glittering muskets looked like a solid mass of steel, moving with the regularity of a pendulum. We passed the Treasury-building, in front of which and of the White House was an immense throng of people, for whom extensive stands had been prepared on both sides of the Avenue. As I neared the brick house opposite the lower corner of Lafayette Square, some one asked me to notice Mr. Seward, who, still feeble and bandaged for his wounds, had been removed there that he might behold the troops. I moved in that direction and took off my hat to Mr. Seward, who sat at an upper window. He recognized the salute, returned it, and then we rode on steadily past the President, saluting with our swords. All on his stand arose and acknowledged the salute. Then, turning into the gate of the Presidential grounds, we left our horses with orderlies, and went upon the stand, where I found Mrs. Sherman, with her father and son. Passing them, I shook hands with the President, General Grant, and each member of the Cabinet. I then took my post on the left of the President, and for six hours and a half stood, while the army passed in the order of the Fifteenth, Seventeenth, Twentieth, and Fourteenth Corps. It was, in my judgment, the most magnificent army in existence — sixty-five thousand men, in splendid *physique*, who had just completed a march of nearly two thousand miles in a hostile country, in good drill, and who realized that they were being closely scrutinized by thousands of their fellow-countrymen and by foreigners. Division after division passed, each commander of an army corps or division coming on the stand during the passage of his command, to be presented to the President, Cabinet, and spectators. The steadiness and firmness of the tread, the careful dress of the guides, the uniform intervals between the companies, all eyes directly to the front, and the tattered and bullet-riven flags, festooned with flowers, all attracted universal notice. Many good people, up to that time, had looked upon our Western army as a sort of mob; but the world then saw, and recognized the fact, that it was an army in the proper sense, well organized, well commanded and disciplined; and there was no wonder that it had swept through the South like a tornado. For six hours and a half that strong tread of the Army of the West resounded along Pennsylvania Avenue; not a soul of that vast crowd of spectators left his place; and when the rear of the column had passed by, thousands of the spectators still lingered to express their sense of confidence in the strength of a government which could claim such an army.

Some little scenes enlivened the day, and called for the laughter and cheers of the crowd. Each division was followed by six ambulances, as a representative of its baggage-train. Some of the division commanders had added, by way of variety, goats, milch-cows, and pack-mules, whose loads consisted of game-cocks, poultry, hams, etc., and some of them had the families of freed slaves along, with the women leading their children. Each division was preceded by its corps of black pioneers, armed with picks and spades. These marched abreast in double ranks, keeping perfect dress and step, and added much to the interest of the occasion. On the whole, the grand review was a splendid success, and was a fitting conclusion to the campaign and the war. — *Gen. Sherman.*

University Press: John Wilson and Son, Cambridge.

EDWARD E. HALE'S WRITINGS.

TEN TIMES ONE IS TEN. 16mo. 75 cents.

CHRISTMAS EVE AND CHRISTMAS DAY: Ten Christ-mas Stories. With Frontispiece by Darley. 16mo. $1.25

UPS AND DOWNS. An Every-day Novel. 16mo. $1.50.

A SUMMER VACATION. Paper covers. 50 cents.

IN HIS NAME. Square 18mo. $1.00.

OUR NEW CRUSADE. Square 18mo. $1.00.

THE MAN WITHOUT A COUNTRY, and other Tales 16mo. $1.25.

THE INGHAM PAPERS. 16mo. $1.25.

WORKINGMEN'S HOMES. Illustrated. 16mo. $1.00.

HOW TO DO IT. 16mo. $1.00.

HIS LEVEL BEST. 16mo. $1.25.

THE GOOD TIME COMING ; or, Our New Crusade. A Temperance Story. Square 18mo. Paper covers. 50 cents

G. T. T. ; or, The Wonderful Adventures of a Pullman. $1.00.

WHAT CAREER? or, The Choice of a Vocation and the Use of Time. 16mo. $1.25.

MRS. MERRIAM'S SCHOLARS. A Story of the "Original Ten." 16mo. $1.00.

For sale by all Booksellers. Mailed, postpaid, by the Publishers,

ROBERTS BROTHERS, BOSTON.

HOW TO DO IT.

By EDWARD EVERETT HALE.

CONTENTS.

How to Talk; How to Write; How to Read; How to go into Society; How to Travel; Life at School and in Vacation; Life Alone; Habits with Children; Life with your Elders; Habits of Reading; Getting Ready.

16MO. PRICE $1.00.

" The little work is intended especially for the benefit of young readers, but it is equally adapted to give pleasure to the older members of the family circle. It is weighty in thought, of acute observation, versatile in its illustrations and examples, affectionate in tone, and racy in expression." — *N. Y. Tribune.*

" This is a very sensible little book. 'How to Do It' means 'how you are to behave in society,' 'how you are to read,' 'how you are to live with your elders,' and 'how with children,' &c. On all these points Mr. Hale gives very shrewd, kindly advice. The first chapter, with its description and reminiscences of Boston as it was, will charm every reader, and tempt him to go further, when indeed he can scarcely fail to get much good." — *London Spectator.*

" It is a mistake to suppose this charming, amusing, and useful little book is only for young people. It is equally needed by multitudes of people who have less knowledge than years; parents who do n t know 'how to do it' any better than their sons and daughters; men and women, well informed in current matters of interest, but who do not know how to read, or write, or talk, or travel, or go into society, or even behave at church, in a proper manner. Let them get this book, and Mr. Hale, in his quaint, humorous, attractive, and sensible way, will tell them exactly how to do all these things, and more. His pages are crowded with good sense and practical wisdom, and bright with anecdote and story, with pleasant talk and words of cheer, which not only show how to do it, but are sure to teach courage to the timid, and modesty to the self-sufficient, in doing it." — *Universalist Quarterly.*

Sold by all Booksellers. Mailed, postpaid, by the Publishers,

ROBERTS BROTHERS, Boston.